CRITICAL INSIGHTS

Albert Camus

CRITICAL
INSIGHTS

Albert Camus

Editor
Steven G. Kellman
University of Texas at San Antonio

Salem Press
Pasadena, California   Hackensack, New Jersey

Library of Congress Cataloging-in-Publication Data
Albert Camus / editor, Steven G. Kellman.
    p. cm. — (Critical insights)
Includes bibliographical references and index.
    ISBN 978-1-58765-825-9 (alk. paper) — ISBN 978-1-58765-821-1 (Crit-
ical insights : alk. paper) — ISBN 978-1-58765-822-8 (set-pack a : alk. paper)
    1. Camus, Albert, 1913-1960—Criticism and interpretation. 2. Camus,
Albert, 1913-1960—Philosophy. I. Kellman, Steven G., 1947-
    PQ2605.A3734Z546122 2012
    848'.91409—dc23
                                                      2011022243

PRINTED IN CANADA

Contents_____

Career, Life, and Influence_____

Critical Contexts_____

Critical Readings_____

Resources

About This Volume_____
Steven G. Kellman

Throughout his career and in the decades following his premature death in 1960, Albert Camus gained a large and avid international readership. But he has also attracted the interest of scholars from many disciplines, specialists in literature, theater, philosophy, theology, political science, history, psychology, medicine, and law. Even drawing exclusively on English-language studies of Camus, the bibliography at the end of this volume testifies both to the mountain of commentaries that his work has inspired and to the wide range of approaches that have been taken toward it. His novels, stories, essays, and plays have been examined within the context of their historical moment, the troubled period before, during, and after World War II. They have been studied for their distinctive, economic styles, their innovative use of narrative perspective, and their thematic preoccupation with alienation and injustice. His work has been read as a contribution to moral and political philosophy and to an understanding of personality disorders, legal theory, and personal identity. In a piece written for this collection, Katherine Stirling even notes the importance of meteorology to an understanding of Camus. At age twenty-four, he held a job collating weather reports from throughout Algeria that reinforced a sensitivity to the nuances of sun and rain evident later in the lyrical essays and the fiction. The tedium of his year-long bureaucratic task, Stirling argues, also gave the nascent author an early inkling of the absurd.

In his survey of the reception of Camus's oeuvre, Matthew H. Bowker identifies ways in which it has been read, themes that have inspired discussion, and points of continuing controversy. Camus's own reaction to his hostile critics, particularly his erstwhile friend Jean-Paul Sartre, led to the bitterness pervading *The Fall* and *Exile and the Kingdom*. After more than seventy years, the accumulated commentary on Camus constitutes a rich and lively conversation to which *Critical Insights: Albert Camus* offers original contributions, while also reprinting a sampling of some of the more trenchant earlier essays about the man and his work.

Biography of literary figures can often be a distraction from texts that make a life worth noting in the first place. However, as a public intellectual active in numerous political causes, Camus lived his work, and, long before he conceived *The First Man*—the autobiographical novel whose unfinished manuscript was found at the scene of the crash that took his life and not published, posthumously, until 1994—Camus's life and work were unusually intertwined. In Scott Mc-Lemee's biographical overview, Camus was decisively shaped by his native Algeria, a North African outpost of France in which, as the French-speaking grandson of European settlers, he remained an outsider. The fact that Camus became famous with the publication of his first novel, *The Stranger*, in 1942, and remained one of Europe's leading literary celebrities had profound effects on his life and work. So, too, did his embrace and subsequent repudiation by Sartre and his coterie of Existentialists. Philip Hallie met him in the final year of his life, 1959, and, in "Camus's Hug," shares a radiant memory of his brief friendship with the famous author. A young instructor of philosophy, Hallie was spending the year in Paris when he encountered Camus at a production of his adaptation of Fyodor Dostoevski's *The Possessed*. During a subsequent private conversation, Camus impressed Hallie with his honesty and clarity as well as his abhorrence of cruelty and abstraction. Hallie locates those same qualities in the works by Camus that he admires. Although Camus's drama—adaptations such as *The Possessed* as well as original plays such as *The Misunderstanding*—has received much less attention than his fiction and essays, he consistently saw himself as primarily a man of the theater—an actor, director, and playwright working in and for a community of shared values. In "Caligula: Camus's Anti-Shaman," Patricia Hopkins examines the author's most important dramatic creation, Caligula, as a demonic parody of the spiritual guide and healer.

Camus is probably best known as the author of a novel in which a European Algerian named Meursault gratuitously murders an Arab on the beach. Setting his fiction again and again in North Africa, he wrote about what he knew best, the *colon* community, descendants of settlers from Europe, and either ignored the indigenous Arabs, Berbers, and Muslims or else tended to render them as nameless, shadowy presences. Inspired by postcolonial theory and resentment, many commentators have faulted Camus for his Eurocentrism and, by denying native Algerians subjectivity and agency, for failing to recognize the full human reality of his non-European characters. However, in "Silence Follows: Albert Camus in Algeria," Robert Zaretsky portrays the author as stymied into silence by the dilemma of having to choose between France and Algeria when he in fact wished to reconcile the two. He recounts Camus's attempt to mediate a truce between the Algerian rebels and the French authorities and emphasizes his continuing distress over its failure.

Reacting against dismissals of Camus as an assimilationist and an apologist for French colonial rule, Christine Margerrison offers an informed and nuanced analysis of his Algerian identity and his acquaintance with the North African communities outside the one into which he was born. In "Algeria's Others," she examines the complexities of Camus's relationships with other kinds of Algerians and traces his developing pessimism about the possibility of creating a secular, tolerant, pluralistic society in his native land. Furthermore, John Randolph LeBlanc and Carolyn M. Jones seek to extract Camus from the binary logic of the conflict between France and Algeria by arguing that, far from embodying and promulgating a colonial mentality, his second published novel actually anticipates postcolonial critiques of French control of Africa. In "Space/Place and Home: Prefiguring Contemporary Political and Religious Discourse in Albert Camus's *The Plague*," LeBlanc and Jones claim that Camus was seeking an alternative to conflict models of discourse. In the intersection of religion, art, and politics that they find in *The Plague*, they see Camus developing a way of thinking about narrative as a model for being at home in a community with others.

After his falling out with Sartre, Camus came to reject the fashionable label "Existentialist" that was often imposed on him, but a vision of an absurd universe nevertheless informs much of his work, fiction and nonfiction. In "Albert Camus and the Metaphor of Absurdity," Brent C. Sleasman uses a belief that the universe exasperates attempts at rational explanation to situate Camus in his historical moment and to interpret stages of his life. Through an analysis of absurdity, he finds affinities between Camus's writing and the works of Blaise Pascal, Søren Kierkegaard, Fyodor Dostoevski, Friedrich Nietzsche, and Franz Kafka. While Sleasman's approach is largely historical and rhetorical, Avi Sagi examines the absurd as a philosophical question, one that is ontological before it is ethical. Defining the absurd as "a yearning for the absolute and a longing for transcendent unity on the hand, and an awareness of the limitations and finality of human ability on the other," Sagi concentrates on *The Myth of Sisyphus*, Camus's most extended and explicit discussion of absurdity. Arguing that for Camus affirming the absurd is a movement toward clarity, he reads the book itself as "the actualization of a process of self-knowledge."

One path toward understanding an author is through examining his or her kinship to other authors. Entire books have been devoted to the Camus-Sartre connection, and much has been written about Camus's literary and philosophical lineage. The influences of Gustave Flaubert, Fyodor Dostoevski, Franz Kafka, and Ernest Hemingway, among others, are often invoked in discussions of his fiction. However, Henry L. Carrigan, Jr., is the first to offer a detailed comparison between Camus and the German writer W. G. Sebald, whose life, like Camus's, ended in a highway accident. Sebald was born in 1944, after Camus had already become famous, and his work was never as politically engaged as Camus's was. Yet, in "Camus and W. G. Sebald: The Search for Home," Carrigan observes that exile shaped the careers of both men and that the theme of home is central to the fiction created by each. By contrast, Yoshinobu Hakutani is not the first to draw comparisons between Camus and Richard Wright, the African American novelist who lived in Paris and in fact knew the French writer. However, in "Richard Wright's *The Outsider* and Albert Camus's *The Stranger*," Hakutani argues that although Wright's 1953 novel focuses on a homicidal rebel, Cross Damon, with a superficial resemblance to Camus's Meursault, the motives for rebellion differ significantly for each. Although both novels constitute eloquent social criticism, it would be a mistake, he contends, to read *The Outsider*, rooted in specifically African American experience, as merely a pallid imitation of Camus's 1942 novel. Through his analysis of the themes of chance, determinism, crime, and guilt, Hakutani offers insights into how the two novels are both similar and distinct.

The Stranger has drawn more attention than any other Camus work, and when *A Happy Death*—the novel that he abandoned in the 1930s and that was not published, as a fragment, until 1971—is discussed at all, it usually is as an earlier version of *The Stranger*. Its protagonist, Patrice Mersault, a French Algerian clerk who kills a man, is clearly a precursor to the later novel's alienated murderer Meursault. However, while noting parallels to works by Fyodor Dostoevski, André Gide, and André Malraux with similar themes of gratuitous homicide, George Strauss reads *A Happy Death* on its own terms, without reference to *The Stranger*. In "A Reading of Camus's *La Mort Heureuse*," he contends that the central issue in Camus's early novel is happiness, how to realize the good life. For Strauss, the work demonstrates that freedom from an absurd universe can be attained through a "willingness to give and receive death without flinching."

A translator into English of the aptly named "L'Hôte" is forced to choose between "The Guest" and "The Host," thereby expunging the title's ambiguity. Published in *Exile and the Kingdom* (1957) as the Algerian War was flaring, this most widely anthologized of Camus's short stories gave its author another opportunity to work out his ambivalence toward Algerian and French identities. In "A Story of Cain: Another Look at 'L'Hôte,'" Elwyn F. Sterling notes that Camus early on considered "Cain" as a title for the story. He analyzes the published work, in which a schoolteacher named Daru is asked to deliver an Arab accused of murder to the authorities, in terms of the Biblical story of Cain. Although the Arab is an obvious parallel to Cain, the killer of his brother Abel, Sterling argues that, after evading responsibility for bringing the man to justice, refusing to be his brother's keeper, Daru, too, bears the guilt of Cain.

The three essays that conclude this volume each deal with the final novel that Camus lived to finish, *The Fall* (1956). Among them, they exhibit some of the range of interests that have been brought to bear on his oeuvre. In "Camus's *The Fall*: The Dynamics of Narrative Unreliability," Amit Marcus applies reader-response theory to what is most distinctive about *The Fall*, its innovative interlocutory structure, in which a cunning narrator who calls himself Jean-Baptiste Clamence tells his humiliating personal story to a stranger, the book's narratee. Marcus argues that, in establishing a dynamic among narrator, narratee, and reader, Camus undercuts the reader's superiority to the unreliable narrator, in effect creating an unreliable reader. Robert C. Solomon complements Marcus's rhetorical analysis of *The Fall* with a philosophical examination of how Camus conceptualizes self, pride, and happiness within his novel. In "Pathologies of Pride in Camus's *The Fall*," he argues that, despite its title, the novel draws on the Christian sin of pride only as a tease, that Aristotle and Friedrich Nietzsche are more helpful in understanding how the work seduces readers into judging themselves and condemning resentful pride. Finally, in "The Popular-Ritual Structural Pattern of Albert Camus's *La Chute*," Evelyn H. Zepp counters the usual reading of Camus as a classicist committed to balance and resolution, analyzing his novel instead as an embodiment of the grotesque. Drawing on Mikhail Bakhtin's theory of carnival, Zepp sees in the polarities created within the narrator Clamence and between him and his interlocutor a simultaneous awarenesss of and dissolution of dualities. The ritual of crowning and discrowning that she sees enacted in *The Fall* creates a cycle that remains as incomplete as any attempt to sum up Camus.

CAREER, LIFE, AND INFLUENCE

On Albert Camus

Camus died today. Or perhaps it was yesterday. In fact, it was on January 4, 1960, but for many readers throughout the world, even those born later, the pain of his sudden, violent end remains raw. Of all the Nobel laureates in literature, Camus spent the briefest amount of time among us. It was an automobile accident, the very prototype of the absurd death that he envisaged as the common fate of all, that cut short Camus's productive life at forty-six. He had been planning to travel back to Paris from the house he had purchased in 1958 in Lourmarin in southeastern France and had in fact already purchased a train ticket. However, his friend and publisher Michel Gallimard persuaded Camus instead to accompany him in Gallimard's sporty new Facel Vega HK500. They had already driven more than 500 kilometers when Gallimard lost control of the car and crashed into a plane tree by the side of a road in Burgundy. Camus's body was returned for burial in Provence, in Lourmarin.

Almost fifty years later, in November 2009, Nicolas Sarkozy proposed completing Camus's journey to the French capital. The president of France recommended that the author's remains be reinterred in Paris, in the Panthéon—to lie beside such other luminaries as Voltaire, Jean-Jacques Rousseau, Victor Hugo, Louis Pasteur, Emile Zola, and Marie Curie. Camus had again become as controversial as he was during the final decade of his life. Many approved of the idea, convinced that Camus had earned a final resting place within the company of the most illustrious thinkers in the history of France. But others contested the move, arguing either that Camus was unworthy of such veneration or else that Sarkozy did not deserve support, that his proposal was a cynical ploy by an unpopular politician to bask in the reflected glory of a great but candid author who, if alive, would have scorned the grandiose gesture. Camus's son, Jean, opposed moving his father's body, and it remains in Lourmarin. As in life, when he was torn between France and Algeria,

Camus in death lies at the margins of two cultures—at the southern edge of Europe and across the Mediterranean from his native North Africa.

As the descendant of European settlers, Camus was never entirely at ease in an Algeria yearning for sovereignty under an independent Arab identity. He was a man who could never go home again, not only because, as a *pied-noir*, the offspring of colonists, he was a stranger in his native land but also because, a ragged interloper among the literary sophisticates of Paris, Camus the provincial always felt himself to be what the British translator of his first published novel chose as its title, *The Outsider*. The only community in which he could claim membership, through the power of his writing, was the borderless realm of Francophonie. "Yes, I have a native land," he declared: "the French language" (Camus, *Notebooks 1935-1951*, 264). Camus was the perfect embodiment of what Edward Said, who spent most of his life in exile from Palestine, called "the intellectual as outsider"—a thinker who "is best exemplified by the condition of exile, the state of never being fully adjusted, always feeling outside the chatty, familiar world inhabited by natives, so to speak, tending to avoid and even dislike the trappings of accommodation and well-being. Exile for the intellectual in this metaphysical sense is restlessness, movement, constantly being unsettled, and unsettling others. You cannot go back to some earlier and perhaps more stable condition of being at home, and, alas, you can never fully arrive, be at one with your new home or situation" (Said 53). The Netherlands (*The Fall*), Czechoslovakia (*The Misunderstanding*), Russia (*The Just Assassins*), Brazil ("The Growing Stone"), Spain (*State of Siege*), and Rome (*Caligula*) are the settings for some of Camus's fictions, but with the possible exception of the story "The Artist at Work," which appears to be set in Paris, everything else takes place in North Africa. Stranded in France after the outbreak of World War II, Camus spent most of his life exiled in a country that, on the evidence of his novels, short stories, and plays, his imagination was never fully invested in. His beloved mother remained in Algiers. The last great project of Camus's life, *The First Man*—like *The Stranger*, *The*

Plague, "The Adulterous Woman," "The Renegade," "The Silent Men," "The Guest," the lyrical essays, and *A Happy Death*—testifies to how much Algeria remained imprinted in his art.

For most of his career, Camus was gifted and plagued by intimations of mortality. At seventeen, he experienced the first symptoms of tuberculosis; throughout the rest of his life, recurring attacks of the deadly disease—for which, at the time, there was no effective treatment or cure—served to remind him that, as his character Tarrou observes in *The Plague*, we all are under sentence of death, that "each of us has the plague within him; no one, no one on Earth is free of it" (Camus, *The Plague* 253). In *The Stranger*, Meursault states that: "Since we're all going to die, it's obvious that when and how don't matter" (Camus, *The Stranger* 114). But when and how we live mattered very much to Camus, despite and because of life's brevity. In a sense, all of his work constituted an extended meditation on how to achieve what, in the title of his first, unpublished novel, he called *A Happy Death*. After his break with Jean-Paul Sartre in 1951, Camus rejected the label "existentialist," but his novels, stories, plays, and essays almost always confront the fundamental truth of individual existence: That it is transitory and devoid of any inherent meaning except what we endow it with. Applying a kind of Cartesian reduction to the contemplation of his own ontology, Camus posits absurdity as the starting point for all philosophical reflection: "I judge the notion of the absurd to be essential and consider that it can stand as the first of my truths. . . . For me the sole datum is the absurd" (Camus, *The Myth of Sisyphus* 23). Seizing upon the Greek myth of Sisyphus as an allegory of the human condition, a futile and pointless attempt to push a boulder up the side of a steep mountain, he nevertheless found solace in the impossible struggle itself and in the awareness of its absurdity: "But Sisyphus teaches the higher fidelity that negates the gods and raises rocks. He too concludes that all is well. This universe henceforth without a master seems to him neither sterile nor futile. Each atom of that stone, each mineral flake of that night filled mountain, in itself forms a world. The struggle itself toward the heights is enough to fill a man's heart. One must imagine Sisyphus happy" (Camus, *The Myth of Sisyphus* 91).

Camus himself was not a happy man in 1957, when he became the seventh Frenchman and the second youngest author (after Rudyard Kipling) to be honored with the Nobel Prize in Literature, for, according to the official citation, "his important literary production, which with clear-sighted earnestness illuminates the problems of the human conscience in our times" ("Nobel"). "Nobel," Camus confided to his journal on October 17, 1958. "Strange feeling of overwhelming pressure and melancholy" (Camus, *Notebooks* 197). Still smarting from the public lashing he had received over his 1951 foray into political philosophy, *The Rebel*, he felt betrayed not only by Francis Jeanson, who excoriated the book in a review for *Les Temps modernes*, but also by Sartre, the magazine's editor and his erstwhile friend, as well as by the entire French intellectual establishment that had exalted and now seemed to be vilifying him. "Trois ans pour faire un livre," he complained, "cinq lignes pour le ridiculiser" (Three years to write a book, five lines to ridicule it, Camus *Carnets II* 27).

Camus had become famous with the publication of his first novel, *The Stranger*, in 1942, and during the following decade fame grew into adulation. Inspired by his writings and the stoic heroism of a man who spoke truth to power, whether imposed by Germany or home-grown, admirers made pilgrimages to the Café de Flore and the Café des Deux Magots on Paris's Left Bank to catch a glimpse of the handsome literary celebrity. His appeal derived not only from his books and plays but also from the moral example of daring to edit an underground newspaper, *Combat*, in defiance of the Nazi occupation and of continuing to speak out against injustices perpetrated after the Liberation. In his journal, Camus defined his role in terms that are at once modest and extravagant: "My job is to make my books and to fight when the freedom of my own and my people is threatened. That's all" (Camus, *Notebooks* 205). For a man on such a mission, it was difficult to adjust from being lionized to being loathed.

During the 1950s, Camus was particularly distraught over the worsening crisis in his Algerian homeland, where a violent liberation movement clashed with the intransigent French administration. Sympathetic both to Algerian aspirations and French cultural hegemony, he attempted to mediate a peaceful solution to an anticolonial insurrection. However, he was rebuffed and ridiculed, scorned by all factions as feckless and out of touch. When a society is polarized, strident shouts tend to drown out the voices of moderation. Camus struggled to find what he called "a third way" between France and Algeria and between the opposing camps of the United States and the U.S.S.R. Uncomfortable with the Manicheanism of the Cold War, Camus, who identified with the left, spoke out against both Soviet oppression and American imperialism, earning him the hostility of erstwhile allies on the left (in Moscow, the magazine *Novy mir* called him a "propagandist of decadent individualism," (Hawes 138)), and the continuing mistrust of the right. The chorus of derision reached a crescendo when the Swedish Academy announced its decision to honor Camus with the world's most prestigious literary prize. Critics insisted that he was too young, that others were more deserving, that his work was already hopelessly passé. But by the time of his death, Camus, once the most prominent intellectual in Europe, was being patronized as a quaint relic of dark times now best laid to rest.

The bitterness of Camus's final years is apparent in the misanthropic harangue delivered by Jean-Baptiste Clamence, the narrator of *The Fall*, who declares that: "A single sentence will suffice for modern man: he fornicated and read the papers" (6-7). And it is there in the ravings of the deranged missionary who, narrating the short story "The Renegade," concludes that "only evil is present, down with Europe, reason, honor, and the cross" (Camus, *Exile and the Kingdom* 54). In his own voice, Camus confided to his diary on January 18, 1956, that "anything is better than this France of resignation and brutality, this swamp where I suffocate" (Camus, *Notebooks* 167). However, he also prided himself on his resiliency, his ability to marshal inner resources to overcome despair: "In the depths of winter," Camus proclaimed, "I finally learned that within me there lay an invincible summer" (Camus, *Lyrical and Critical Essays* 169). Like Dr. Bernard Rieux, the narrator of *The Plague*, he was able to conclude that "there are more things to admire in men than to despise" (Camus, *The Plague* 308). As early as 1954, he had begun working on an ambitious project that would lead him in a dramatically new direction. Propelled from the car that crashed in Lourmarin was a briefcase containing Camus's notebooks and French translations of Friedrich Nietzsche's *The Gay Science* and William Shakespeare's *Othello*, as well as 144 pages of an uncompleted autobiographical epic. Camus's heirs jealously shielded the manuscript from the eyes of editors and scholars. But when they finally published *Le Premier Homme* (*The First Man*, 1997) in 1996, the extensive fragments hinted at a more expansive and introspective direction in his work.

During the 1980s and 1990s, the ascendancy of Les Nouveaux Philosophes (the New Philosophers), a loose constellation of thinkers that included André Glucksmann, Alain Finkelkraut, and Bernard-Henri Lévy, helped rehabilitate Camus's tarnished reputation. Shocked by Aleksandr Solzhenitsyn's revelations about the horrors of the gulag, they repudiated their own Marxist roots and rejected authoritarian systems and philosophies. In the ancient quarrel between Sartre and Camus, they sided with Camus, who had dared speak out against Stalinist atrocities at a time when any criticism of the Soviet Union was considered a betrayal of the left, aid and comfort to the forces of reaction. By 1999, when the French newspaper *Le Monde* and the retail chain Fnac polled readers on which books had left the most indelible imprints on their memory, the consensus first choice was Camus's *The Stranger*, just ahead of fiction by Proust and Kafka ("Les Cent Livres"). Earlier in Britain, male readers of the *Manchester Guardian* had named *The Stranger* as the book that most changed their lives. And though Camus's body was never transferred to the Panthéon, his literary corpus was canonized in 2006 by publication in a prestigious, definitive Pléiade edition. In that same year, Camus's alma mater, the University of Algiers, hosted an international conference on his impact on Algerian literature. In places as far-flung as Japan, Israel, and Argentina, Camus was read widely and avidly. In Britain, the rock group the Cure scored a hit with their debut single, "Killing an Arab," a musical variation on the plot of Camus's first novel. Like such classics as *The Odyssey*, *The Divine Comedy*, and *Don Quixote*, which are continually being retranslated, *The Stranger* has so far been rendered into English three times—by Stuart Gilbert (1946), Joseph Laredo (1982), and Matthew Ward (1988). It has been translated into forty-five languages, *The Plague* into twenty-eight, while other Camus works have been translated dozens of times each, assuring the author millions of readers around the world.

"Those who write obscurely have great luck; they will have commentators," Camus, a paragon of lucidity, wrote; "The others will have only readers, and this, it seems, is worthy of scorn" (Camus, *Notebooks 1935-1951* 251). Like Joseph Grand, the clerk in *The Plague* who strives to write one perfect sentence, Camus left nothing to luck and scorned misguided scorn for clarity. Despite his stubborn dedication to writing limpid, candid prose, transparent texts that, at least for his early work, the influential critic Roland Barthes hailed as "white writing," "the zero degree of writing," "a style of absence that is almost an ideal absence of style" (Barthes, 77), Camus has attracted both readers and commentators in abundance. Only a snob or a boor would begrudge his ability to appeal to both.

As soon as they were published, Camus's works regularly showed up on bestseller lists, and today, when book store offerings barely possess the shelf life of yogurt and books in general seem to many quaint relics of a technologically primitive age, they remain in print and relevant to readers in the twenty-first century. At least one story, "The Guest," survives in almost every anthology of short fiction. Posthumous publication of unfinished fiction and collections of essays continues to ensure that Camus remains prolific and popular.

However, Camus has inspired not just readers but commentators as well. A recent check of the Modern Language Association Bibliography revealed 2,673 entries—articles, dissertations, monographs—on Albert Camus. He has been the subject of three full-scale biographies—by Herbert R. Lottman (1979), Patrick McCarthy (1982), and Olivier Todd (2000)—as well as many more memoirs and assorted biographical studies, and his works have been analyzed by formalists, feminists, Marxists, structuralists, postcolonialists, and critics of every other theoretical persuasion. Camus has drawn the professional attention not only of scholars of literature and of Francophone culture but also of philosophers, theologians, political scientists, and historians. Medical ethicists have seized on *The Plague* as a key text for examining the responsibilities of physicians. In addition, Camus has inspired the founding of organizations devoted to the study of his work. Based in France, La Société des Etudes Camusiennes has branches in Japan and the United States. The Albert Camus Society, which publishes the *Journal of the Albert Camus Society*, is active in both the United Kingdom and the United States. At the same time that it continues to be read by nonspecialists, the Camus oeuvre—particularly the three novels completed and published within his lifetime, *The Stranger* (1942), *The Plague* (1947), and *The Fall* (1956)—is widely studied in high schools, colleges, seminaries, and medical schools. It is the cultural heritage of scholars as well as general readers.

"All our troubles," Tarrou observes in *The Plague*, "spring from our failure to use plain, clear-cut language" (Camus, *The Plague* 254). Some of the appeal of the Camus novels derives from their author's fastidious concern with clarity. There are several Camus styles—the affectless text of *The Stranger*, the rhapsodic evocations of the lyrical essays, the barbed rhetoric of *The Fall*, the impassioned logic of Camus the polemicist. But it is his talent for terse epigrammatic formulations that earned him a generous space in anthologies of quotations. "You know what charm is," says Jean-Baptiste Clamence in a quip that itself exerts a chilling charm: "a way of getting the answer yes without having asked any clear question" (Camus, *The Fall* 56-57). Also distinctive about the completed Camus novels is their canny narrative constructions, different in each of the three books. *The Stranger* comes to us in the voice of a pathologically disconnected narrator, almost simultaneous with the events he recounts. *The Plague* is told in retrospect and in third person by a narrator who conceals his identity until the final pages. And with *The Fall*, Camus creates a second-person narrative, a cunning story told by Jean-Baptiste Clamence to a stranger who wanders into a bar in Amsterdam named Mexico City. For his 2007 novel *The Reluctant Fundamentalist*, Mohsin Hamid adapted Camus's format so that it becomes an enigmatic Pakistani who tells his story to a stranger who wanders into the marketplace in Lahore.

While his status has fluctuated in France, Camusophilia quickly assumed and maintained epidemic proportions in the United States. "Kafka arouses pity and terror, Joyce admiration, Proust and Gide respect, but no modern writer that I can think of except Camus, has aroused love," wrote Susan Sontag in 1966, when Camus's reputation had dimmed in France but still blazed brilliantly across the Atlantic (Sontag 11). Novelist William Styron stated: "Camus was a great cleanser of my intellect, ridding me of countless sluggish ideas and, through some of the most unsettling pessimism I had ever encountered, causing me to be aroused anew by life's enigmatic promise" (Styron 21-22). Particularly for Americans who came of age during the decades following World War II, Camus was an icon of integrity. Like *The Catcher in the Rye* (1951), *Catch-22* (1961), and *One Flew Over the Cuckoo's Nest* (1962), the Camus novels appealed to young Americans for their rejection of cant, their defiance of the "phony" world that drove Holden Caulfield, Yossarian, and Chief Bromden crazy. "The truth. The truth!" is Camus's solitary diary entry for July 23, 1957 (Camus, *Notebooks 1951-1959* 188). Truth and freedom were rallying points for a generation coming of age in America in opposition to the repressions and evasions of its elders, and in the Nobel banquet speech that he delivered in Stockholm on December 10, 1957, he identified "the two tasks that constitute the greatness of his craft: the service of truth and the service of liberty" (Camus, "Banquet"). Like *Lord of the Flies* (1954), Camus's fiction, in its somber vision of human possibility, offered a counterweight to a prosperous society's dominant creed of smug cheer. Camus, who adapted William Faulkner's *Requiem for a Nun* to the stage, acknowledged his debt to Ernest Hemingway, James M. Cain, and other American authors of frank and frugal prose, which in a sense means that, in the spare and unsparing sentences of *The Stranger*, *The Plague*, and *The Fall*, American readers were receiving American fiction recycled back through France.

Encouraged by the prospect that Camus's austere sentences would be accessible long before the ornate texts of Proust or Balzac, American students even took up French. The fact that readers in the United States have felt a special affinity with Camus led the French author Serge Doubrovsky to observe that he "is a great American writer even more than a French one, inasmuch as the public makes the writer" (Doubrovsky 16). That public included Randy Shilts, who modeled his history of the deadly spread of human immunodeficiency virus (HIV), *And the Band Played On: Politics, People, and the AIDS Epidemic* (1987), after *The Plague* and even appropriated epigraphs for four of his book's nine sections from Camus's novel, as well as Brad Pitt, who tattooed "Life is Absurd" on his left forearm. It also included Paul Goodman, whose *Growing Up Absurd* (1960), a manifesto for resistance to an inauthentic adult society that was a vade mecum for the American youth culture of the 1960s, appropriated terms and themes from Camus. According to journalist Jack Newfield, a close friend of Robert F. Kennedy, the senator always traveled with a copy of Camus's writing: "He discovered Camus when he was thirty-eight, in the months of solitude and grief after his brother's death. By 1968, he had read, and reread, all of Camus's essays, dramas, and novels. But he more than just read Camus. He memorized him, meditated about him, quoted him, and was changed by him" (Newfield, 58-59). A very different American politician stepped forward as a Camus aficionado when, in August 2006, countering his image as an intellectual lightweight, George W. Bush reported that he had taken up *The Stranger* as summer reading at his Crawford ranch. The claim led some to question the appropriateness of waging war against an Arab country while reading about a man who murders an Arab on the beach.

A man of many arts, Camus was a journalist, editor, actor, director, playwright, novelist, short story writer, essayist, and philosopher. His fiction and essays seem most likely to last. However, from the 1930s in Algeria through the 1950s in France, Camus was deeply committed to theater, the most communal of the literary arts. *Caligula* (1944) is his most frequently produced play, in France and abroad, but neither it nor *The Misunderstanding* (1943), *The State of Siege* (1948), *The Just Assassins* (1949), nor his adaptation from Dostoevski or from Faulkner has found as secure a place in the world's theatrical repertoire as such other contemporary French dramas as Jean-Paul Sartre's *No Exit* (1944), Eugene Ionesco's *The Bald Soprano* (1950), and Samuel Beckett's *Waiting for Godot* (1953) have. Outside France at least, Camus as a playwright is more likely to be encountered in a book than on the stage. Camus was banned in Haiti under the dictatorship of Papa Doc Duvalier, but at the outset of her reflections on the artist in exile, *Create Dangerously: The Immigrant Artist at Work* (2010), Edwidge Danticat recounts attempts by young Haitian dissidents to perform *Caligula* clandestinely in a Creole translation. She explains (Danticat 6) that she chose the title of her book from an exhortation that Camus delivered during a lecture at the University of Uppsala in December 1957 and that was later published posthumously in the volume *Resistance, Rebellion, and Death: Essays* (1960). "Create dangerously," insisted Camus, the former editor of *Combat*, who believed that art worthy of the effort must always in some way put the artist at risk.

Camus lived in perilous, violent times, but the dangers did not vanish with the independence of Algeria two years after his death, in 1962. In his Nobel Prize banquet speech, Camus, brooding over concentration camps and atomic bombs, conceded that the writer cannot reform the world, only at best keep it from destroying itself. It is as if the writer—like Sisyphus, condemned to push a boulder toward a peak it will forever fall short of reaching—is tasked with again and again pulling humanity back from the brink of self-annihilation. For the writer, burdened with an awesome responsibility, it is not enough simply to fulfill Joseph Grand's ambition in *The Plague* to craft a perfect sentence.

It is a measure of Camus's enduring authority that one is tempted to speculate on what, if he had survived the drive from Lourmarin to Paris, he might have had to say about the Cuban missile crisis, the Vietnam War, the Prague Spring, the 1968 Paris uprising, the Cultural Revolution, and the fall of the Berlin Wall. If he had lived into his late eighties, Camus, disturbed anew by the same urge to polarize that he had resisted during the Cold War, surely would have commented on "the clash of civilizations" between Islam and the secular West. The author of *The Just Assassins* —a play that questions whether noble ends can justify brutal means, whether the sacrifice of innocent children is acceptable "collateral damage" in pursuit of a greater good— and of *The Plague*—in which Dr. Bernard Rieux proclaims: "until my dying day I shall refuse to love a scheme of things in which children are put to torture" (Camus, *The Plague* 218)—would have had much to say about the spread of terrorism and the violent reactions to it. The creator of Jean-Baptiste Clamence, the scourge of urbane hypocrisy, might have commented on the ease with which civilized nations abandon their principles in order to torture and exterminate strangers.

One of the causes that Camus felt most passionate about was the campaign to abolish capital punishment, and he certainly would have rejoiced at France's decision in 1981 to end all executions and at the policy later adopted by the European Union of denying membership to any nation that still imposes the death penalty. Following the Liberation, when France embarked on a binge of reprisals against collaborators with the Nazi occupation, Camus argued strenuously to spare the lives even of heinous traitors. "In such a world of conflict, a world of victims and executioners," he would later write, "it is the job of think-ing people not to be on the side of the executioners" (Camus, *Resis-tance, Rebellion, and Death* 147). On several occasions, he recalled the family memory of how his father, who died when he was still an in-fant, returned home traumatized from witnessing a convicted man put to death. Meursault's impending encounter with the guillotine con-cludes *The Stranger*, and in *The Plague*, Jean Tarrou, who ran away from home over his lawyer father's complicity in the machinery of sentencing defendants to death, wanders the world crusading against institutionalized murder. "This, and only this," he explains, "can bring relief to men and, if not save them, at least do them the least harm pos-sible and even, sometimes, a little good. So that is why I resolved to have no truck with anything which, directly or indirectly, for good rea-sons or for bad, brings death to anyone or justifies others' putting him to death" (Camus, *The Plague* 252-53). As "judge-penitent," Jean-Baptiste Clamence reminds us that no one is innocent, hence that no one is entitled to condemn anyone else. In his 1957 essay "Reflections on the Guillotine," Camus argues that: "Capital punishment is the most premeditated of murders, to which no criminal's deed, however calcu-lated, can be compared. For there to be an equivalency, the death pen-alty would have to punish a criminal who had warned his victim of the date on which he would inflict a horrible death on him and who, from that moment onward, had confined him at his mercy for months. Such a monster is not to be encountered in private life" (Camus, *Resis-tance* 199).

Camus wrestled with many monsters, including abject poverty, re-current illness, war, and fame, during his relatively brief life. Heir to the rich French tradition of *philosophes*, men (before Camus's time, there were few such women) of letters who enlisted their pens in the service not of pleasure or art but truth, he began a review of Jean-Paul Sartre's *Nausea* (1938) by declaring that: "A novel is never anything but a philosophy expressed in images" (Camus, *Lyrical and Critical Essays*, 199). He devoted his art to addressing fundamental questions of identity and responsibility. A freelance thinker not tied to any academic institution, he wrote for general readers and to advance the common good. Camus would today be called a "public intellectual," though the preferred term in his time was *engagé*; he was commited to the struggle for social progress. Given his working-class origins and his discomfort with the Parisian intelligentsia, he might also have been what Italian philosopher Antonio Gramsci called an "organic intellectual," a thinker and activist rooted in the proletariat. Like Michel de Montaigne, Voltaire, Victor Hugo, and Emile Zola, Camus dared to speak out against injustice. Like such committed contemporaries as Hannah Arendt, Arthur Koestler, George Orwell, and Ignacio Silone, he wrote to keep a roiled world from destroying itself. His work at *Combat* made important contributions to the French Resistance during World War II, and he later spoke out frequently on behalf of human rights, opposing the harsh Soviet response to a workers' strike in Berlin in 1953 and to the Hungarian Revolution of 1956. He protested the decision to admit Spain as a member of the United Nations, despite the continuing abuses of Francisco Franco's right-wing regime, by terminating his service to UNESCO. Active in the movement toward federation that eventually, after his death, led to the creation of the European Union, he founded the Comité Français pour la Féderation Européene (CFFE), the French Committee for European Federation. And he of course attempted to intervene to resolve the conflict over Algeria.

In *The Myth of Sisyphus*, Camus declares that "the absurd joy par excellence is creation" (Camus, *Myth of Sisyphus* 69). And, though the statement is unaccountably omitted from the book's English translation, he adds: "Créer c'est vivre deux fois" (Camus, *Mythe de Sisyphe* 171)—To create is to live twice. Albert Camus was a man of his own troubled times but ours as well. The trenchant, limpid works he created during the forty-six years available to him before the car crash in Burgundy will lead more than one afterlife.

Works Cited

Barthes, Roland. *Writing Degree Zero and Elements of Semiology*. Trans. Annette Lavers and Colin Smith. Boston: Beacon, 1970.

Camus, Albert. "Banquet Speech." Nobelprize.org. http://nobelprize.org/nobel _prizes/literature/laureates/1957/camus-speech-e.html.

_____. *Carnets II: Janvier 1942-mars 1951*. Paris: Gallimard, 1964.

_____. *Exile and the Kingdom*. Trans. Justin O'Brien. New York: Vintage, 1958.

_____. *The Fall*. Trans. Justin O'Brien. New York: Vintage, 1956.

_____. *Lyrical and Critical Essays*. Ed. Philip Thody. Trans. Ellen Conroy Kennedy. New York: Vintage, 1970.

_____. *The Myth of Sisyphus and Other Essays*. Justin O'Brien, trans. New York: Vintage, 1955.

_____. *Le Mythe de Sisyphe*. Paris: Gallimard, 1942.

_____. *Notebooks 1935-1951*. Trans. Philip Thody. New York: Marlowe & Co., 1998.

_____. *Notebooks 1951-1959*. Trans. Ryan Bloom. Chicago: Ivan R. Dee, 2008.

_____. *The Plague*. Trans. Stuart Gilbert. New York: Vintage International, 1991.

_____. *Resistance, Rebellion, and Death: Essays*. Trans. Justin O'Brien. New York: Vintage International, 1995.

_____. *The Stranger*. Trans. Matthew Ward. New York: Vintage International, 1989.

Danticat, Edwidge. *Create Dangerously: The Immigrant Artist at Work*. Princeton, NJ: Princeton UP, 2010.

Doubrovsky, Serge. "Camus in America." Germaine Brée, ed. *Camus: A Collection of Critical Essays*. Englewood Cliffs, NJ: Prentice-Hall, 1962.

Hawes, Elizabeth. *Camus, a Romance*. New York: Grove, 2009.

Newfield, Jack. *Robert Kennedy: A Memoir*. New York: E. P. Dutton, 1969.

"The Nobel Prize in Literature 1957." Nobelprize.org. http://nobelprize.org/nobel _prizes/literature/laureates/1957.

Said, Edward. *Representations of the Intellectual: The 1999 Reith Lectures*. New York: Vintage, 1996.

Sontag, Susan. *Against Interpretation*. New York: Farrar, Straus and Giroux, 1966.

Styron, William. *Darkness Visible: A Memoir of Madness*. New York: Random House, 1990.

Biography of Albert Camus_____

Scott McLemee

Albert Camus wrote in a variety of literary forms: fiction, drama, philosophical essay, and journalistic commentary. But if a single label could sum up his role as an author, it would be *moralist*. The word in this case comes without the usual overtones it has in English— someone with a sharp, even dogmatic sense of right and wrong—but rather the French tradition of writers seeking to define human nature and the conditions for the good life. While Camus scorned the idea that an author's work is necessarily autobiographical, readers of his work are left with the sense of a strong and complex personality.

Camus was born on November 7, 1913, in Mondovi, a town in the North African country of Algeria, which had been under French control since 1830. The younger of two sons, he grew up in a family of modest means. His father, an Algerian-born Frenchman, was called into service at the start of World War I and died in battle before Albert's first birthday. The future winner of the Nobel Prize in Literature was raised by his mother, an illiterate cleaning woman for whom life was a struggle. Her memory and her stoic example would haunt Camus's writings.

Although he was raised in the Catholic Church, Camus was never pious, and the stronger influence on his moral code seems to have been the sense of sportsmanship he learned in adolescence as a swimmer and soccer player. A talented student as well as an athlete, he was encouraged by a teacher in elementary school to prepare to pursue further education—despite the expectation of family members that he get a job as soon as possible. In 1924, he received a scholarship to the Lycée Bugeaud, a selective preparatory school.

There Camus came under the influence of a philosophy teacher, Jean Grenier, who encouraged his literary and intellectual interests and became his lifelong friend. Besides giving Camus a solid grounding in the history of philosophy and recommending works of contemporary literature for him to read, Grenier was editor of a cultural journal, *Sud*, in which the young author published his first essays.

In 1930, Camus was diagnosed with tuberculosis. Although his formal studies were interrupted as he convalesced while living with his uncle, Camus continued to read and write, and to enjoy as much of a bohemian life as his health would permit. By 1933, he was able to enroll at the University of Algiers. The following year, he married Simone Hié and joined the Communist Party not long afterward. In each case it proved an unhappy alliance—with the marriage lasting one year and his party membership about three. In 1936, he received his degree in philosophy, submitting a thesis on "Neoplatonism and Christian Thought."

During this period, Camus began working in the theater—helping to form two theater groups and trying his hand at writing plays. He contributed political and literary articles to *Alger-Républicain*, a left-wing newspaper, and worked on a novel, *A Happy Death*, that appeared posthumously. In 1937, he published his first book, *The Wrong Side and the Right Side*, consisting of personal essays by turns lyrical and ironic. A second collection of similar pieces on the landscape of North Africa, *Nuptials*, appeared the following year. These volumes appeared in small editions in Algeria and were reissued only after Camus won the Nobel Prize—by which point he was somewhat embarrassed by them.

In 1939—with World War II approaching—Camus was exempted from military service because of his health. Growing censorship in Algeria made life impossible at the newspaper where Camus worked, and in 1940 he moved to France to write for the daily *Paris-Soir*. The city was occupied by the German army in June. In December of that year, he married Francine Faure—a development that seems not to have distracted him too much from a fairly strenuous romantic life with numerous other women. Following a return to Algeria in early 1941, he taught high school while revising his novel *The Stranger* and completing his philosophical essay *The Myth of Sisyphus*.

Meursault, the central character in *The Stranger*, is an affectless figure who kills an Arab during a quarrel and receives a death sentence; he faces death with as much indifference as he has life. In *Sisyphus*, Camus poses the question of whether suicide is a necessary response to the fundamental sense of life's absurdity given the collapse of transcendental certainties. The novel was published in 1942 and the book-length essay in 1943—both by Gallimard, the most prestigious literary press in France.

In 1942, Camus relocated to Paris, where he soon joined Gallimard as an editor. By 1943, he was involved in a more clandestine form of publishing work, joining the staff of the underground Resistance newspaper *Combat*, where he published under a pseudonym until the liberation from Nazi occupation in the fall of 1944. During this period he formed a friendship with the philosopher and novelist Jean-Paul Sartre, a fellow Gallimard author.

Sartre's review-essay on *The Stranger* offered a brilliant assessment of Camus's literary style and philosophical perspective. Camus would later insist on the differences between his sense of the absurd and Sartre's version of existentialism. But such nuances mattered little to the public. The authors' names were closely linked in the minds of readers, both in France and abroad—their work regarded as expressions of the bleak but courageous worldview of a generation disillusioned by war and occupation. A remarkably photogenic man (particularly given his striking profile while dressed, like Humphrey Bogart, in a trench coat), Camus became one of France's most recognizable literary figures.

His play *The Misunderstanding* was staged in Paris in 1944, just at the time he was taking over as editor-in-chief of *Combat*. His earlier historical drama *Caligula*—which Camus regarded as part of a "trilogy of the absurd" that included his novel and philosophical essay—was staged the following year. Reunited with his wife, who had remained in Algeria during the war, he became the father of twin girls in 1945.

The following year, Camus undertook a lecture tour of the United States, where there was great fascination with existentialism in literary circles. An English translation of his debut novel was published in 1946. When *The Plague* appeared in France in 1947, it was promptly translated. A thinly veiled allegory of life in France under the occupation, it was—like his play *The State of Siege*, published in 1948—an effort to depict heroism and solidarity in the face of contemporary political horrors.

The political essays Camus published in the immediate postwar period gave voice to a radicalism that, while often expressed in socialist terms, reflected a pronounced strain of anarchism. *The Just Assassins*, his play about Russian revolutionaries in 1905, was performed in 1949 and expressed his preoccupation with questions about political violence and moral responsibility.

Reflection on these problems would lead Camus to undertake a study of the historical and philosophical sources of totalitarianism. But first he had to endure another wave of tuberculosis attacks, making the final decade of his life difficult and at times depressing. *The Rebel*, published in 1951, reflected deep revulsion at how revolutionary theories had been used to justify mass murder. Its publication at the height of the Cold War showed just how profound were the differences between Camus and Sartre, who, while critical of Soviet dogmatism, considered it necessary to support the French Communist Party.

In spite of this tension, a degree of mutual affection remained between them—at least until 1952, when Sartre's magazine *Les Temps modernes* (Modern Times) published a devastating review of *The Rebel* by a young philosopher named Francis Jeanson. Camus wrote a bitter open letter addressed to Sartre, the editor-in-chief, whom he held responsible for the attack on his book. Sartre responded in kind. This controversy drew international attention and marked a turning point for both authors—with Sartre becoming ever more committed to revolutionary politics, while Camus moved towards a kind of pacifism marked by absolute opposition to the death penalty.

Despite great personal misery in the wake of the conflict with Sartre—as well as the strain of his chronic ill health and the distractions of a complicated love-life—Camus wrote a number of short stories in the mid-1950s. He also adapted works by other authors for the stage. In 1954 he published *Summer*, a volume of essays. His third novel, *The Fall*—a wry, perplexing monologue by a guilt-riddled narrator—appeared in 1956 (Interpreters have found in it echoes of the debate with Sartre). He spoke out in support of the Hungarian revolutionaries whose uprising was crushed by Soviet troops in 1956. A collection of his short fiction, *Exile and the Kingdom*, appeared in 1957. That same year, he collaborated with Arthur Koestler on a book denouncing capital punishment.

In October 1957, at the age of forty-four, Camus was named winner of the Nobel Prize in Literature. If he felt pleasure at this, he seems to have been averse to expressing it—insisting that it should have gone to the novelist André Malraux instead. There was more to this than modesty, for Camus was suffering from bouts of writer's block, and the honor aroused the animosity of much of the French literary community.

Another complicating factor was the situation in Algeria, where a nationalist guerrilla movement had been fighting for self-determination for the country's Arab majority. As a young man, Camus had supported independence from France. Indeed, his break with the Communist Party in the 1930s had been, in part, a matter of frustration with its lack of vigor in pursuing national liberation. But he also was, by background, a *pied-noir*—that is, a descendant of Europeans who had settled in Algeria in the nineteenth century and who regarded the country as their home.

Trying to assume a nuanced position between the independence movement and those who wanted Algeria to remain part of France, Camus satisfied nobody. His situation only became worse in the wake of an exchange with students at Stockholm University following his acceptance of the Nobel. "I have always condemned terrorism," he said in remarks that soon appeared in the newspapers, "and I must condemn a terrorism that works blindly in the streets of Algiers and one day might strike at my mother and my family. I believe in justice, but I will defend my mother before justice."

His adaptation of Dostoevski's novel *The Possessed* was staged in 1959, to mixed reviews but sufficient public interest to sustain six hundred performances. He worked on *The First Man*, a novel drawing on his memories of growing up in poverty in Algeria.

He expected this to be his longest work of fiction. The manuscript had reached the length of about 150 pages by January 4, 1960, when he took it with him when setting out by car to Paris from southern France. The driver, his friend and publisher Michel Gallimard, took a curve too fast and crashed into a tree. The briefcase containing the manuscript survived, but not the occupants of the car. Camus was forty-six years old. It was impossible not to recall the example he had once given of the absurd in its purest form: death in an automobile crash.

Bibliography

Aronson, Ronald. *Camus and Sartre: The Story of a Friendship and the Quarrel that Ended It*. Chicago: U of Chicago P, 2004. Dual biography throwing light on the work of both writers through a careful reconstruction of their friendship and conflict.

Bloom, Harold, ed. *Albert Camus's "The Stranger."* Philadelphia: Chelsea House, 2001. Selected essays on the author's first novel.

Brée, Germaine, ed. *Camus: A Collection of Critical Essays*. Englewood Cliffs, NJ: Prentice-Hall, 1962. Early collection of critical studies with particular focus on author's literary works.

Bronner, Stephen Eric. *Camus: Portrait of a Moralist*. 2d ed. Chicago: U of Chicago P, 2009. A work of "intellectual history with a political intent," first published in 1999. New edition includes afterword revisiting the book in the wake of the September 11, 2001, terrorist attacks and the Iraq War.

Carroll, David. *Albert Camus, the Algerian: Colonialism, Terrorism, Justice*. New York: Columbia University Press, 2007. Close reading of fiction and essays from postcolonial perspective.

Ellison, David R. *Understanding Albert Camus*. Columbia: U of South Carolina P, 1990. Compact overview of the author's life and work.

Fitch, Brian T. *The Fall: A Matter of Guilt*. New York: Twayne, 1995. Handbook on themes and reception of Camus's third and most puzzling novel.

Hughes, Edward J., ed. *The Cambridge Companion to Camus*. New York: Cambridge UP, 2007. Collection of new critical essays covering Camus's literary, philosophical, and journalistic writings.

Judt, Tony. *The Burden of Responsibility: Blum, Camus, Aron, and the French Twentieth Century*. Chicago: U of Chicago P, 1998. A study situating Camus in the intellectual history of the non-communist Left in France of the middle of the twentieth century.

Lottman, Herbert R. *Albert Camus: A Biography*. New York: Doubleday, 1979. The first authoritative biography of the author.

McCarthy, Patrick. *Albert Camus: The Stranger*. 2d ed. New York: Cambridge UP, 2004. A thorough examination of the style, themes, and context of Camus's first novel. Originally published in 1988.

Sprintzen, David A., and Adrian Van Den Hoven, eds. *Sartre and Camus: A Historic Confrontation*. Amherst, NY: Humanity Books, 2004. An edition of documents from the conflict between Camus and Sartre following publication of *The Rebel*, plus critical essays on the dispute by historians.

Tarrow, Susan. *Exile from the Kingdom: A Political Rereading of Albert Camus*. Tuscaloosa: U of Alabama P, 1985. Traces the stages of Camus's political thinking and commitments from the 1930s through the 1950s.

Todd, Olivier. *Albert Camus: A Life*. New York: Alfred A. Knopf, 1997. An abridged translation of the major biography of Camus in French, published in 1996.

Zaretsky, Robert. *Albert Camus: Elements of a Life*. Ithaca, NY: Cornell UP, 2010. A succinct treatment of the author's major writings, with an eye to their contemporary interest.

the PARIS
REVIEW

The *Paris Review* Perspective

Katherine Stirling for *The Paris Review*

In 1937, the physicist Jean Coulomb, director of the Institut de Météorologie et de Physique du Globe in Paris, wrote to a twenty-four-year-old Albert Camus, "Would you be willing to undertake a job that has nothing literary about it, and isn't even interesting?" Camus was eager to leave his life in Algeria for Paris (as Coulomb himself had), but he also needed a day job, and accepted; for nearly a year, he busied himself with the collation of meteorological data gathered from 355 weather stations across Algeria. It was not a field assignment but rather an office job: Each day, he put on a long white smock, climbed into the stacks, and cross-referenced the weather readings from the previous twenty-five years. (Camus's contribution to meteorology is recorded in the acknowledgements of Paul Seltzer's 1946 book *Le Climat de l'Algérie.*) The young aide devised a new, improved system for calculating average rainfall but noted in his journal that any such effort to quantify atmospheric conditions merely captured "an arbitrary slice out of reality." Soon after he began working at the institute, Camus wrote a story in his journal about a young office worker "who seemed destined for a brilliant career" and who spends his weekends gazing out the window, making note of the changes in weather. "And so on all year long," Camus wrote. "He waits. He waits to die."

And so a philosophy of the absurd was born. Like Kafka and Melville, authors to whom Camus refers frequently in his journals, Camus spent a portion of his writerly life as a functionary, and the experience informed his work. His stint at the institute also marked the beginning of his extraordinary attentiveness to weather, which formed a part of the descriptive and symbolic fabric of his writing from that point forward. It is comparatively rare for a twentieth-century writer to dwell so consistently and lovingly on descriptions of climate; and yet, weather is not, for Camus, merely a device for encapsulating a mood. It precedes plot and character and is the starting point for much of his writing.

In 1938, just after he left the Institut de Météorologie, Camus wrote elegiacally about Algerian climate in "Nuptials at Tipasa." The essay begins, "In springtime, Tipasa is inhabited by gods and the gods speak in the sun and the scent of absinthe leaves, in the silver armor of the sea, in the raw blue sky, the flower-covered ruins, and the great bubbles of light among the heaps of stone. At certain hours of the day the countryside is black with sunlight." "Black with sunlight"—It's a lovely and unintuitive phrase, and the kind of simple, evocative description that makes his novels viscerally resonant as well as philosophically engaging. In three words, Camus conjures the harsh, clear backlighting that makes everything in its path appear pitch-dark by contrast.

A young writer who had not yet made a name for himself, Camus was already aware of the power of the landscape, and capable of capturing it in his writing. In "Nuptials," he celebrates "a life that tastes of warm stone, that is full of the sighs of the sea and the rising song of the crickets"—brimming with the physical pleasures bestowed by nature. He concludes the essay with a description of his love affair with the terrain, the light, the air of his homeland: "It was neither I nor the world that counted, but solely the harmony and silence that gave birth to the love between us. A love I was not foolish enough to claim for myself alone, proudly aware that I shared it with a whole race born in the sun and sea, alive and spirited, drawing greatness from its simplicity, and upright on the beaches, smiling in complicity at the brilliance of its skies."

Camus revisited his earlier text in 1952 when he wrote "Return to Tipasa." It begins, "For five days rain had been falling ceaselessly on Algiers and had finally wet the sea itself. From an apparently inexhaustible sky, constant downpours, viscous in their density, streamed down upon the gulf. Gray and soft as a huge sponge, the sea rose slowly in the ill-defined bay. But the surface of the water seemed almost motionless under the steady rain. . . . In front of the soaked sea I walked and waited in that December Algiers, which was for me the city of summers. I had fled Europe's night, the winter of faces. But the summer city herself had been emptied of her laughter and offered me only bent and shining backs." In fourteen years, everything has changed: the blazing sun has given way to implacable precipitation. Camus had conquered Europe on his own terms; he was returning to Tipasa as a Resistance hero, an internationally renowned author, and, quite simply, a celebrity. Still, nothing felt familiar to him in this homecoming. He found himself alienated from the most fundamental, the originary sensation of his life: the Algerian summer.

Near the end of this later essay, he writes: "I have again left Tipasa; I have returned to Europe and its struggles. . . . I have not been able to disown the light into which I was born and yet I have not wanted to reject the servitudes of this time." Visceral belonging was at odds with his cerebral quest. As early as 1943, he explained the growing distance between himself and his existentialist compatriot Jean-Paul Sartre to the "simple fact that our climates are incompatible. From the artistic point of view, let's just say that the sky over Le Havre is not that of Algiers." Camus shied away from the roles thrust upon him in Paris; he was, he insisted, neither a philosopher nor a political figure, but a writer.

In his paean to classical values and beauty, "Helen's Exile" (1948), Camus set up the juxtaposition most succinctly, "The Mediterranean sun has something tragic about it, quite different from the tragedy of fogs." He was unable to adjust himself to the tragedy of fogs, and Algeria never stopped exerting its seductive pull on him. The sun, the sea, the rain, they are everywhere in his descriptions of Algeria, and some of his most beautiful writing is devoted to the description—at once meticulous and poetic—of the place where he was born. Camus knew from experience that the soul of a place lay, at least in part, in what people see and smell and feel when they are there. Each "arbitrary slice of reality" has a story to tell, and Camus never lost sight of that in his writing.

In his final, unfinished autobiographical novel, *Le Premier Homme*, Camus wrote, "So it was each time he left Paris for Africa, a quiet jubilation, his spirit opening wide, the satisfaction of someone who has just made a neat escape and who laughs when he thinks of the faces of the guards." He never did escape, though. He died, in a car accident, at the age of forty-six, in Burgundy, and he is buried in Lourmain, along the Cote d'Azur.

Copyright © 2012 by Katherine Stirling.

Works Consulted

Camus, Albert. "Helen's Exile" and "Return to Tipasa." In *The Myth of Sisyphus and Other Essays*. Trans. Justin O'Brien. New York: Vintage International, 1955.

_____. "Noces à Tipasa." In *Noces*. Paris: Charlot, 1945.

Judt, Tony. *The Burden of Responsibility: Blum, Camus, Aron, and the French Twentieth Century*. Chicago: U of Chicago P, 1998.

Lottman, Herbert R. *Albert Camus: A Biography*. Corte Madera, CA: Gingko Press, 1997.

CRITICAL
CONTEXTS

Algeria's Others

Christine Margerrison

Did you ever say Yes to one joy? O my friends, then you said Yes to *all* woe as well.

—Friedrich Nietzsche

The charge that Camus evades history is so familiar that we are likely to accept it as self-evident; after all, there is little focus on Arab or Berber characters in his fiction, and little sign of the growing militancy that will lead to the Algerian war. Although there is no necessary connection between these two propositions, this first claim has become a cornerstone of the second, upon which psychologizing arguments have been constructed that depict Camus as an isolated figure, out of touch and suffering from a vague colonial malaise. This leaves him unwilling to confront those facts of history that would demonstrate him to be a stranger in the land of his birth: that he and his kind are on the verge of extinction. Such is the "logic" of history, retrospectively defined.

Ironically, the proponents of such arguments rarely display more than a superficial interest in Algerian history themselves. Instead, a highly abstract and generic "colonialism" substitutes for concrete analysis of a particular historical context. Edward Said, for example, accuses Camus of ignoring history (211) while himself decontextualizing it, as in his bald statement that Arabic was declared a foreign language on March 8, 1938 (217). One might ask to which Arabic Said is referring; if his reference is to the dialectal Arabic of Algeria, the declaration appears to make no sense.[1] Said's statement is entirely divorced from the historical context during the 1930s of the growing Islamic movement called Salafism, which attempted to impose Egyptian Arabic on the population (one fifth of whom were Berbers, whose first language was not Arabic in any case). The decree concerned the closure of unauthorized private schools run by those Ulemas who introduced these new Salafist doctrines to Algeria (Ageron 339, 347), but Said's isolated snippets of information bypass the social context, thus distorting the complexities and contradictory currents of historical processes. Said's point is political and not historical, as is confirmed by his apparent assumption that the people of Oran were mainly Arabs when Camus wrote *The Plague* (217). As Jean Sarocchi has remarked, the majority of commentators seem entirely unaware that the central part of Oran was almost exclusively European (1995: 150); 75 percent of the total population was of European origin, as was also the case in the Algiers of Camus's childhood—facts of which Conor Cruise O'Brien seems likewise unaware.

Although O'Brien observed that European criticism was ethnocentric (10), he becomes, ironically, the illustration of his own point when he is surprised by the existence of a district in Oran called the "negro village," and queries whether there were any black people there at all (89 n.8). He might have been enlightened by knowledge of the trans-Saharan slave trade, but history is not his concern. O'Brien was writing forty years ago, and his ignorance of the Algerian social context is perhaps more understandable. Said's curiously dated comments in *Culture and Imperialism* were first published in 1993, five years *after* the rioting in Algiers that was a precursor to the bloody civil war of the 1990s. He, nevertheless, blocks off this inconvenient knowledge in favor of an Algerian of his own invention who will tell him what he wants to hear—that 1962 was the "triumphant inauguration of a new phase" (212). The Algerian writer Assia Djebar, on the other hand, speaks of the return of the Janissaries of pre-colonial times, electing their new dey in secret (1999: 177), while Gilbert Meynier likewise compares the power structure of independent Algeria to a new form of *beylikate*.[2] As he demonstrates: "The FLN was never a revolutionary party—neither of the avant-garde nor the élite. It bore the essential mark of militarisation" (684). Without an extraordinary degree of indifference to the fate of *real* Algerians, it is difficult to view as a triumph the installation in 1962 of a one-party state with military backing but no democratic mandate. There is little to learn from such specious arguments (although, for some of us, much to unlearn).

Well over 70 percent of the indigenous population lived in the rural areas under colonialism, whereas the majority of French Algerians were urban, and it has never seemed surprising to me that Camus wrote about those who peopled his daily life, segregated as it was. (The same might be said of Djebar's *L'Amour, la Fantasia*, whose narrator understandably describes a childhood where French Algerians remain mostly shadowy figures.) Camus's relationships with individual Algerians appear to have resulted from his political activities as a young communist and as a journalist for *Alger Républicain* during the 1930s rather than from purely social interactions—a factor that relates as much to cultural and religious taboos as to colonial divisions. There are no shared memories of childhood friendships. His early piece of youthful writing, "The Moorish House" (1933), is permeated by an underlying atmosphere of hostility emanating from an unknown community from which the young narrator is excluded, despite his claims to the contrary. This is confirmed in Camus's last, unfinished work, *The First Man*, which describes this gulf between the two communities; in the evenings Jacques Cormery's aunt bolts the doors and windows of her isolated farm against that "constant danger no one spoke of," a gesture reciprocated in the town by:

> [T]his people, alluring yet disturbing, near and separate, you were around them all day long, and sometimes friendship was born, or camaraderie, and at evening they still withdrew to their closed houses, where you never entered, barricaded also with their women you never saw . . . , and they were so numerous in the neighbourhoods where they were concentrated . . . they caused an invisible menace that you could scent on the air some evenings on the streets when a fight would break out between a Frenchman and an Arab. (*FM*, 217, t.a.: *PH*, 257-58)

Friendships might be born, but there are few shared social spaces or activities where they might flourish. In the countryside, where hostilities are at their height, friendships based on long familiarity might be glimpsed, as in the relationship between Veillard and Tamzal, whose son disappeared after being taken away by the army, accused of supplying the FLN. Asked whether he *had* supported them, "What can you expect, it's war," replies Veillard (*FM*, 142: *PH*, 170). Through shared activity and experience are such relationships forged—as is likewise intimated in "The Adulterous Woman" (1957), where the soldiers of that border region physically resemble the Arabs of the town by virtue of a shared geography and way of life. Such glimpses are rare and fleeting, while the acknowledgement of mutual collective suspicions underlying social relations overshadows *The First Man*. Since his days as a young communist, Camus had condemned colonialism; in 1958 he had written that "The time of colonialism is over, it is necessary only to know this and draw the consequences" (*E*, 898). The appendix to *The First Man* draws these consequences: "Title: The Nomads. Begins with a move and ends with the evacuation from Algerian land" (*FM*, 232: *PH*, 282). Jean Sarocchi bleakly observes: "To have lived for nothing: this will be a crucial theme of *The First Man*" (2009: 269). The novel is no attempted political intervention, as some commentators have suggested, but an acceptance of the coming exile. "They passed unknown across this land. But *my* role is that through my book their shadow will still remain after their passage over this land" (*OC4*, 948).

In an apparent reflection of Camus's own experience, Jacques Cormery's now fractured friendship with Saddok in *The First Man* grew out of past political alliances. Saddok's political development since the days of their youth has led him to embrace terrorism and the Arabo-Islamic ideology espoused by the FLN (*PH*, 314). The two men discuss his imminent marriage to a woman he does not know, and when asked why he consents to a tradition he himself considers cruel, Saddok replies:

Because my people are identified with this tradition, they have nothing else, they are locked into it, and to part with that tradition is to part with them. That is why I will go into that room tomorrow, and I will strip a stranger of her clothes, and I will rape her to the sound of gunshots. (*FM*, 250, t.a.: *PH*, 313)

One might contrast to these words Assia Djebar's female narrator in *L'Amour, la fantasia*, who rejects this custom as barbaric (124); or compare Amar Ouzegane, Camus's comrade from the Communist Party, who later approved cutting off the noses of those who smoked during Ramadan (Margerrison, 2010). As far as I am aware, the above quotation is the sole instance in all of Camus's work where the inequality of Muslim women is raised. The conversation with Saddok is the most telling criticism in Camus's literary writings, striking at one of the religion's greatest sources of inequality and potential division, but the unfinished nature of the draft makes it impossible to know how this might have developed.

Until the 1950s Camus's public comments on Islam are not only very rare, they are also noncommittal. This restraint is (at least initially) the product not only of his secularism but of ignorance, for as a young reporter at *Alger Républicain* his support in 1939 for the Ulema leader Tayeb el Okbi, accused of involvement in the murder of an established religious figure, does him little credit. Camus appears indifferent to the religious conflicts of which this trial was an important symbol. During the 1950s, though, this position appears to change, and privately Camus increasingly saw Islam as the most significant source of cultural division. According to Jean Daniel, Camus regarded Algerian society as being composed not of plural communities but of "Muslims and the others" (Daniel 15). In certain respects, this opinion is supported by the findings of modern historians, who record that in the eyes of most grassroots Muslim activists this same distinction applied; Islam *was* "the nation" and there was no other (Meynier 91-93; Harbi, 1975, 67-68; 1996, 66). However, just as Muslim activists do not represent the entire population, it would be a mistake to believe that Camus saw cultural divisions in such crude terms. He was well aware that Islam in Algeria did not speak with one voice, as his later literary writings show. If one might adopt Daniel's term "Muslims" as a category, this was no monolithic entity; on the contrary, forms of religious worship and religious belief were diverse and often contested. In this sense, Islam in Algeria contained its own sets of internal "others," as did the European community.

During the early 1950s, Camus was also thinking more deeply about Islamic history in North Africa. In December 1952, he paid his first visit to the Algerian south, a journey that inspired many of the short stories in his 1957 collection, *Exile and the Kingdom*. In 1954 he began writing the second of these stories, "The Renegade," which was based on his visit to Ghardaïa, one of the walled cities of the Mozab onto which his fictional town, Taghâsa, was transposed. He was also reading Eugène Fromentin's account of his travels, *Un Été dans le Sahara* (1857), and expressed the intention of reading *Le Grand Désert* by Eugène Daumas (*C3* 93). This book, published in 1848 (the year France outlawed slavery in its colonial possessions), foregrounds the continuing trans-Saharan slave trade, first established after the Arab conquest of North Africa in the seventh century. As I have shown elsewhere, the Taghâsa of Camus's "The Renegade" was not the product of the author's imagination, as is generally supposed, but a real historical location lying on the central Saharan slave route from Timbuktu (2008, 244-245: 2010).[3]

Its rulers were a Berber tribe called the Messufa, and (climate change permitting) this salt mine existed for centuries until its destruction in the late sixteenth century. The comment in "The Renegade" that "each slab of salt that is cut out is worth one man" (*EK* 36, ta: *TRN* 1584) is not immediately obvious unless one understands that because there was no salt in the sub-Saharan regions this had a very high value and was crucially important as a means of exchange in the purchase of slaves. Olivier Pétré-Grenouilleau views the salt of Teghaza as one important factor in the commercial take-off of the Islamic empire before the twelfth century (543-44). Still in the nineteenth century, Arab traders were exchanging salt for African slaves (Daumas, 139), who were then exported across the desert to the great slave markets of the East. Although the term "surreal" is frequently applied to this story, the reference to Taghâsa roots it in the real—with its buildings made from salt and its generations of unknown African slaves who, over the course of almost a millenium, were worked to death in the mine. Centuries later, Camus alone traces the shadow of their passage over this Earth.

The Berber Mozabites of Ghardaïa were descended from the Ibadites, who had virtually monopolised this slave trade after the eighth century. Known as the "puritans of the desert" in contemporary Algeria, they had withdrawn from the "faithless" wider society in the eleventh century, retiring into their walled desert cities where all outsiders (Arabs, Jews and others) were forbidden to live. The depiction of Taghâsa as a closed society hostile to outsiders seems partly inspired by this example, but this description might also apply to the growing Salafist movement intent on the "purification" of Islam through a return to the supposed original purity of the times of Muhammad and his companions, the *Salaf* of the seventh century. These literalist Ulemas are often called the first nationalists, but their principal targets were traditional, mystical forms of Islam, which they condemned as pagan and corrupted by contact with the West. As Ageron observes, these "gendarmes of the Faith" were intransigent missionaries whose actions destroyed or impoverished popular forms of the religion (347-48). Followers of El Okbi, the particularly uncompromising Wahhabi leader in Algiers, regularly disrupted funerals because they disapproved of the custom of chanting verses from the Qur'ān, thus arrogating to themselves the authority to determine correct practice (Christelow 261-62). The fictional Taghâsans:

> [G]ive orders, they strike, they say that they are a single people, that their god is the true god, and that one must obey. They are my lords, they know no pity and, like lords, they want to be alone, to advance alone, to rule alone. (*EK* 36, t.a.: *TRN* 1584)

This insistence on being a "single people" recalls, in particular, the Salafists' stance towards the Berbers (the original inhabitants of Algeria), who were redefined as Arabs: equally, those claiming a specific Berber identity were successively "purged" from the nationalist movements.

Like Algerian democrats such as Aziz Kessous or Ferhat Abbas, Camus had once imagined a secular, pluralist Algeria (an "Algerian Algeria") in which those of all faiths and none might live in equality. As late as July 1955, Camus briefly revives an argument first made in 1937, writing in *L'Express* of the Mediterranean as that space where a fusion of East and West is possible (*E*, 1875), but it seems unlikely that he believed this[4]—especially as by 1954 he was already writing "The Renegade," which silently voices the death of such hopes. This death of hope is expressed, I suggest, in the traumatized slave's faith in the invincibility of his masters and their religion of conquest:

> O my masters, they will then conquer the soldiers, they'll conquer the world and love, they'll spread over the deserts, cross the seas, fill the light of Europe with their black veils . . . , sow their salt on the continent, all vegetation, all youth will be extinguished, and mute crowds with shackled feet will plod beside me in the desert of the world under the cruel sun of the true faith, I'll no longer be alone. (*EK*, 47, t.a.: *TRN*, 1592)

This is no harmonious fusion of East and West. Instead, here is announced a new theme in Camus's fictional writings; the theme not simply of defeat but of an apocalyptic ending, the death of the West. It is not my wish to impose a single meaning on Camus's work, which may be interpreted on many levels, and it is important to remember that the Cold War was also at its height. Indeed, it is in response to this in the late 1940s that Camus is first beset by fears of a coming conflict threatening the West. Communism is also targeted in "The Renegade" as one form of messianic faith rooted in Christian doctrines. This is the subject of Camus's brief explanation of "The Renegade," that it concerned the communist intellectual who ends up adoring "the religion of evil" to expiate his own feelings of guilt (Grenier 197). Equally, these comments on religion might be taken literally, especially as in this same conversation he stated that he had *wanted* the story's meaning to be "hidden." My aim is not to deny alternative interpretations, but to follow that thread arising from the recognition that Teghaza was no fictional town, and that in basing this strange story on the real, Camus begins in North African history itself. This is the fundamental *fact* of "The Renegade," which cannot be ignored.

In 1947, Camus's "Short Guide to Towns Without a Past" had spoken of the beauty of Algeria's young people:

> [T]he Arabs, of course, and then the others. The French of Algeria are a bastard race, made up of unforeseen mixtures. Spaniards and Alsatians, Italians, Maltese, Jews and Greeks have come together there. As in America this brutal interbreeding has had happy results. (*SEN*, 133)

But, as has often been pointed out, Camus refers specifically here to "the others": The "Arabs, of course" are not included in this melting pot. What of the "Arabs" in 1947? In 1937, when the young Camus was first speaking of the Mediterranean as the meeting place of East and West, the Ulema leader, Ben Badis, was insisting that the Algerians were a "single people," a Muslim people of Arab heritage: "Whoever tries to assimilate it is attempting the impossible" (Merad 365). These are the doctrines that took root amongst the nationalists, despite their looming "Berber crisis" of 1949, when some objected to the movement's increasingly Islamic rhetoric as well as the use of the term "Arab," arguing in vain for a secular and "Algerian" Algeria. On the political level in 1947, despite the extension of the vote to Muslim women, the hopes of Algerian democrats were dashed as the French Fourth Republic gained a reputation for electoral fraud.

Is a new Mediterranean culture possible, Camus had asked in 1937, on the eve of the second World War. In 1957, he asks the question again in *Exile and the Kingdom* with greater seriousness and knowledge. The previous year he had complained that according to the FLN, unless the French Algerians converted to Islam they would be considered foreigners in an independent Algeria (Grenier 182). In other words, they would be considered *dhimmi*, occupying a traditionally inferior position, their personal status protected as "people of the Book," but with no political rights. This is indeed what happened to non-Muslims after 1962 (Meynier 92, 256, 257). What, therefore, might the notion of cultural fusion mean, especially in the context of a rapidly growing demographic imbalance between these cultures? In 1830, the indigenous population had numbered between two and three million: by the late 1950s, it was approaching nine million. This demographic explosion, to which Camus refers in his 1958 *Actuelles III: Chronique Algérienne, 1939-1958* (*E*, 897-1018), was sometimes called "the revenge of the cradle," but it continued unabated after independence, with all the social and economic problems this entailed.

I have suggested that "The Renegade" contains a hidden critique of the Salafist, pan-Islamic trend in 1950s Algeria—"hidden" in the sense that Camus had declared this as his wish with regard to the story's meaning, and because, as far as I am aware, he did not reveal the significance of Teghaza as a historical site. The religious militancy of the Taghâsans is not, however, the only allusion to Islam here. The story's protagonist was a European trainee priest who had travelled to Taghâsa against the advice of his teachers in order to convert its inhabitants to Catholicism. Ironically, despite his wish to preach the Word, after his arrival he never speaks again—initially because of his terror, subsequently because his tongue is cut out. He is received in silence, then imprisoned in the House of the Fetish. When the door of his cell eventually is opened, he is confronted by the Sorcerer:

[W]ith his raffia hair, his chest covered with a breastplate of pearls, his legs bare under a straw skirt, wearing a mask of reeds and wire with two square openings for the eyes. He was followed by musicians and women wearing heavy motley gowns that revealed nothing of their bodies. They danced . . . , and finally the Sorceror opened the little door behind me . . . , I turned around and saw the Fetish, his double axe-head, his iron nose twisted like a snake. (*EK* 38: *TRN* 1585-586)

After his brutal ritual consecration to the Fetish, he is subsequently forced to witness, with his face turned to the wall, nightly scenes of violence and bestiality. But the slave's dedication to his new god, the Fetish, is completely confirmed only after his tongue has been cut out, when finally "I surrendered to him and approved his maleficent order, I adored in him the evil principle of the world" (*EK* 43).

Although these descriptions seem out of place here, they represent an extreme version of precisely those charges leveled by the Salafists against the traditional diversity of Islam; that such forms of worship were animist, polytheistic, idolatrous, the "survivals of a distant pagan past" (Merad 144). However, the insistence on a distant pagan past entirely overlooks the legacy of slavery in North Africa. I earlier noted O'Brien's perplexity at the "negro village" in Oran. It was in these quarters that the relatively few descendants of African slaves often had lived (Dermenghem, 285-86),[5] while black "colonies" of slave descendants also were to be found in the south. Over the centuries, a number of black religious associations developed, which, while professing Islam, understandably retained elements of their own religious practices. At the same time, these practices found a reflection in pre-Islamic beliefs within the wider population, with which they became assimilated (260). Thus, I suggest, this view of Islam as multifaceted lies at the center of Taghâsa itself. Although this particular allusion is elusive precisely because it requires specific knowledge of the social and historical context, the final story of *Exile and the Kingdom* lends further weight to the proposition that Camus is examining such forms of cultural "fusion" in this collection. In "The Growing Stone," the protagonist, D'Arrast, encounters a similar example of a syncretic religion, with a similar historical background of slavery, in the form of the Afro-

Brazilian *macumba* ceremony—a fusion of traditional African and Catholic beliefs.[6]

Particularly as one overarching theme of "The Renegade" concerns forms of enslavement (ideological and literal), one might conclude that the depiction of Taghâsa delivers a particularly severe verdict on Islam. The story seems to allude to both elements of the contemporary religious conflict in Algeria, but, rather than being opposed, they are indistinguishable, each integral to the whole. Thus an enduring conflict at the heart of the religion is established (especially as the Mozabites originally were a product of Islam's first split after the death of Muhammad). The insistence on "purity" and the rejection of the (Islamic) Other characterizes the Mozabites and the Salafists alike, while slavery and conquest are the very means by which such so-called impurities are introduced. In his journalism, Camus had spoken of the Ulemas as being engaged in a "rational" reform of the religion; there is no reason to suppose he believes that here, or in his 1958 introduction to his *Actuelles III: Chronique Algérienne, 1939-1958*, in which he condemned Egyptian pan-Islam and dreams of an Islamic empire (*E* 901, 979). The Salafists identified the West as a source of corruption, but the same might be said of Africa, for here is presented an entirely different example of "cultural fusion," which the Salafists thoroughly condemned but which their earlier historical counterparts, the Mozabites, had helped to create. As Sarocchi (1988) has pointed out, the general theme of *Exile and the Kingdom* concerns confrontations with Otherness—the Other with whom there is no common ground, no shared values, who is inassimilable. In "The Renegade," Camus seems to be suggesting that the inassimilable Other Culture also is at war with its own internal Others.

I have here focused specifically on Islam as *the* central thread that runs through "The Renegade," and this has led me to bypass (but not to contest) alternative emphases on Christianity or left-wing politics: after all, in one of his lives the protagonist *is* a trainee priest, and Camus frequently equated Marxism with Christianity. I have chosen to focus on the protagonist's other life as a slave because, as I noted earlier, by placing his story in a real historical location, Camus clearly situates it in Islamic history itself. This is, I believe, the starting point for interpretation, which necessitates a different reading. Unlike Said or O'Brien, I would insist that knowledge of the social and historical context is indispensable to this story in particular, of which Roger Quilliot, the first editor of the *Pléiade* edition of Camus's work, said "Mysterious to read, 'The Renegade' remains so after critical study" (*TRN* 2043).

In his *Carnets* of 1951, Camus had cited Louis Guilloux: "In the end, one does not write in order to speak, but in order *not to speak*" (*C2* 291). This, I believe, was Camus's intention in "The Renegade." The entire story takes the form of an internal monologue delivered by a slave whose tongue has been cut out—who is *unable* to speak. Only the final line deviates from this narrative form, as the voice of the narrator tells us with heavy irony that "A handful of salt fills the mouth of the garrulous slave" (*EK* 49: *TRN* 1593). He is hardly garrulous: he *never speaks*. Yet, the impression persists that in some way something has changed, as is reinforced by the comments of this story's editor in the new *Pléiade* edition of Camus's work: "the character seems finally to realise his mistake before being definitively reduced to silence by the Sorcerer, who puts a handful of salt in his mouth . . ." (*OC4* 1347). Salt, the very *taste* of slavery, provides the most bitterly ironic confirmation that nothing whatsoever has changed; it *does not matter* whether he changes his mind (who cares what a slave thinks about—dreams about?), whether he is alive or dead (there are always replacements), even whether he has killed a priest (French policy will not be swayed by the death of one mere priest). From the day of his arrival in Taghâsa, the slave has no further impact on history or life. Indeed, I believe that this entire monologue is presented as irrelevant. During the 1950s, with the outbreak of war and the fall into silence of Algerian democrats (because, fearful of FLN reprisals, they are *afraid* of death), Camus, with the taste of salt already in his own mouth, writes this story in order *not* to speak.

His condemnation of the colonial system in Algeria always had been based on secular principles, but the increasing Islamic rhetoric of the FLN, who used religion both as a means of control and as a means of establishing an Arabo-Islamic national identity in an otherwise diverse population with little understanding of the notion of "nation," brought into sharp relief the religious dimension of the conflict, which was based precisely on the distinction between "Muslims and the others." (Jews, who were amongst the oldest inhabitants, were included in this category of "others.") Camus is often referred to as an "assimilationist" without due regard to the meaning of this term. *Exile and the Kingdom* is the closest he comes to expressing a judgement on this subject. His depictions of already existing forms of cultural "fusion" in "The Renegade" (and "The Growing Stone") do not suggest, I think, an optimistic prognosis for the future of cultural assimilation in Algeria.

The pessimism of *Exile and the Kingdom* is not, however, Camus's final word on this subject, even though *The First Man* was cut short by his untimely death. Taken as a whole, the drafts and notes of this unwritten novel suggest that the proposition that the French Algerians had "lived for nothing" is far less significant than the glimpses of other, major themes that have permeated Camus's literary writings. Camus was above all a creative writer whose most haunting work is driven not by logical argument but by those "obscure forces of the soul" that leave him feeling that it is not he but his pen that writes, tapping into those underground sources of inspiration of which he speaks in *The First Man*. I began this chapter with a quotation from Nietzsche, who has accompanied Camus from the first days of his literary career. To say "Yes" to one joy, Nietzsche suggests, entails the acceptance of *all* woe as well—of life in all its light and shade. As he sits in his prison cell during what are probably the last days of his life, Meursault, the protagonist of *The Stranger*, is asked what life he imagines after his death: "A life in which I can remember this life" (*TO* 117: *TRN* 1210). This is the life he has been remembering and reliving, every moment of it in his prison cell, since those first words: "Today Maman died." And so Camus, in the last years of French Algeria, follows his first protagonist's lead and remembers his life, and the lives of those first immigrants, the "conquerors" struggling to survive, fighting against illness, poverty and death. The autobiographical component of *The First Man* is necessary to the acceptance of the fact that the life into which we are all born has changed beyond recognition by the time we leave it. Like all those other empires in history, the West will die and others—other races, other cultures—will claim the soil we once called our own. Reflecting that constant preoccupation with history that pervades Camus's work, the novel resituates that single life of the author himself—of no greater value than that of the Teghazan slave—into the greater cycles of history and time. Yes, the Algeria Camus knew is on the verge of extinction, but *The First Man* is no work of mourning for what will be lost. The autobiographical focus illustrates an affirmation and a choice—of *this* life, this history, with all of its joys and woes. They did not live for nothing precisely because they *lived*, leaving their shadow across this earth. I suggest that like Meursault, and like Nietzsche's Zarathustra, Camus finally chooses the earth:

I shall return with this sun, with this earth, with this eagle, with this serpent—not to a new life, or a better life, or a similar life: I shall return eternally to this identical and self-same life, in the greatest things and in the smallest. (Nietzsche 237-38)

Notes

1. As Said cites no evidence, it is difficult to evaluate this particular claim, especially as I can find no reference to it either in the historical research cited in this chapter, or in any other contemporary history. Ageron's discussion of this decree does not mention it. Although Said recommends that Camus's assumptions about Algeria should be tested against histories written by Algerians after independence (212), after 1962 this discipline was strictly censored and reduced to the repetition of official discourse (Margerrison, 2010).

2. The political structure of the Ottoman Empire in Algeria, based on the theoreti-

cal authority of the *dey* of Algiers, was divided into *beyliks*, each ruled over by a *bey* and backed by military power.

3. As is to be expected, the name of this town has been transcribed in a number of ways over the centuries, but the predominant spelling today seems to be "Teghaza."

4. Although the (Greek) Mediterranean has a significant mythological role in his work, I think it very doubtful that Camus ever seriously believed in such a "fusion." At the time of his speech at the "Maison de la culture" (*E*, 1321-327) the twenty-three-year-old Camus was still a member of the Communist Party, for whom the threat of fascism had become paramount—as is illustrated by Camus's rejection of the notion of a "Latin" West, associated with Charles Maurras. For an insightful assessment of Camus's speech, see Jean Sarocchi's "La Méditerranée est un songe, monsieur" (2005), and for an overview of this subject and its ideological predecessors, see Dunwoodie (2007).

5. It would be very surprising if Camus knew nothing of such matters, and neither is there reason to suppose that Camus was not familiar with this book by Dermenghem, whose work was recommended to him by Jean Grenier. Camus cites one of Dermenghem's books in *L'Homme révolté* (*E*, 596).

6. Although his discussion of religion is confined to Christianity, David H. Walker (1998) provides an excellent discussion of "The Growing Stone" and the symbolic significance of the stone itself. His edition of *L'Exil et le royaume* likewise provides a clear introduction to the stories as a whole (1981).

Works Cited

Ageron, Charles-Robert. *Histoire de l'Algérie contemporaine: De l'insurrection de 1871 au déclenchement de la guerre de libération 1954, II.* Paris: PUF, 1979.

Christelow, Allan. "Ritual, Culture and Politics of Islamic Reformism in Algeria." *Middle Eastern Studies* 23.3 (July 1987): 255-73.

Daniel, Jean. "*Le Premier Homme*, la religion, le siècle." *Narcisse* Special Edition: *Encore Camus? Camus Encore!* 16 (1996): 9-16.

Daumas, Eugène, and Ausone de Chancel. *Le Grand Désert ou itinéraire d'une caravane du Sahara au pays des nègres.* Paris: Napoléon Chaix, 1848.

Dermenghem, Émile. *Le Culte des saints dans l'Islam maghrébin.* 3d ed. Paris: Gallimard, 1954.

Djebar, Assia. *L'Amour, la fantasia.* Paris: Albin Michel, 1995.

_____. *Ces Voix qui m'assiègent . . . en marge de ma francophonie.* Paris: Albin Michel, 1999.

Dunwoodie, Peter. "From *Noces* to *L'Étranger*." *The Cambridge Companion to Camus.* Ed. Edward J. Hughes. New York: Cambridge UP, 2007.

Grenier, Jean. *Jean Grenier: Carnets 1944-1971.* Ed. Claire Paulhan. Paris: Seghers, 1991.

Harbi, Mohammed. *Aux Origines du Front de Libération Nationale.* Paris: Bourgois, 1975.

_____. "Les Fondements culturels de la nation Algérienne." *Algérie: Comprendre la crise*. Ed. Gilles Manceron, et al. Brussels: Complexe, 1996.

Margerrison, Christine. *"Ces Forces obscures de l'âme": Women, Race and Origins in the Writings of Albert Camus*. Amsterdam, Atlanta: Rodopi, 2008.

_____. "History, Ideology and Camus's 'Le Renégat,'" *French Studies* 64.4 (2010): 423-37.

Merad, Ali. *Le Réformisme musulman en Algérie de 1925 à 1940*. Paris: Mouton, 1967.

Meynier, Gilbert. *Histoire intérieure du FLN*. Paris: Fayard, 2002.

Nietzsche, Friedrich. *Thus Spoke Zarathustra:A Book for Everyone and No One*. Trans. R. J. Hollingdale. Harmondsworth, England: Penguin, 1969.

Pétré-Grenouilleau, Olivier. *Les Traites négrières: essai d'histoire globale*. Paris: Gallimard, 2004.

Sarocchi, Jean. "L'Autre et les autres." *Albert Camus' "L'Exil et le royaume": The Third Decade*. Ed. Anthony Rizzuto. Toronto: Paratexte, 1988.

_____. *Camus le Juste?* Biarritz, France: Séguier, 2009.

_____. *Le Dernier Camus ou Le Premier Homme*. Paris: Nizet, 1995.

_____. *Variations Camus*. Paris: Séguier, 2005.

Walker, David H. "Albert Camus: 'La Pierre qui Pousse.'" *Short French Fiction: Essays on the Short Story in France in the Twentieth Century*. Ed. John Ernest Flower. Exeter: University of Exeter Press, 1998.

_____, ed. *Albert Camus:L'Exil et le royaume*. London: Harrap, 1981.

Abbreviations used

E: *Essais*. Ed. Roger Quilliot and Louis Faucon. Paris: Gallimard, 1965.

TRN: *Théâtre, Récits, Nouvelles*. Preface by Jean Grenier, ed. Roger Quilliot Paris: Gallimard, 1962.

C2: *Albert Camus: Carnets II 1942-1951* . Paris: Gallimard, 1964.

C3: *Albert Camus: Carnets III 1951-1959*. Paris: Gallimard, 1989.

PH: *Le Premier homme*. Cahiers Albert Camus 7. Paris: Gallimard, 1994.

OC4: *Albert Camus: Œuvres complètes IV 1957-1959*. Ed. Raymond Gay-Crosier, et al, Paris: Gallimard, 2008.

TO: *The Outsider*. Trans. Stuart Gilbert. Harmondsworth, England: Penguin, 1964.

EK: *Exile and the Kingdom*. Trans. Justin O'Brien. Harmondsworth, England: Penguin, 1962.

FM: *The First Man*. Trans. David Hapgood. London: Hamish Hamilton, 1995.

SEN: *Selected Essays and Notebooks*. Ed. and trans. Philip Thody. Harmondsworth, England: Penguin, 1979.

Albert Camus and the Metaphor of Absurdity

Brent C. Sleasman

Absurdity, for Albert Camus, represented "the conclusion arrived at by those who had assumed the possibility of a total explanation of existence by the mind but who discover instead an unbridgeable gulf between rationality and experience" (Cruickshank 49). Out of this tension between the way one desires the world to appear and the harsh truth of human existence emerges the metaphor of the absurd. The understanding of the term "metaphor," as used in this essay, is informed by the work of Paul Ricoeur, who writes, "[T]his is the function of metaphor, to instruct by suddenly combining elements that have not been put together before" (33). In many ways this notion of metaphor can be understood as a sort of interruption to the routine of daily living.

Michael Hyde, in his work addressing "rhetorical interruptions," suggests, "[S]hould it not be the case that when conscience calls, rhetoric ought to answer, even if the word of the poet is yet to come and even if what one has to say is out of step with the party line?" (77). Combining these ideas, one comes to the conclusion that this understanding of metaphor allows the world to be reinterpreted in a new and different fashion. Camus's use of the metaphor of the absurd serves such a purpose: to provide a unique lens through which one can make better sense of human existence. This interaction between Albert Camus and the metaphor of the absurd provides the framework for the central question guiding this essay: "How does Albert Camus's use of the metaphor of the absurd assist one in engaging the contemporary historical moment, a time of narrative and virtue contention, from an existential ethical perspective?"

Introduction

In contemporary usage, "absurd" means something that is "utterly or obviously senseless, illogical, or untrue; contrary to all reason or common sense; laughably foolish or false." Emerging from this definition is a sense that in order for one's actions to be considered absurd, they must be in conflict with everyday common sense. An absurd act, therefore, can be understood as something that is out of order when compared to the surroundings. But what happens when these absurd actions become so commonplace that they no longer stand out as odd? What happens when the once-acceptable standards of living are called into question and "common sense" is no longer common? Some scholars use the terms "postmodern" to describe this era defined by the decline of these agreed-upon approaches to life. For example, Jean-François Lyotard famously wrote that "the grand narrative [of modernity] has lost its credibility" and therefore the question of knowledge is open for debate and disagreement (37). But can a moment of absurdity be defined by a single term? While Lyotard and others suggested "postmodern" as an appropriate label for the human condition, some scholars observe that the term "postmodern" is no longer a sufficient description of our current historical moment. Annette Holba writes, "We have taken our postmodernism and embraced it and we have now moved clearly beyond it" (20). Regardless of the terminology one uses, life provides ample opportunities to illustrate an existence defined by contradiction and uncertainty.

Turning to the life and work of Albert Camus provides insight into how to navigate through an absurd historical moment. Camus's role as a journalist, playwright, actor, essayist, philosopher, and novelist allowed him to engage a complex world in a variety of capacities and offer an array of interpretations of his time. Many of the formative experiences of his life—including his father's death in World War I, his role in the French Resistance (against Germany) during World War II, and his efforts at offering a vision for rebuilding France following the German occupation at the conclusion of World War II—were not unique to his existence. But the culmination of his experiences allowed him to provide a distinctive insight into how to make a way within a world of chaos and disorder. The metaphor of the absurd is not exclusively found within the domain of philosophy, since it is deeply tied to one's experience. But the reverse is true as well; absurdity is not merely a metaphor concerned with human existence, having no philosophical justification. While a fuller biography of Camus's life is offered elsewhere in this volume, the following section suggests that Camus was both a product of and a shaper of his own moment in history.

Albert Camus: His Life and Times

Albert Camus was born on November 7, 1913, in Mondovi, Algeria, and died on January 4, 1960, in Villeblevin, France. At the time of his birth, Algeria was a colony of France and, therefore, male adults were subject to service in the French military. On October 11, 1914, less than a year after Albert's birth, his father was fatally wounded in the First Battle of Marne (France) during World War I. After the death of her husband, Catherine Camus, Albert's mother, moved him and his brother into the home of his grandmother. "Grandmother Catherine Sintes was a harsh woman . . . the return of Catherine Camus with two infants exceeded her understanding. . . . The children's mother was a passive witness to the brawling and beating, restrained by fatigue, by fear of the old woman, and the inability to express herself sharply and effectively" (Lottman 21). The absurdity of losing one's father and being raised by an illiterate mother and grandmother formed the early years of Camus's life (Lottman 18). If any opportunities were to come for Camus, he would have to overcome the family circumstances and create them for himself, despite the absurdity of the situation. Joseph McBride writes, "For Camus, then, it is not the world but the human condition that is absurd. The world itself is simply unintelligible" (5).

A further example of the potential absurdity of human existence occurred when, at seventeen years old, Camus experienced his first symptoms of tuberculosis (Lottman 43). Camus had been an avid soccer player, but from that point on, life "in the sense he knew it seemed to come to an end, when it should just be beginning" (Lottman 45). Although he was not yet writing about absurdity, Camus was gaining experiential knowledge about the concept that would come to define his work. This unexpected interruption of tuberculosis forced Camus to experience the absurd firsthand; many life circumstances defy explanation and, quite often, any ultimate meaning remains hidden from human sight.

Through these early years, Camus's main engagement with absurdity came within his experiences. As he continued his academic training, these personal experiences would be expanded as he encountered ideas of many thinkers, including St. Augustine and Fyodor Dostoevski. From 1918 through 1923, Camus attended primary school. Upon completion of this phase of his education, he held various jobs, including selling spare parts for cars and working in a marine broker's office (Cruickshank 13). He completed his formal education in 1936 with a dissertation that addressed the beliefs of Plotinus as they related to the Christian faith of St. Augustine. Although Camus never embraced the Christian faith, he remained sympathetic to Christian beliefs throughout his life. While completing his education, Camus also was building a reputation for his skills and interest in the theater. In 1935, he founded the Théâtre du Travail (later reorganized into the Théâtre de l'Equipe). Within this context, Camus first adapted and performed works by Dostoevski. Although it was not published until 1944 or performed until 1945, Camus wrote the play *Caligula* during this time of productivity in the theater as well.

Camus moved to mainland France in 1940 when he accepted a job working as a reporter at the newspaper *Paris-Soir*. This occurred only months before the German offensive in northeast France, beginning Camus's journey into the French Resistance movement in the early stages of World War II. After the German occupation of Paris, Camus remained in the French capital. It was during this time, in 1943, that he met Jean-Paul Sartre, a major influence through the duration of Camus's life. During this time, Camus edited and wrote for the underground newspaper *Combat*. Following the liberation of Paris by the Allied forces, Camus offered his vision for postwar France. His commitment to ethical practice was evident when he wrote on September 4, 1944, "[T]he affairs of this country should be managed by those who paid and answered for it. In other words, we are determined to replace politics with morality. That is what we call a revolution" ("Morality" 28). This overwhelming burden that Camus felt for the future of postwar France did not immobilize him, leaving him incapable of making a decision about how to act in a given moment. He sought the freedom to respond to the moment as was necessary and rejected being labeled by any one particular system of belief. He did not "belong to any school of thought" and held, along with Franz Kafka, a "marked dissatisfaction with traditional philosophy [which was] superficial, academic, and remote from life" (Kaufmann 12). Camus had a keen interest in the implications of deeply philosophical ideas revealed within everyday life accompanied by his commitment to an ethical philosophy.

Thus far in his life, Camus's personal meeting with the absurd included the loss of his father at a very early age (a theme that would later serve as a foundation in his posthumously published *The First Man*), his recurring attacks of tuberculosis, and an unanticipated role in the French Resistance movement. During this time, his growing relationship with Sartre also provided the foundation for a defining moment in Camus's life, a dispute that arose from a review of Camus's *The Rebel*, a publication that represents his attempt at navigating the post-World War II European turbulence of the 1940s and 1950s. After the collapse of the totalitarianism of Nazi Germany, the two political systems competing for the support of Europeans were democratic capitalism (best exemplified by the United States of America) and communism (best exemplified by the Soviet Union). Although Camus had some early sympathy for communism (in fact, he was briefly a member of the Communist Party), he came to see that the best hope for the future of Europe was a "third way," or an approach that did not fully embrace either political structure. While he saved his greatest criticisms for communism, Camus also leveled criticisms at the United States for the perceived acceptance of unbridled capitalism.

In the introduction to *The Rebel*, Camus meets the absurdity of his moment head-on as he writes, "The purpose of this essay is once again to face the reality of the present . . . it is an attempt to understand the times in which we live" (3). Camus, along with many others of his era, could have chosen to ignore "a period which, in a space of fifty years, uproots, enslaves, or kills seventy million human beings" (*Rebel* 3). But instead of ignoring the moment, Camus believed that he had to make the choice to engage the moment as it actually appeared before him, although he lacked the clarity of what the long-term implications of those actions may be. Ronald C. Arnett and Pat Arneson write, "We are not saying that one must like or approve of a given historical moment. We are suggesting, however, that any historical moment must be taken seriously and responded to, rather than ignored" (37). *The Rebel* was one of Camus's entrances into the ongoing conversation of his historical moment and represents his attempt to "face the reality of the present" by recognizing the atrocities committed during World War II and attempting to provide a vision for the future of mainland Europe.

With the publication of *The Rebel*, Camus's criticisms of Soviet communism brought him into direct conflict with his friend of more than ten years, Jean-Paul Sartre. By this point, Sartre had become one of many "apologists for Stalin" (Lottman 523), while Camus was growing more and more hostile towards communism. "The author's [Camus's] unambiguous stand against Stalinism was bound to receive sympathy and approval from conservatives, from anti-communists of all types" (Lottman 522). Camus worked from a position situated within a larger context or narrative, and he came to embody the particular narrative that he represented. Camus's commitment to living out his political and philosophical beliefs despite the absurdity of his historical moment, while contributing to his eventual broken relationship with Sartre, demonstrated his belief that words and actions should be consistent with each other. Aronson writes, "In the end Camus and

Sartre split not only because they took opposing sides but because each became his own side's intellectual leader" (2). Perhaps in less turbulent times the two could have remained friends, but the politics of their everyday lives and the situation in post-war France made that option impossible. In our current moment many would simply "agree to disagree," but within a moment possessing an "unbridgeable gulf between rationality and existence" (Cruickshank 49), this split further accentuated the absurdity of their time. Eventually the two differing approaches to post-World War II France led to a permanent end to the friendship:

> In a philosophically intense and personally brutal argument, the two main voices of postwar France intellectual life publicly destroyed almost ten years of friendship. At first reluctantly and hesitantly, and then with a rush that seemed uncontrollable, Sartre and Camus also shattered their political milieu and any traces of what was once their common project of creating an independent Left. (Aronson 2)

While a full explication of the differences between Camus and Sartre are beyond the purpose of this essay, what becomes evident is that Camus was greatly influenced by the unintended consequences that emerged as he took action in his moment of absurdity. He knew that he and Sartre viewed the world through different lenses, but the significance of these differences was not fully evident until after the publication of *The Rebel*. Following Cruickshank's suggestion that absurdity can be understood as a longing for clarity, Camus continued to take action without full knowledge of the outcome of his acts.

The final act of absurdity for Camus during his life is illustrated through the manner in which he died. On January 4, 1960, while traveling with his good friend and publisher, Michel Gallimard, Camus was killed in a car accident that had no apparent explanation (Lottman 698). In some ways it seems appropriate that one, who was so deeply influenced by the metaphor of absurdity, should have his life permanently interrupted through this tragically unexplainable event.

Albert Camus: His Legacy

How does an understanding of Camus's engagement with his own historical moment assist one in navigating through the contemporary historical moment? Like Albert Camus, we live in an age of recognized absurdity, defined by contradiction and contention of narrative and virtue structures of the past. When living in such a time, one can be greatly informed by seeking out those passionate voices who have navigated through similar circumstances. Many voices from such moments in human history provide first-hand insights into how to navigate such a time. Many of the influences on Camus approached life with radically different agendas from their contemporaries while living through their own eras of uncertainty and contradiction. As will be demonstrated shortly, these voices from the past include Blaise Pascal, Søren Kierkegaard, Fyodor Dostoevski, Friedrich Nietzsche, and Franz Kafka. While each of those individuals just listed offers vast wisdom for our time, the focus of the present study, Albert Camus, provides a perspective for navigating through our own historical moment of contradiction. When considering absurdity as a metaphor that accurately describes the contemporary moment, one is invited into a conversation about how the work of Albert Camus can inform an existential ethical response within a postmodern moment of narrative and virtue contention.

Living in an absurd historical moment challenges one to steer clear of attempting to implement a template from a past narrative within the contemporary, and often very different, narrative structure. It is not uncommon to find many people within our contemporary American culture who become overly concerned with convenience and finding a "quick fix" while lacking a willingness to take the time to find an appropriate and ethical response to everyday situations. What the life and writing of Camus suggest is not that the world should always be viewed through the lens of the metaphor of the absurd but that we should allow space for the emergence of metaphors that help make sense of the moment before us. Camus recognized the absurdity of his own historical moment and sought out the voices (such as Kierke-gaard, Dostoevski, and Kafka) that helped him make sense of his own moment in history. Arnett and Arneson write, "applying concepts [metaphors] from a historical era other than our own requires concepts from a given theory to meet the needs (answer commonsense questions) of the present historical moment or we invite an interpretation of communication that is static and dangerously anachronistic" (32). These unreflective decisions often emerge out of a longing to satisfy personal desires and are motivated by nothing more than personal preference, lacking any connection to or consideration of a larger life narrative. These decisions could be considered groundless, thus leaving one with only personal preference. If someone does not work from a grounded standpoint, in future moments he will be tempted to either implement the previously successful model, or he will again be tempted to work from personal preference. Alasdair MacIntyre uses the term "emotivism" to indicate decision-making that is *nothing* but expressions of preference, expressions of attitude or feeling" (*After Virtue* 12). Either way, one will lack the coherence and fidelity suggested by Walter R. Fisher that gives meaning to one's personal narrative and, in turn, his life. The goal of the following section is to provide constructive connections between the historical moment of Albert Camus and our present age, thus suggesting what his legacy can be for those who seek to follow his example.

While many lessons can be drawn from Camus's life and work, three major themes will be explored: first, his willingness to draw upon the ideas of relevant voices that preceded him; second, his effort to engage life as it actually existed and not as he wished it to appear; and third, a realization that sometimes ideas are more important than relationships. A common thread throughout all three of these lessons is the notion that Albert Camus can function as a philosopher of communication with deep ethical commitments and therefore assist us in navigating through our own historical moment of absurdity.

Camus provides an example of a person working from a constructive perspective, as he was willing to draw upon the thought of many contemporaries and great thinkers from the past while engaging his own time in history. Of those who influenced Camus's thinking about the absurd, there are five names that appear to have greatly impacted not only his life's work, but more importantly his understanding of the absurd: Blaise Pascal (1623-1662), Søren Kierkegaard (1813-1855), Fyodor Dostoevski (1821-1881), Friedrich Nietzsche (1844-1900), and Franz Kafka (1883-1924). The following was the age of each upon his death: Pascal was thirty-nine, Kierkegaard was forty-two, Dostoevski was fifty-nine, Nietzsche was forty-four at the time of his well-documented mental breakdown and fifty-five at the time of his death, and Kafka was forty years old at the time of his death. The average age at the time of death for the five men mentioned above is forty-seven years old—the same age that Camus would have been if he had lived to experience his next birthday. While it is a fruitless and unproductive effort to ask "what might have been?" it is interesting to note the tragically short lives of each and how they were able to gather around the common theme of absurdity. One could consider the idea that brilliant scholars who live abbreviated lives represent an aspect of Camus's absurdity, illustrating that life is without order and one must make the most of the time one is given. An overview of the thought of each of these men is provided next as his ideas relate to Camus's use of the absurd.

Pascal's influence on Camus and his writings may be explained in terms of individualism, choice, and the paradoxes of the human condition. It is through the outworking of these ideas that Pascal is considered one of the precursors to existentialism. The paradox of living is what provided the foundation for Camus's understanding of the absurd. One of Pascal's most well-known portions of the *Pensees* is commonly referred to as "Pascal's Wager" in which he provides a choice between a belief in God or a denial of God's existence. Cruickshank wrote, "Having faced a dilemma similar to part of the dilemma outlined by Pascal, Camus wagers in the opposite direction. . . . [H]is decision to stake everything on immediate physical life is the result of arbitrary choice" (35). Lavine describes Pascal as "expressive of absurdity" during the time of Descartes (331). Camus praised this "beloved philosopher" in a letter to a friend; Camus wrote, "If you knew how ravishing Pascal is . . . clear, profound, and unforgettable about the human heart and in his despairing glory" (Todd 30). While Camus did not share the religious convictions of Pascal, it is evident in *The Stranger* that Camus shared with Pascal an interest in the individual's reaction to the human condition.

The influence of Kierkegaard, "widely known as the 'father of existentialism'" (Eller 57), can be traced to his early existential themes of the response of the individual to the human condition as hopeless and full of anxiety and despair. The publishing of Camus's *The Stranger* was critiqued as "the sign of Kierkegaard's arrival in France" (Lottman 268). Lavine explains Kierkegaard's view of life as "inexplicable, and wholly absurd" (331). Kierkegaard's writings were responding to crisis, and what ought to be done. Much like Camus, Kierkegaard's writings demonstrated an interest in how one responds to everyday events, and while deeply philosophical, his ideas were not esoteric and unrelated to the lived situation. While Camus did not directly cite Kierkegaard when discussing despair in *The Rebel*, Kierkegaard's exploration of the topic provides helpful insights into an understanding of the topic. Kierkegaard wrote in *The Sickness Unto Death*, a text dedicated to the question of despair, "If there is to be any question of a sickness unto death in the strictest sense, it must be a sickness of which the end is death and death is the end. This is precisely what despair is" (17). One way in which Kierkegaard makes use of the metaphor of despair "is abandoning the project of achieving the salient good because one finds oneself powerless to achieve it" (Hannay and Marino 331). When engaging absurdity, one does not respond with "I'll never . . ." but seeks to encounter life on its own terms and respond in an ethical and productive manner without falling into a perpetual state of despair.

Camus commented that Dostoevski's novel *The Possessed* "is one of the four or five works that I rank above all others" ("Foreword," *The Possessed*). Camus adapted this work for the theater and it represents one of his most personally cherished publications. As he worked through the implications of the absurd in *The Myth of Sisyphus* Camus wrote, "And probably no one so much as Dostoevski has managed to give the absurd world such familiar and tormenting charms" (110). While Camus himself was an atheist, he could constructively work with the religious themes of Dostoevski's novels. Camus wrote, "It is possible to be Christian and absurd" ("Myth" 112). While Camus never accepted the narrative of the Christian faith for himself, when speaking to a group of Christians he stated that he believed the tension of the differences allowed for "real dialogue, [and] that falsehood is just as much the opposite of dialogue as is silence, and that the only possible dialogue is the kind between people who remain what they are and speak their minds" ("Unbeliever" 70). With Dostoevski, Camus shared an interest in humanizing the ideals of the absurd, as seen in his memorable characters in *The Stranger* and *The Plague*.

Nietzsche provided great inspiration for Camus. For Camus, Nietzsche "nourished his suspicions of all traditional morality" (Todd 142). Camus's concern with responding to the historical moment turned more so on morality than philosophy. In exploring this notion, Camus searched for a way one should live in such an absurd world. "Trying to sketch out a morality, he turned back to Nietzsche: 'What matters is not eternal life but eternal liveliness'"(Todd 145). Much like Kierkegaard, Nietzsche was responding to crisis and prescribing what ought to be done, which can be understood as a concern for the ethical response to the historical moment. Lavine comments:

For Kierkegaard and Nietzsche, and for the existentialism which follows them, the crisis of the modern world is a problem concerning the individual, the human self. The consciousness of the human subject is the only key to the diagnosis and possible cure of the problems of the modern era. (326)

Kaufmann found that Camus's *The Myth of Sisyphus* "sounds like a distant echo of Nietzsche" (21). Camus shared with Nietzsche an interest in not only the implications of one's philosophical position but also a deep concern for ethical conduct in the midst of daily living. One major difference between Camus and Nietzsche was that Camus did not give into despair and succumb to the dead end of nihilism. Camus did not become immobilized by his understanding of absurdity but discovered that the meaning found in one's life is created by the individual, thus moving him towards greater productivity and away from total cynicism.

The final influence, Franz Kafka, created the most problems for Camus during his lifetime. Since Kafka was a Jewish writer, a chapter on Kafka's work within the original version of *The Myth of Sisyphus* had to be eliminated before it was allowed to be published in German-occupied France in 1941 (Lottman 262). This essay would appear later in "a free zone magazine" and in subsequent editions of the text (Lottman 265). Two themes of interest to Camus are evident in the writings of Kafka. First, Camus comments that within Kafka's work "You recognize a theme familiar to existential philosophy: truth contrary to morality" ("Myth" 133). Second, he is captured by Kafka's interest in maintaining hope in an effort to overcome the despair that often presents itself in the absurd conditions of everyday life. Camus wrote, "Within the limits of the human condition, what greater hope than the hope that allows an escape from that condition" ("Myth" 135). Camus's work in the French underground demonstrates his commitment to perform what he thought was the truthful, ethical act even when illegal. This concern for legality provides evidence that Camus recognized the limits that one's situatedness presents. While Camus searched for meaning in life, he never abandoned the notion that a realistic hope existed. After suffering in several concentration camps during World War II, Viktor Frankl wrote, "the sudden loss of hope and courage can have a deadly effect" (75). Camus, along with Kafka and Frankl, represent a commitment to a hope that takes the challenges of life head-on, and maintains hope in spite of the absurdity of the moment.

While the personal notebooks of Camus reveal a variety of different influences upon his work, it is primarily through the ideas of Pascal, Kierkegaard, Dostoevski, Nietzsche, and Kafka that Camus discovered the most texture for his understanding of the metaphor of the absurd. The variety of ideas and metaphors that he engaged through his own reading of the work of other novelists and philosophers allowed him to respond to his historical moment in a more appropriate manner. By his constructive use of the ideas of others, Camus demonstrated the significance of the absurd for his own moment, as well as providing insight into how the absurd is connected to our own postmodern moment; thus, allowing himself to serve as a voice to provide wisdom for ways to make our way through the contemporary moment.

The second major contribution left by Albert Camus is demonstrated by his willingness to engage an ever-changing historical moment on its own terms; for Camus this meant rejecting a Christian faith that would have provided an objective position from which to judge the chaos experienced in life. He accepted the absurdity of his historical circumstances and allowed an organic metaphor of absurdity to emerge from within the turmoil of his moment. Camus did not interpret the evil that he witnessed in spiritual terms but believed that humans are capable of creating the meaning of their existence, whether for good or evil. These evil actions could be manifested through both attacks on people and attacks on clarity of idea. He wrote, "[N]ever perhaps at any time has the attack on reason been more violent than in ours" (*Myth* 22). The metaphor of the absurd emerged and expanded as Camus engaged his particular historical circumstances through his activity as an advocate for his homeland Algeria and as a participant in the French Resistance movement during World War II. This moment revealed itself as a moment of narrative and virtue contention while at the same time being unpredictable, irrational, and violent—a time much like our own.

Throughout his life's work, Albert Camus made use of metaphorical distinctions to emphasize the general themes of his writings. These metaphors emerged at a relevant moment in history in which they connected Camus's own experience with historical circumstances. Camus's ideas were grounded in everyday living as he worked out the implications of the metaphor of the absurd. For example, Camus's first cycle of work exploring absurdity includes the novel *The Stranger*, the philosophical essay *The Myth of Sisyphus*, and the plays *The Misunderstanding* and *Caligula*. As Camus's historical moment changed, he began working more explicitly with the metaphor of revolt leading to the publication of his second cycle of work including the novel *The Plague*, the philosophical essay *The Rebel*, and the play *The Just Assassins*. This move should not be viewed as a turning away from engaging absurdity but as a way of adding further nuance to his understanding of absurdity. Camus did not encourage an optimistic outlook that held unrealistic expectations for living. Arnett and Arneson write, "A wedding of hope and cynicism within a dialogic perspective is guided by a metaphor, not of unlimited potential, but of hope within limits" (25-6). When one willingly recognizes the limits of a given moment while at the same time attempting to respond ethically and productively, one is walking in the land of Martin Buber's "unity of contraries." This dialectical tension is "lived out in the confusion of contradictions, not in the certainty of YES or NO" (Arnett and Arneson 142). Resignation and hope went hand in hand for Camus through his recognition that those who took action in the world were capable of great evil; nevertheless, he attempted to build a vision for the world that encouraged one to take action in spite of the absurdity of life. This tension helps each keep the other portion healthy and provides limits within the optimism or unrealistic hope that many possess while engaging absurd circumstances.

The final lesson to be drawn from Camus's work is that, sometimes, ideas are more important than relationships. Along with the contributors to *Communication Ethics in an Age of Diversity*, a text that explores the implications of taking ethical action in the contemporary historical moment, Camus sought to "develop constructive responses to the challenges of [his] unique age" (Makau and Arnett viii). Sometimes these constructive responses result in the destruction of an interpersonal relationship. As stated earlier, Camus's engagement with his historical moment eventually led to a conflict of philosophical positions with celebrated individuals such as Jean-Paul Sartre and Simone de Beauvoir. Camus's friendship-ending disagreement with Sartre was driven by a difference in philosophical beliefs as opposed to a breakdown in the interpersonal dynamics of the relationship. But it was also driven by a different vision for post-World War II France; Sartre was a staunch supporter of the Soviet-style communism while Camus was seeking a "third way" between the communism of the East and the capitalist system of the West.

Whatever one calls the contemporary historical moment—a moment of absurdity, a postmodern moment, a moment of contention over virtue and narrative—one of the by-products of living in such a moment can be interpersonal conflict. As the events of the twentieth century unfolded, leading to the end of the modern era, more and more voices began seeking an answer to the question of whether meaning was found within metanarratives or within human experience and relationships. His break with Sartre is a brief glimpse of how Camus foreshadowed the coming postmodern era. Sometimes when one embraces a narrative or story over a relationship, he or she will find that particular relationship no longer sustainable in light of the new commitments.

Conclusion and Implications

One of the goals of this essay is to provide one with options for making a reflective existential ethical choice as an informed participant in the contemporary historical moment. Albert Camus provides insight into how one can benefit from listening to relevant voices from previous generations. We must allow the time to familiarize ourselves with those who sought answers to similar questions that we are asking. For Camus, this meant discovering how others engaged an absurd historical moment. For us, this means listening to the voice of Albert Camus, as he represents the closest historical perspective on how to make sense of a world that has radically changed since both World Wars of the twentieth century. This is an intentional choice and only comes through an investment of time and energy in the ideas of others. Camus also sought answers to his questions by engaging people and ideas and not by seeking something outside of human existence, such as religious framework, to serve as his interpretive lens. This does not invalidate the existence or acceptance of a religious worldview, but it should serve as a reminder that life is best understood by embracing life and not attempting to explain it away by looking at something (such as an afterlife) that occurs outside of our everyday existence. Finally, Camus's personal experience helped him understand that there are times when support for certain ideas comes into conflict with particular relationships. This break with Sartre demonstrates one final way in which Camus was both a product of and a shaper of his own historical moment. As such, Albert Camus can be regarded as a philosopher of communication with deep ethical commitments. A better understanding of his work provides a glimpse into a way in which one can better navigate the tensions of living within our contemporary age of absurdity.

Works Cited

Arnett, Ronald C., and Pat Arneson. *Dialogic Civility in a Cynical Age: Community, Hope, and Interpersonal Relationships*. Albany: State U of New York P, 1999.

Aronson, Ronald. *Camus and Sartre: The Story of a Friendship and the Quarrel That Ended It*. Chicago: U of Chicago P, 2004.

Buber, Martin. *I and Thou*. Trans. Walter Kaufman. New York: Charles Scribner's Sons, 1958.

_____. *The Knowledge of Man: A Philosophy of the Interhuman*. New York: Harper and Row, 1966.

Camus, Albert. "Caligula." *Caligula and Three Other Plays*. Trans. Stuart Gilbert. New York: Vintage, 1962.

_____. *The First Man*. Trans. David Hapgood. New York, Vintage, 1995.

_____. "The Just Assassins." *Caligula, and Three Other Plays*. Trans. Stuart Gilbert. New York: Vintage, 1962.

_____. "The Misunderstanding." *Caligula, and Three Other Plays*. Trans. Stuart Gilbert. New York: Vintage, 1962.

_____. "Morality and Politics." *Camus at Combat: Writing 1944-1947*. Trans. Arthur Goldhammer. Princeton, NJ: Princeton UP, 2006.

_____. "The Myth of Sisyphus." *The Myth of Sisyphus*. Trans. Justin O'Brien. New York: Vintage, 1991.

_____. *The Plague*. Trans. Stuart Gilbert. New York: Vintage, 1948.

_____. *The Rebel: An Essay on Man in Revolt*. Trans. Anthony Bower. New York: Vintage, 1956.

_____. *The Stranger*. Trans. Matthew Ward. New York: Vintage, 1989.

_____. "The Unbeliever and Christians." *Resistance, Rebellion, and Death*. Trans. Justin O'Brien. New York: Vintage, 1960.

Cruickshank, John. *Albert Camus and the Literature of Revolt*. New York: Oxford UP, 1960.

Dictionary.com. "Absurd." *Dictionary.com Unabridged 1.1*. 25 Mar. 2008. http://dictionary.reference.com/browse/absurd.

Eller, Vernard. "Ellul and Kierkegaard: Closer than Brothers" *Jacques Ellul: Interpretive Essays*. Ed. Clifford G. Christians and Jay M. Van Hook. Urbana: U of Illinois P, 1981.

Fisher, Walter R. *Human Communication as Narration: Toward a Philosophy of Reason, Value and Action*. Columbia: U of South Carolina P, 1987.

Frankl, Viktor. *Man's Search for Meaning*. Trans. Ilse Lasch. Boston: Beacon, 2006.

Gadamer, Hans-Georg. *Philosophical Hermeneutics*. Trans. David E. Linge. Berkeley: U of California P, 1976.

_____. *Truth and Method*. 2d rev. ed. Trans. Joel Weinsheimer and Donald G. Marshall. New York: Continuum, 2000.

Hannay, Alastair, and Gordon D. Marino, eds. *The Cambridge Companion to Kierkegaard*. New York: Cambridge UP, 1999.

Holba, Annette. *Philosophical Leisure: Recuperative Praxis for Human Communication*. Milwaukee, WI: Marquette UP, 2007.

Hyde, Michael. *The Call of Conscience*. Columbia: U of South Carolina P, 2001.

Kaufmann, Walter. *Existentialism: From Dostoevsky to Sartre*. New York: Meridian, 1975.

Kierkegaard, Soren. *The Sickness Unto Death*. Princeton, NJ: Princeton UP, 1983.

Lavine, T. Z. *From Socrates to Sartre: The Philosophical Quest*. New York: Bantam, 1984.

Lottman, Herbert R. *Albert Camus: A Biography*. Corte Madera, CA: Ginko Press, 1997.

Lyotard, Jean-Francois. *The Postmodern Condition: A Report on Knowledge*.

Trans. Geoff Bennington and Brian Massumi. Minneapolis: U of Minnesota P, 1984.

McBride, Joseph. *Albert Camus: Philosopher and Litterateur*. New York: St. Martin's Press, 1992.

MacIntyre, Alasdair. *After Virtue*. Notre Dame, IN: U of Notre Dame P, 1984.

Magnus, Bernd, and Kathleen Higgins. *Cambridge Guide to Nietzsche*. New York: Cambridge UP, 1996.

Makau, Josina M., and Ronald C. Arnett, eds. *Communication Ethics in an Age* of Diversity. Urbana: U of Illinois P, 1997.

Nietzsche, Fredrich. *The Will to Power*. Trans. Walter Kaufman. New York: Vintage, 1968.

Pascal, Blaise. *Pensees and Other Writings*. Trans. Honor Levi. New York: Oxford UP, 1995.

Ricoeur, Paul. *The Rule of Metaphor: Multidisciplinary Studies of the Creation of Meaning in Language*. Trans. Robert Czerny, Kathleen McLaughlin, and John Costello. Toronto: U of Toronto P, 1975.

Albert Camus and W. G. Sebald:
The Search for Home _____

Henry L. Carrigan, Jr.

Not long after *Austerlitz* was published in 2001, W. G. Sebald was killed in a car accident, robbing modern literature of one of its most distinctive voices. Critics hailed his work, which became more popular in America and Britain than in his native Germany. The late cultural and literary critic Susan Sontag wondered whether literary greatness is still possible and what a noble literary enterprise would look like. She proclaimed that W. G. Sebald's work provided one of the few answers to these questions. Like Günter Grass, Sebald explores the political despair, social chaos, and individual guilt of post-World War II Germany, especially as individuals attempt to come to terms with loss and search to find explanations for the crimes perpetrated against Jews. Like Kafka, Sebald offers us portraits of outsiders living in exile, continually trying to find their way into the castle or beyond the gates of the law. Like Proust, Sebald explores the halls of memory but interrogates its facility to be a repository of truth and examines its power to distort. Like Stendhal, Sebald exploits autobiography and twists it into fictional narratives. Like Borges, Sebald playfully manipulates the borders between truth and imagination.

In his four "novels," Sebald explores themes of memory, identity, history and truth, beauty and transience, and exile. Sebald questions the boundaries of realism by weaving photographs, real people's names, and fictional characters in his "novels." His writings in many ways resemble Rilke's notebooks, with the narrators observing the activities of a variety of characters, including themselves. The narrators of Sebald's books, who are often doubles of himself, find themselves wandering through various urban and rural landscapes in search of their identities. Often, though, they end up circling and circling, wending their way down tortuous paths to self-identity. Outsiders, they circle through time and space in search of themselves and for some kind

---

of home. In various ways, all of Sebald's books explore the nature of identity and the function of memory.

When Sebald was killed in 2001, his untimely death evoked the life, work, and death of another novelist and essayist whose life was also cut short in an automobile accident: Albert Camus. The French Algerian Camus examined many of the same themes that Sebald explores, but Camus's works grow out of a political engagement that is absent from Sebald's novels and essays. Camus was born into a settler family in French Algeria, and as a child he lived with his mother in a poor section of Algiers. By the time he was twenty-two, Camus already was active politically, joining first the French Communist Party and then, one year later, the Algerian People's Party. Although he later rejected communism, he continued to be active politically, joining the French Resistance during World War II. Almost all of his novels and essays explore in some manner or other the notion of resistance, rebellion, alienation, exile, and moral courage in the face of possible defeat and death. All of his works deal with individuals struggling with themselves as they search for ways to fashion meaning in their world. These individuals also struggle with ways to create their own identities amid communities that alienate them because they are different or that attempt to ordain identities for these individuals by asking them to live by a certain set of rules that define the nature of humanity and selfhood.

Although he rejected the label, Camus has been most closely associated with the philosophical school called existentialism. This philosophy holds that existence precedes essence; that is, individuals do not possess preordained essential qualities or traits that somehow define them as individuals. Rather, each person must make choices regarding his or her actions and thus define himself or herself through these actions. Thus, for an existentialist, courage is an abstract quality against which soldiers are measured in wartime; according to this view, all soldiers who join the military and fight in a war possess the quality of courage. An existentialist would simply argue that courage does not exist apart from the decision to be courageous and that one's choice to perform a courageous act then marks one as courageous. While Camus certainly thought that humans cannot be defined by essential qualities—and his writings do emphasize that individuals are either free or not free to act in certain ways—his philosophical attitudes were more defined by the search for meaning in life. How, given that we know that life can often be meaningless, can we create meaning in our lives? How, in the midst of exile (strangers living in a strange land), is it possible to live a meaningful life? If we are in search of a meaningful life and we're not able to discover the ways to live such a life, should we commit suicide? What is the meaning of suicide, and is it ever an act that is meaningful? That is, does meaning arise out of an absurd response to an absurd and meaningless life? Although Camus's questions regarding suicide prompted an intense debate among philosophers and critics, he left the theme of suicide behind not long after his early work *The Myth of Sisyphus* (*Le Mythe de Sisyphe*, 1942), even though thoughts of suicide fill the minds of many of the characters in his novels, such as *The Stranger* (*L'Étranger*, 1942) and *The Plague* (*La Peste*, 1947).

Camus's writings grow out of his deep engagement with his political activities, and his own body of work is defined by his direct experience of Nazi occupation. In *The Plague*, for example, the Algerian port town of Oran is quarantined because a plague has invaded the town. Some of the characters are not even residents of the town, yet they must remain in its confines until the quarantine is lifted. Many interpreters have read the plague to be an infestation of Nazism, and the Nazis are compared to vermin who carry the plague of death into an innocent town. In his first sermon to the town, the local priest even accuses the townsfolk of bringing the plague on themselves because of their inattentiveness to the evil around them (much as, in this critical reading, various European communities were inattentive to the Nazi evil spreading around them). Both *The Stranger* and *The Fall* (*La Chute*, 1956), although focused on single individuals rather than on a group of people, raise questions about the nature of humanity and its ability to resist evil. In what ways does society define evil, and in what ways do individuals either capitulate to society's teachings or resist such teachings? *The Stranger*, for example, asks the question whether it is more evil to kill someone (even though Meursault tries to justify the killing by telling the judge that the Arab is a stranger and Meursault is a French citizen) or to feel no regret or pity about your mother's death.

Unlike Camus, W. G. Sebald was not directly politically engaged, even though many interpreters read his novels as attempts to come to terms with and to understand the meaning of the Holocaust. Although he learned about the Holocaust in school and although his teachers showed him and his classes pictures of the camps, his teachers were never able to explain the meaning of these events to Sebald and his classmates. Such a lack of information prompted Sebald to leave Germany to study German literature in Switzerland, and he eventually moved to England, where he taught German literature at the University of East Anglia and where he spent the rest of his life. Sebald's writings, however, deal only marginally with the Holocaust, and explore in a fuller way the journeys of individuals searching for an identity in a strange land and also searching for home (*Heimat*). More than anything, Sebald's characters spend their time wandering from place to place looking for home. The German title—*Die Ausgewanderten*—of Sebald's novel, *The Emigrants* (1996), nicely echoes this central theme of Sebald's work.

Even though the fashion and untimely nature of Camus's and Sebald's deaths are similar, and even though Sebald's death brought immediately to mind the death of Camus, their work appears on the surface to be more different than similar. Indeed, no critical articles comparing or contrasting the lives and works of these two writers have been written. Camus tends to be read and understood as a writer of his time, responding to the vagaries of war and weaving themes of resistance and revolt into his fiction; Sebald is often read as a writer whose blend of fact and fiction—many of his novels feature historical or liv-

---

ing people (Stendhal, Thomas Browne, Michael Hamburger) as characters—blurs the lines of the fictive and asks questions about the nature of reality. Camus was famous for writing collections of essays that he thought served as companions to his novels; Sebald, on the other hand, wrote essays on literature as a part of his occupation as a university professor, and these essays range from works on the German Expressionist playwright Carl Sternheim to critical interpretations of the Swiss novelist Robert Walser and the Czech writer Franz Kafka. Sebald's essays offer no insight into the structure of his novels, but they do deal with many of the same themes—digression, distraction, exile, homelessness, wandering—that can be found in his novels. Camus's novels tend to be realistic in the sense that they can be read from beginning to end and readers can follow a plot, or several aspects of a plot. *The Fall* is an exception to this structure, since in that novel readers must follow the meandering thoughts of the main character. Sebald's novels are more character-driven and are plotless. In his four novels, one of which takes its very title from the main character (*Austerlitz*, 2001), readers embark on a journey through history and space with one character or a set of characters. Sometimes there is a narrator who accompanies readers on the journey to explain the main characters' feelings and thoughts; sometimes the main character narrates his own journey. On yet another level, Camus's and Sebald's works display more differences than similarities. Although it is clear that Camus was very familiar with literatures other than French—he wrote in *The Myth of Sisyphus* about Dostoevski and Kafka, and he wrote about Herman Melville and William Faulkner in another set of critical essays—his own writing demonstrates a kinship with themes of historical, political, and philosophical struggle so characteristic of the French literary tradition, ranging from Flaubert and Zola to Balzac, Stendhal, and Voltaire. Sebald's novels do follow a more German literary lineage where—with the exception perhaps of Robert Musil's *The Man Without Qualities*—philosophical and literary questions trump social and political questions. Sebald's novels resemble more nearly those of Goethe (*Wilhelm Meister's Travel Years*; *Elective Affinities*), Hermann Hesse (*Journey to the East*), Kafka (*Amerika: The Missing Person*), or Robert Walser (*The Tanners*) where the main characters embark on a quest to find meaning in life, or to discover their homeland. Perhaps the greatest difference between the two writers—and this arises out of the literary traditions of their individual cultures—is Camus's persistent emphasis on morality (What constitutes a lie? What is the nature of evil?) and Sebald's apparent indifference to such moral questions. Many interpreters read Camus's novels as moral treatises that offer a particular solution to specific moral questions ("Is suffering a sign of having committed an evil act?"). Sebald's novels, however, do not propose particular answers to particular questions of morality, even though the events in which the characters participate may have moral gravity. In other words, while Camus is often called a moralist because his novels and essays focus explicitly on moral issues, Sebald's writings explore moral issues only where such issues arise in the context of the character's other struggles, and Sebald offers no guidance regarding a solution to such moral crises.

In spite of the many and significant differences between the two writers and their work, however, the works of Camus and Sebald are similar in some minor ways and in one major way. First, both writers owe a great debt to Franz Kafka and each admits as much in various essays. In a brilliant essay on hope and the absurd in Kafka's works in *The Myth of Sisyphus*, Camus declares that the whole art of Franz Kafka is in forcing the reader to reread. According to Camus, Kafka's novels and his stories are full of paradoxes that reveal to the reader both the absurdity (a character waking to find himself metamorphosed into a giant bug; a clerk arrested one morning without any explanation who must then wend his way through a labyrinthine legal system with no satisfaction) and the hope of human existence. Although two essays ("To the Brothel by Way of Switzerland: Kafka's Travel Diaries" and "Kafka Goes to the Movies") appear in English in the collection of essays titled *Campo Santo* (2006), Sebald's essay on work, messianism, and exile in Kafka ("Der Gesetz der Schande: Macht, Messianismus, und Exil in Kafkas *Schloss*") appears in a yet-to-be translated work on Eastern European literature, *Unheimliche Heimat: Essays zür österreichischen Literatur* (Gloomy Homeland: Essays on Eastern European Literature). In this latter essay, Sebald discusses the function of hope in the midst of exile in Kafka's *The Castle*. Second, both writers explore the acts and the consequences of a political regime that forces individuals to leave their homeland, or to be strangers in their own land (as in *The Plague*, in which the unfamiliar traps individuals in their own town with little hope and, at least initially, no promise of escape). Sebald's novel *The Emigrants* focuses on some characters whose emigration is the result of the actions of a regime hostile to the religious and social identity of the characters themselves. Finally, the one major theme that runs through both Camus's and Sebald's works is the search for home. In both cases, the search is lonely and confusing; in Camus's case, the search may result in an individual's recognition of an identity though that identity is confused. In Sebald's case, though, the search is never-ending, though each individual may find a temporary resting place. Camus's *The Stranger* and *The Plague* provide the clearest examinations of the theme of home in his writings; each of Sebald's four novels explores this theme in various ways, but *The Emigrants* and *The Rings of Saturn* provide perhaps the most forceful examples of this theme in Sebald's writings.

In Camus's *The Stranger*, the narrator, Meursault, searches for some understanding of society's codes of conduct regarding human relationships. As the novel opens, Meursault is attending his mother's funeral. He doesn't know how to express his emotions or what kinds of emotions that society expects him to express on such an occasion. He doesn't recognize that society expects him to engage in a certain period of mourning for his mother, for soon after his mother's death he ponders a sexual relationship. Meursault also wants to rise higher in his profession, and his thoughts turn to his success rather than to his mother's death. In the second part of the novel, Meursault spends the day at the beach, basking in the hot Mediterranean sun. His afternoon at the beach culminates when he shoots and kills an Arab. Of course, all kinds of questions arise from this event. To whom does this land belong? Is Meursault the interloper here as a French Algerian? That is, he feels that this is his home, but as the occupier, (French) Algeria is really not his home. Camus's descriptions of the sun turning Meursault into a particular shade of brown raise such questions to a new level: How much is Meursault like the Arab? Is Meursault homeless as a result of these actions? The questions that Camus raises in the novel deal with the guilt arising from the murder. Was Meursault's action premeditated? He is convicted of murder, but less on the evidence that the act was premeditated and more on the fact that he had failed to understand society's codes of conduct. Meursault ends the novel as a homeless creature who paradoxically feels at home in the benign indifference of the universe. As he opens himself to this gentle indifference, he experiences a feeling of happiness and hopes that his fraternal fellowship with the universe provides.

The Plague is set in the Algerian port town of Oran. Oran is an ordinary town where everyone is bored and where the town's citizens work only to get rich. Commerce is the habit most cultivated in Oran, and winter is the most pleasant season, for in other seasons the sun bakes the houses or the streets are filled with mud from constant rains. One day in Oran rats start to appear in the streets and die. Someone notices that these rats have grapefruit-sized tumors; it's not long before the doctor in the town sees his first human patient, who has a large tumor similar to the ones that appeared in the rats. Soon, a few individuals in the town die from the plague; the town is quarantined and its citizens must endure this trial as best they can. The novel focuses on a group of characters who find themselves thrown together in their efforts to resist the plague. Of all the members of this little group, Rambert, the journalist, an outsider, is the one who most wishes to escape and go home to his mistress, for his happiness lies elsewhere. In the early days of the plague, the journalist tells the narrator that he is sick of hearing about people who die for an idea; one must live and die because of what one loves. Even though Rambert decides to stay and help Rieux and the others fight the plague, his decision does not erase his earlier sentiments regarding his homelessness in Oran. The narrator (and he is not revealed as the narrator until late in the novel), Dr. Rieux, also is trapped in this port city, but he decides early during the plague that he will fight the pestilence with all his energy, even though he has a sick wife, who has left Oran for a sanatorium outside the city, to whom he would like to attend. Rieux's longing for home is as powerful as the others who wish to leave Oran for home, but he is consumed by a moral energy to help the sick in Oran. Rieux is not a religious man, but his attitude toward good and evil, suffering and redemption provide a contrast to the town priest, Father Paneloux, who, initially at least, lays the blame for the plague on the town's sins. Rieux's tireless heroism and moral courage in the face of the plague make him a secular saint whose identity is formed in the crucible of physical suffering. Father Paneloux preaches two sermons in the novel; in the first, he blames the people for bringing the plague upon themselves through their evil actions. The church is full as he lambastes the gathered listeners, and they trudge home weary and hopeless following his sermon. By the time of his second sermon, though, Paneloux has witnessed the death of a child to the plague, and he struggles to explain the suffering of innocents. When he preaches his second sermon, there are few citizens in the church for they have realized that the only optimism and hope they have in the face of this epidemic is to band together as a community to eradicate it. In this novel, the search for home takes many forms. The journalist yearns for his home only to realize that perhaps he has found it in the humanity of Oran. The citizens of Oran—who once thought of home as an ordinary place marked by the day-to-day activity of making money—now recognize that home becomes a meaningful place when that home becomes a true community of like-minded individuals fighting for, or against, a common cause.

In W. G. Sebald's novels, the search for home takes different forms and often involves individuals who literally wander out in search of themselves and home. Like Kafka and Robert Walser, Sebald records the experiences of individuals who wander though their lives searching the past for some clues about their identity. These characters often drift through broken landscapes littered with the debris of shattered families, madness, and the shards of history as they try to remember how they came to their particular historical moment and discern ways to live within that moment. More than any other contemporary German novelist, Sebald explores the ways that individuals manage to carry— or cannot manage to bear—the unbearable weight of history in their lives. Although all of Sebald's novels explore the themes of exile, homelessness, and the function of memory and forgetting as ways of approaching these issues, *The Emigrants* and *The Rings of Saturn*, in particular, provide clear expressions of these themes.

Sebald's *The Emigrants* follows the lives of individuals who are "wandering out" (*Ausgewanderten*) in search of their identities. Although the characters in the four sketches that make up the novel must confront the loneliness and isolation that emigration brings, they have voluntarily migrated from their homelands to various places in Europe. Each character desires to start life in this new place, but as in all of Sebald's novels the longing for home (*Heimat*) is unbearable. In contract to Camus's characters, who often embrace the loneliness of their settings, Sebald's characters are melancholics, longing wistfully for the homes they have left. In *The Emigrants*, each of these individuals commits suicide as a result of this unbearable heaviness of longing, and each tale thus becomes a cautious reflection on the burden of memory and the hope associated with emigration. As in Camus, suicide becomes in Sebald a response to the paradox of loss and belonging, and, although Sebald's narrators never articulate this in the same philosophical fashion as Camus's narrators might, suicide becomes a way of creating meaning in a meaningless world.

In the first story, the narrator meets Henry Selwyn, a Lithuanian Jew who had emigrated to London quite by accident. Through a series of conversations with various other characters, Selwyn reveals that he has kept his Jewish identity a secret (his real name is Hersch Serewyn) even from his wife, and he realizes that he must come to terms with the guilt of his past; that is, he feels guilty for keeping his Jewish identity a secret and emigrating and leaving behind his friends to be persecuted and killed by the Nazis. When he realizes he can never be free from these memories, he ends his life, and the narrator uses this death as the starting point for his own reflections on the nature of memory and the weight of the past. The second story focuses on schoolteacher Paul Bereyter, who adores his students but also reviles them for their disrespectful attitude toward art, music, and literature. While Paul considers his students the hope for a more open future—without the prejudices that characterize the nationalistic pride of Germany—he also is disheartened by his students' failures to recognize or understand beauty. Sebald likely modeled this on one of his own teachers. The third story is a family tale of Great Uncle Ambros Adelwarth (perhaps Sebald's own uncle), who emigrates to New York, works for a wealthy family, becomes the lover of the family's younger son, loses his lover to death, and goes through a deep depression leading to his own death. In the end, Adelworth is exiled not only from his community but from himself. Sebald modeled the main character of the final story, Max Ferber, on the English Jewish painter Frank Auerbach. The narrator of this story—who may be Sebald—meets Ferber in Manchester, England, where Ferber has been living for twenty-two years. As the two begin to talk about the present and the past, they offer each other the community of exiles in a strange place. Only after Ferber's death does the narrator understand the gravity of the secrets Ferber has kept hidden and the horrors from which neither his exile nor his memory would allow him to escape. Much like Camus's *The Plague*, then, Sebald's *The Emigrants* demonstrates that the loss of community often provides the impulse for the creation of community. Like the citizens of Oran, who have been exiled from their own community, the pestilence, these emigrants, who have tried to fashion a new homeland in unfamiliar places, discover that the individual search for a new homeland often fails. For it is only when individuals work together—a group of emigrants—that they can achieve true community and establish a new home, even though the longing for the old home will never be quenched.

The Rings of Saturn

Like Homer's *Odyssey*, Dante's *Divine Comedy*, and Joyce's *Ulysses*, among others, Sebald's *The Rings of Saturn* depicts a journey or a quest to find one's way back home or to move out of a mysterious stage of life into a place where new directions for life are revealed. In fact, the full title of the novel is *The Rings of Saturn: An English Pilgrimage* (although the subtitle was inexplicably omitted from the English translation). The novel defies easy plot summary, for it consists of ten episodes, each connected by the presence of the narrator and his reflections on his walking tour. Like other Sebald novels, *The Rings of Saturn* is a dazzling display of intertextuality—the underlying texts range from Thomas Browne to Rembrandt to Joseph Conrad to Dante—and the novel contains his typical mix of "fact," photographs, and fiction. On one level, the novel resembles a kind of Dantean *Inferno*, with each chapter representing a circle of the inferno. In this case, there is not a single Virgil to lead him through a particular landscape, but there is some person—living or dead—who acts as a guide on each of the narrator's rambles. On another level, the novel resembles the *Wanderjahre* of Goethe, Hesse, and innumerable nineteenth-century German Romantics. On yet another level, the novel resembles almost any of Kafka's novels with their sense of displacement; K and Karl Rossman undergo continual displacement, even when they think they have arrived at the place they had intended their journeys to take them (Law, Castle, America). On still yet another level, the novel resembles the destiny-less destiny of novels such as Robert Walser's *Der Gehülfe* (*The Assistant*) and Robert Musil's *Der Mann ohne Eigenschaften* (*The Man Without Qualities*).

The novel opens in August 1992 with the dog days of summer drawing to an end. The narrator sets off to walk the county of Suffolk in hopes of dispelling the emptiness that he feels after having just completed a writing project. As he ambles through the countryside, the narrator feels a joyous sense of freedom in Nature but also a revulsion when he encounters destruction in Nature, primarily from the bombings of World War II. One year after he has begun his walking tour, he is taken into a hospital in Norwich in a state of almost total immobility. During his hospitalization, he recalls, he begins in his thoughts to write the pages that will eventually make up the novel. Although he does not set pen to paper until one year after his discharge from the hospital, he has begun almost immediately to cast his reflections in terms of unveiling and sight. In fact, apart from the images associated with walking in the novel, the predominant images in the novel revolve around sight, seeing, gaze, lightness, and darkness. Although he can now see the world only from a small window in his hospital room, his desire to assure himself of a reality he feared had vanished forever causes him to pull himself over to the window and drag himself up to the sill in the tortured posture of a creature that has raised himself erect for the first time to look outside the window. These images of light and darkness, sight and blindness, point to the desire on the narrator's part to participate in a process of revelation that will disclose to him new meanings about his relationship to the natural world. As the narrator learns, however, the journey toward transformation and revelation is never-ending. Much as in both *The Stranger* and *The Plague*, nature becomes in *The Rings of Saturn* the setting for the main characters' attempts to find themselves at home in the world. Much as Meursault allows himself to be embraced by the benign indifference of the universe, Sebald's narrator finds his home not in the society of humans which is responsible for the destruction he sees around him but in the natural world. In a late scene in the novel, the narrator tells a tale about silkworms and the ways that these creatures construct community; the silkworms function as a metaphor for the acceptance of one's place in the natural world. The human place within the natural world also dominates Camus's *The Plague*. In that novel, humanity arises anew out of the destruction brought on by nature, and individuals begin the process not only of rethinking their relationships with one another but also their relationship to the natural world.

In spite of the many differences between the lives and work of Albert Camus and W. G. Sebald, both of these novelists are preoccupied with the search for home—indeed, a longing for home—in the midst of the twentieth century, when homelessness (and both of these writers experienced their own variety of homelessness) and exile defined the human experience. Each writer responded in his own way to the Nazi regime and its forceful expulsion of Jews from various homelands and the Nazi extermination of the Jews; Camus literally joined the French resistance in his resistance to the forms that fascism was taking in France and French Algeria, and in his writings he emphasized that individuals must join together in resisting evil. Sebald looks wistfully over a landscape destroyed by a Holocaust and portrays the emigrants who will be forever wandering in search of a new home while always looking over their shoulders with a melancholy gaze at their old home now lost.

Bibliography

Apter, Emily. "Out of Character: Camus's French Algerian Subjects." *Continental Drift: From National Characters to Virtual Subjects*. Chicago: U of Chicago P, 1999.

Blackler, Deane. *Reading W. G. Sebald: Adventure and Disobedience*. Rochester, NY: Camden House, 2007.

Brée, Germaine, and Margaret Guiton. *The French Novel from Gide to Camus*. New York: Harcourt, Brace & World, 1962.

Doctorow, E. L. *Creationists: Essays, 1993-2006*. New York: Random House, 2006.

Hawes, Elizabeth. *Camus, A Romance*. New York: Grove P, 2009.

Hughes, Edward J., ed. *The Cambridge Companion to Camus*. New York: Cambridge U P, 2007.

Judt, Tony. *The Burden of Responsibility: Blum, Camus, Aron and the French Twentieth Century*. Chicago: U of Chicago P, 1998.

Knapp, Bettina, ed. *Critical Essays on Albert Camus*. Boston: G. K. Hall, 1988.

Long, J. J. *W. G. Sebald: Image, Archive, Modernity*. New York: Columbia UP, 2008.

Long, J. J., and Anne Whitehead, eds. *W. G. Sebald: A Critical Companion*. Seattle: U of Washington P, 2004.

Lottman, Herbert. *Albert Camus: A Biography*. Garden City, New York: Doubleday, 1979.

McCulloh, Mark R. *Understanding W. G. Sebald*. Columbia: U of South Carolina P, 2003.

Patt, Lise, and Christel Dillbohner. *Searching for Sebald: Photography After W. G. Sebald*. Los Angeles: Institute of Cultural Inquiry and ICI Press, 2007.

Santner, Eric L. *On Creaturely Life: Rilke, Benjamin, Sebald*. Chicago: U of Chicago P, 2006.

Schwartz, Lynne Sharon, ed. *The Emergence of Memory: Conversations with W. G. Sebald*. New York: Seven Stories Press, 2007.

Todd, Olivier. *Albert Camus: A Life*. Trans. Benajmin Ivry. New York: Knopf, 1997.

Albert Camus's Critical Reception:
From Celebration to Controversy_____

Matthew H. Bowker

Much as Walt Whitman's poetry captured the tumultuous spirit of democracy and change in mid-nineteenth-century America, Albert Camus's ambitious work articulated the moral and intellectual crisis that tested mid-twentieth-century Europe. And like Whitman, Camus contained multitudes, for while his fiction plumbed the depths of absurdity, his philosophical essays and journalistic writings defended ethical action, meaningful dialogue, and a cosmopolitan ideal of justice. In nearly all areas of his life and work, Camus met with both acclaim and condemnation: While some praised his original literary voice, many protested his sentimental style, his inexact philosophizing, and his unconventional political message. All of these forces have come to define contemporary critical debates about Albert Camus: his celebrity, his complexities, and the public controversies in which he found himself embroiled.

Absurdity is undoubtedly Camus's central concept, and although the idea of "absurdity" may be traced back to Søren Kierkegaard, Friedrich Nietzsche, or even the Book of Ecclesiastes, Camus's writings were the first serious attempts to explore absurdity's meaning in a systematic way. Camus's early triad of works, *The Stranger*, *The Myth of Sisyphus*, and *Caligula*, all confronted absurdity, but not in the manner of Surrealists or dramatists of the absurd. As Martin Esslin pointed out in his landmark study of the latter: "If Camus argued that in our disillusioned age the world has ceased to make sense, he did so in the elegantly rationalistic and discursive style of an eighteenth-century moralist" (24). This stylistic choice alone may help to explain why Camus is remembered equally as a philosopher and a writer of literature, and why Camus's plays are among the least celebrated aspects of his *oeuvre*.

In addition to *The Stranger* and *The Myth of Sisyphus*, Camus's novel of occupation and resistance, *The Plague*, his essay on revolt and revolution, *The Rebel*, and his introspective novel about guilt, vanity, and vice, *The Fall*, spoke to shared experiences of struggle, loss, and meaninglessness set off by the terrors of the mid-twentieth century. In fact, Camus's "*actualité*" (a French word meaning both relevance and current-ness) was very much a part of his early success. In 1945, Camus was considered "France's leading public intellectual . . . the moral voice of his era" (Judt 88), partly for his fiction and philosophy, partly for his writing in the French Resistance journal *Combat*. In the 1940s and 1950s, the publication of a new book by Camus was a worldwide literary event (Brée 4). In 1952, the Jewish German philosopher Hannah Arendt wrote that Camus was "undoubtedly, the best man now in France . . . head and shoulders above the other intellectuals" (qtd. in Judt 87). In 1957, the Swedish Academy agreed, and, at the age of only forty-four, Camus was awarded the Nobel Prize in Literature.

Such victories, however, almost always were accompanied by controversy and critical setbacks. Particularly damaging to Camus's reputation were his rejection of communist doctrine, his public rift with Jean-Paul Sartre, and his profoundly unpopular stance on Algerian independence. Beside Camus's "*actualité*," therefore, we must place his "*inactualité*": the degree to which he was out of step with the political movements and intellectual fashions of his time. Especially near the end of his life, critics from all sides "fell over one another to bury [Camus]" for his "philosophical naïveté" (qtd. in Judt 88), while his moralistic tone, once the source of his esteem, ultimately earned him mockery as a "secular saint" (qtd. in Todd 374). Jacques Laurent described Camus's Nobel Prize as the crowning of "a finished oeuvre" (qtd. in Judt 87), while Lucien Rebatet wrote cruelly that "this prize which falls most often to septuagenarians is not at all premature in this case, because since his allegorical *La Peste*, Camus has been diagnosed with an arteriosclerosis of style" (qtd. in Todd 373).

Further muddying Camus's reputation was a persistent confusion of his work with that of famous existentialists, such as Jean-Paul Sartre. In response, Camus made several public comments, such as: "I am not an existentialist. Sartre and I . . . have even thought of publishing a short statement in which the undersigned declare that they have nothing in common with each other. . . . It's a joke, actually. Sartre and I published all our books . . . before we had ever met. When we did get to know each other, it was to realize how much we differed" (*Lyrical and Critical* 345). In fact, one would not be wrong to consider *The Myth of Sisyphus* a direct attack upon existentialism. Sartre recognized this, being among the first to insist that Camus belonged not in the tradition of existentialist philosophers but alongside moralists such as Michel de Montaigne, Blaise Pascal, Voltaire, Jean-Jacques Rousseau, and André Gide. In 1952, the weight of political events proved too much for Camus's and Sartre's fragile friendship, and the differences between the two men erupted into a bitter public quarrel.

Today, Camus's books have been translated and read throughout the world. His novels are taught regularly in French and Francophone schools, where they have earned him the status of a modern master. Even in Germany, the nation whose intellectual and political culture Camus often denounced, no foreign writer of the postwar era "achieved a greater or more immediate popularity" than Camus (Ziolkowski 132). And Avi Sagi has noted that, in Israel, a country contending with extraordinary violence and conflict, Camus's thought has "found paths to the hearts of young men and women thirsty for a human voice at once consoling and demanding" (3). Yet, Camus's work remains relevant not because it is universally adored, but because it addresses, and sometimes raises, troubling ethical and political questions. Indeed, the posthumous (1994) publication of Camus's unfinished autobiographical novel, *The First Man*, reignited debates about Camus's colonial and racial politics, in part because it coincided with a period of renewed Western political and military intervention in Muslim countries. Insofar as questions of occupation, colonialism, terrorism, and cultural misunderstanding are at the forefront of contemporary consciousness, even half a century after his death, Camus seems to have something significant, and often controversial, to contribute to the discussion.

But to understand contemporary debates in context, we must begin with the earliest questions posed by Camus's critics and readers. This chapter does not attempt to answer these questions definitively, but rather to trace the evolution of critical attention to Camus's work across three domains: the meaning of absurdity in Camus's early work; the reception of Camus's political message in the second "cycle" of his career; and the controversy over Algerian independence that survived Camus's tragic death in 1960.

The Meaning of Absurdity

While many writers struggle in obscurity for decades or even entire lifetimes, fame came quickly and abundantly to the young Camus upon the 1942 publication of *The Stranger*. When Jean-Paul Sartre, certainly among the world's most respected intellectuals at the time, wrote a favorable review of the novel, Camus was welcomed into European literary and philosophical circles as something of a new hero.

Like much of Camus's work, *The Stranger* seemed to captivate readers' imaginations because it addressed questions both timely and eternal. In the wake of the violence and terror of World War II, Meursault's absurd behavior evoked a familiar feeling of shell-shock, but it also recalled a more distant, Eastern quietism. Meursault's clear estrangement from his society invited both lofty philosophical reflection on the nature of humanity and political commentary about the effects of modernity and alienation. Perhaps readers were equally curious about Camus, himself: a young man educated in the French system, but a foreigner born and raised in the North African colony of Algeria. Camus's unique voice was both youthful and weary of the trials of poverty, war, and suffering.

These complexities in Camus's life and work, coupled with the immensely conflictual political events of Camus's era, most notably the rise of the Nazi Party and the German occupation of France, seemed destined to produce in Camus what John Cruickshank called an "inevitable attitude" of absurdity (6). Camus described his own writing as an effort to contend with the absurd experience of his generation, one that had seen "too many contradictory, irreconcilable things" (qtd. in Cruickshank 4). Germaine Brée understood Camus's absurd art as a direct reflection of the cultural, intellectual, and moral crisis of the day, a crisis she boldly compared with the end of the Roman Empire. Brée therefore found Camus's notion of absurdity to be representative of "a whole trend of twentieth-century European thought which grew out of a painful awareness of the impossibility of finding a rational justification for any system of moral values" (26).

Yet, in spite of its powerful moral and emotional resonance, many readers found Camus's notion of absurdity to be unfortunately ambiguous. John Cruickshank claimed that Camus's theory of absurdity contained circular arguments, and that Camus's "different meanings of the term 'absurd' involve three different kinds of relationship and are both confused and confusing" (63). In his authoritative biography, Olivier Todd agreed that Camus's thought-process in *The Myth of Sisyphus* was most often "rapid, punchy, and fluid. [Camus] sought a certain lucidity without quite attaining it" (144).

Over the years, vastly different interpretations of Camus's "absurdity" have been offered, from Robert de Luppé's claim that absurdity is "the meaninglessness of life," indeed, the meaninglessness of "everything" (5), to Jean Onimus's explanation of absurdity as the condition represented by the life of Christ, but only if "the final pages of the gospel are ripped out" (49). To be fair, Camus, himself, was not terribly clear about the scope and application of the concept. In the first essay of *The Myth of Sisyphus* alone, Camus described absurdity in an astounding variety of ways, including: "a feeling that deprives the mind of sleep" (6), an "odd state of soul in which the void becomes eloquent" (12), "the confrontation between the human need and the unreasonable silence of the world" (28), a "contradiction" (18), a "passion" (22), a "revolt" (25), an "equation" (50), and a "wager" (52).

Thus, critics have often infused Camus's vision of absurdity with their own. Sartre's influential review, "An Explication of *The Stranger*," praised Camus for having articulated the "facts" of absurdity: that "the world is chaos," that "tomorrow does not exist," and that "man is *not* the world" (110, *emphasis in original*). This reading drew heavily upon Sartre's own philosophy in which human consciousness is superfluous in a non-rational world. It also drew upon Sartre's argument that *The Myth of Sisyphus* was Camus's "precise commentary upon [*The Stranger*]" (108). Sartre's linking of the two texts together has likely guided more interpretations of Camus's work than any other.

Roger Quilliot's study, *The Sea and Prisons*, saw Meursault as simple, indifferent, and even primal, yet "born to duplicity," for "between that smile that he tries to express and the grimace that his tin plate flashes back to him, there is a kind of rift; already, a fall from innocence" (81-82). Quilliot saw in Meursault a moral complexity that is a source of much critical disagreement. For instance, Donald Lazere argued that "Meursault is not in the least disturbed by his subjectivity . . . he is more an object than a subject" (154). In his description of Meursault as a "distorting mirror held up to us" (83), Quilliot's characterization of Meursault may be equally appropriate to Clamence, the hero of *The Fall*, who so memorably struggles with duplicity and self-consciousness.

Although Sartre's and Quilliot's interpretations were influential, Camus was particularly upset by critics such as Wyndham Lewis, Pierre Lafue, and Aimé Patri, who saw Meursault as "'a schizophrenic,' or 'a moron,' or . . . an example of the mechanization and depersonalization of modern life" (*Lyrical and Critical* 336n). Such approaches to Meursault have remained common. For instance, Arthur Scherr has argued that Meursault had "low self-esteem" and "thwarted ambition" attributable to his unloving mother (150), while Colin Wilson recently described Meursault as "basically a brainless idiot" (qtd. in Scherr

150). Camus replied to this sort of criticism in his *Preface* to the American University Edition of *The Stranger*: "Meursault is not a piece of social wreckage, but a poor and naked man enamored of a sun that leaves no shadows. Far from being bereft of all feeling, he is animated by a passion that is deep because it is stubborn, a passion for the absolute and for truth" (*Lyrical and Critical* 336).

Most critics today understand Meursault's absurdity, and the idea of absurdity in general, as the lack of correspondence between human culture and the natural world. John Cruickshank's seminal work, *Albert Camus and the Literature of Revolt*, attempted to clarify Camus's absurdity in just this way, as "something which arises from a confrontation between the human desire for coherence, for understanding, and the irrationality, the opacity, of the world" (xiii). Cruickshank's interpretation of absurdity as a kind of intellectual disappointment has influenced many, if not most, subsequent critical readings of Camus.

Yet, debates about the meaning of absurdity were not, and are not, merely academic. At stake has been the question of absurdity's consequence: To what type of action does absurdity *lead*? Thus, while the ambiguity of Camus's idea of absurdity certainly impacted his critical reception, disagreements about the appropriate moral and political consequences of absurdity have played an even more significant role in shaping Camus's legacy.

Resistance, Revolt, or Rebellion?

No single argument in Camus's life was more widely publicized than the quarrel between Sartre and Camus that began with the 1952 publication of an unsparing critique of *The Rebel* in Sartre's literary journal, *Les Temps modernes*. If, in our day, it is difficult to imagine great popular interest in a squabble between two philosophers, at the time it had something of a tabloid attraction, perhaps not entirely unlike the fever surrounding a scandalous Hollywood divorce.

The review, written by Sartre's disciple, Francis Jeanson, accused

Camus of being "separated from reality" and of having become "an unrepentant idealist" who had lost touch with history (qtd. in Aronson 143). Against these charges, Camus wrote a bitter reply defending his book and accusing Jeanson and Sartre of intentionally misreading it. Sartre then retorted by "publicly flay[ing] Camus in the most personal terms," by "explain[ing] Camus's anti-communism as an evasion of personal growth and a refusal to fully live in the changing and demanding real world," and by leveling charges that Camus's response evinced "a racism of moral beauty" (qtd. in Aronson 148-149). "You rebelled against death," Sartre wrote, "but in the industrial belts which surround cities, other men rebelled against social conditions that raise the mortality rates. When a child died, you blamed the absurdity of the world and the deaf and blind God that you created in order to be able to spit in his face. But the child's father, if he was unemployed or an unskilled laborer, blamed men. He knew very well that the absurdity of our condition is not the same in Passy as in Billancourt" (qtd. in Aronson 153).

Here, it is possible to see how a disagreement about the scope and meaning of absurdity informed a much more heated debate about the appropriateness of moral and political action. In *The Rebel*, Camus had attacked the practice of historical revolution and the justifications of violence offered by revolutionary thought, while Sartre and his companions, especially those in the Communist Party, championed "the revolutionary . . . [who] is actively concerned to change the world of which he disapproves" (Cruickshank 103), even if that change demanded violence. Sartre and the Communists held great influence over progressive opinion in France at the time, and their advocacy of violent means to achieve a communist end was, at least momentarily, the orthodoxy of the radical Left. Thus, Camus's refusal of this position, which concerned first the legitimacy of communist revolution, and later, the proper course of action in Algeria, was shocking to his contemporaries, and has since become one of the most significant topics of critical attention to Camus's work.

Camus's hesitancy to endorse revolutionary violence was at times attributed to a secret conservatism on Camus's part, at times to a loss of nerve. Camus's second novel, *The Plague*, had drawn criticism along the same lines because its explicit subject was a natural occurrence, a disease, rather than a war or military occupation. Conservative voices praised the book, while many of Camus's allies were confused if not dismayed by its message (Zaretsky 79-80). Since the novel clearly referred to the recent war and to France's occupation by Germany, critics such as Roland Barthes and Simone de Beauvoir found its symbolism dangerously misleading. Why write an allegory of a plague, they asked, which denounces no historical evils and which oversimplifies the dilemmas of resistance and revolution? Camus defended his novel in a well-known letter to Barthes that claimed that *The Plague* was applicable to "any resistance against any tyranny" because "terror has several faces" (*Lyrical and Critical* 340).

At issue here was whether Camus's philosophy of absurdity could support a strong ethical and political stance, or whether it condemned one to indecisiveness, passivity, or bourgeois complacency. There is a valid theoretical debate at the heart of this issue, one clarified by John Cruickshank, Herbert Hochberg, and others who have fairly criticized Camus for confusing his descriptive account of the absurdity of the human condition with his normative account of the ethic appropriate to absurd individuals. Yet some critics have offered solutions, such as Donald Lazere's postulate that absurdity suggests the supreme importance of individual life. "Once we affirm every individual consciousness as an absolute value," Lazere wrote, "we become bound to seek a social system that promotes maximal length, intensity, and freedom for each individual's life. Hence we must oppose war, capital punishment, and any ideology that subordinates human flesh and blood to abstractions such as nationalism or bourgeois property" (138).

Fred Willhoite Jr.'s *Beyond Nihilism: Albert Camus's Contribution to Political Thought* remains a greatly influential interpretation of Camus's work in which Camus's political aim is defined as "dialogic communion," drawn in part from Martin Buber's ideas of dialogue and intersubjective relationships (64-69). The appropriate attitude of the absurd person, according to this view, is that of the "genuinely free dialogic attitude that exalts and enhances life" as opposed to the "monological hardness and fanaticism that leads to death" (66).

Jeffrey Isaac's well-known *Arendt, Camus and Modern Rebellion* argues that Camus's goal was to find a way between all or nothing, to discover a relative ethical stance that could withstand the pressures of both absolutism and nihilism. Isaac's book contends that Camus endorsed democratic politics, dialogic communities, and a posture of ethical reflexivity. "Absurdity involves, then, not just the absence of an ultimate answer, but a question, as well as a questioner, whose inquiry attests to the value of human life and to the importance of the freedom to ask elusive questions and dream elusive dreams" (120).

Some attempts to resolve Camus's ethical and political dilemmas have been even more complex. As we explore absurdity, says the philosopher Avi Sagi, we are elaborating a kind of self-knowledge, which is "ethical, in the sense of a return to concrete existence moulded by acquaintance with its foundations" (282). Other critics, however, have seen in absurdity only an evil to be combated. For example, Thomas Merton claimed that "[Camus] wants his reader to recognize 'the absurd' in order to resist it" (182). Absurdity, for Merton, was "simply one face of 'the plague' which we must resist in all its aspects" (182).

Curiously, the question of *which* absurdities to reject and *which* absurdities to accept was the question that defined Camus's career. Most recently, this question has been examined in the context of French colonialism and the Algerian War for independence (1954-1962). Although a child of Europeans and a citizen of France, Camus was deeply connected to Algeria, the land of his birth. So when the longstanding conflict over independence erupted into full-scale violence, Camus found himself in an extremely difficult position.

The Algerian Controversy:
What If Camus Was Wrong?

Today, it is not uncommon for discussions of Camus to pass over his most celebrated fiction and essays, concentrating instead on his journalism, his letters and reports on Algeria, and his unfinished novel, *The First Man*. But these seemingly unusual points of focus are not without justification, for Camus's position on Algerian independence was complex and, by most contemporary standards, lamentable. At various points in his career, Camus both criticized the idea of complete Algerian independence and sought to rectify the deplorable conditions of Arab Algerians living under French rule. He denounced the use of terrorism as a tactic of the National Liberation Front (FLN), but also criticized the repressive methods of the French administration (*Resistance* 115). He advocated moderate steps toward peaceful resolution, but also desired to keep the French colonial system intact, even claiming that it was necessary for Algeria to be "conquered a second time" (Hughes 2). What Camus meant by this most unfortunate phrase, however, was that the full rights of French citizenship should be extended to *all* Algerians: Europeans, Arabs, and Berbers.

For several decades, critics have decried Camus's position as vacillation, collaboration, even racism. Raymond Aron's lament that Camus was simply unable to escape the attitude of a "well-intentioned colonizer" (Judt 119), has become a common contemporary assessment of Camus's writings and speeches of the time. In 1957, after several passionate editorials, speeches, and failed attempts to intercede, Camus refused to make any more public statements about Algeria at all. Of course, critics then took issue with Camus's silence. Simone de Beauvoir at first denounced Camus's "hollow" language on the Algerian conflict, then later declared herself "revolted by [Camus'] refusal to speak" (qtd. in Zaretsky 140-142).

The question that informs critical fascination with Camus's Algerian politics is really the question of how Camus, hero of the French Resistance, untiring advocate of justice, and passionate moralist of *The*

Plague and *The Rebel* could reasonably defend colonization and the permanent occupation of a foreign land. If Camus was "wrong" on this matter, then what are readers to make of his moral intuition, his political writing, and his overall contribution? On his own account, Camus had been "wrong" before, particularly in supporting the capital punishment of Nazi collaborators such as Robert Brasillach (Zaretsky 63-74; Foley 34). In Camus's later retraction of his position on Brasillach, one may remark the beginnings of Camus's developing political stance, from his immoderate demand for justice on behalf of the liberated French nation to his measured and arguably timid solution to the war for Algeria's independence.

Many critics take issue not only with Camus's political writings on Algeria, but with his novels and stories for their treatment of colonial problems of power, race, and identity. Albert Memmi and Pierre Nora argued that colonialist racism and sadism could be read between the lines of Camus's fiction, and since then, numerous critics have followed suit. While it is true that critics tend to read Camus quite selectively on this issue, many have found Camus's fiction to be emblematic of a Eurocentric mindset unable to confront the realities of inequality, systematic violence, and racism in North Africa and, by extension, elsewhere around the globe.

Conor Cruise O'Brien's *Albert Camus of Europe and Africa* has made the greatest impact in examining issues of colonialism with respect to Camus's life and work. Like many others, O'Brien was puzzled that Camus could recognize the injustice of Germany's invasion of France, and the injustice of the plague's invasion of Oran, while ignoring the French invasion and colonization of North Africa. Few would maintain that Camus consciously sought to perpetuate injustice, but O'Brien argued that Camus was blinded by his proximity to the French/Algerian issue, perhaps even resorting to a willful self-delusion to justify his colonial stance.

More than anything else, it was Camus's idea of an Algeria to which *he* belonged that was the source of O'Brien's and, later, Edward Said's famous indictments. Said's *Culture and Imperialism* accused Camus of being an oppressor of indigenous Algerians and, effectively, a usurper of their homeland, while O'Brien argued that Camus drew the wrong conclusions about Algeria because he suffered from the colonial hallucination of a shared cultural heritage. Subsequently, and rather cleverly, referred to as his "*nostalgérie*" (Carroll 2007 15), Camus's "idealized . . . fantasy of 'Mediterranean man,'" has been criticized often as a dangerous delusion, one Camus should have discarded amidst the extreme desperation and violence of the Algerian War (Apter 508).

Critics have noted that Arabs are often depicted as little more than "stick figures holding up the scenery" in Camus's fiction (Apter 503). O'Brien went further, describing Camus's treatment of Arabs in *The Plague* as Camus's "artistic final solution of the problem of the Arabs of Oran" (56). In *The Stranger*, it is true that Meursault's victim, "*l'Arabe*," is given no other name in the text; like many other Arab Algerian characters in Camus's work, he is little more than a ghost. Similarly, in *The Plague*, the Arab quarter is ravaged by pestilence but is almost completely ignored; even the heroes of the tale, Rieux and Tarrou, do not carry their struggle against the plague that far.

Although O'Brien, Said, and others have been correct in claiming that Camus was unable to imagine an Algeria without him (and other European settlers) in it, there has been a recent attempt to rescue Camus from the condemnations of postcolonial criticism. Notably, David Carroll has described Camus's vision of a unifying Algerian identity more generously as one of "an original sharing and being-together before separation, difference, and conflict" ("Camus's Algeria" 529). And Carroll's recent book, *Albert Camus the Algerian*, both departs from and extends this effort by examining Camus in terms of his "Algerianness." John Foley's recent book *Albert Camus: From the Absurd to Revolt* also lays out a fair critique of O'Brien and Said, defending Camus against many of their accusations.

Perhaps surprisingly, in spite of his controversial stance, Camus now is claimed by Algerian writers such as Assia Djebar as a national literary hero and one of their own (Djebar; Kelly). At the same time, French President Nicolas Sarkozy led a controversial effort to move Camus's body to the Pantheon, Paris's mausoleum for the greatest contributors to French life and culture. At the time of this writing, it seems doubtful that Camus will be memorialized alongside Voltaire, Rousseau, Zola, and others. But the controversy itself serves as a reminder that, even amid vocal criticism of his work, possession of Camus's legacy is still sought after by the many traditions, cultures, and ideologies in which his complex work took part. Perhaps the most one can say about the future of Camus's critical reception, therefore, is that the controversies of his life and death have not detracted from his celebrity but have become an integral part of it, attracting new generations of readers to Camus who are likely to discover in his work the same originality, complexity, and *actualité* that has engaged readers for nearly seventy years.

Works Cited

Apter, Emily. "Out of Character: Camus's French Algerian Subjects." *MLN* 112.4 (1997): 499-516.

Aronson, Ronald. *Camus and Sartre: The Story of a Friendship and the Quarrel That Ended It*. Chicago: U of Chicago P, 2004. Brée, Germaine. *Camus*. Revised ed. New Brunswick, NJ: Rutgers U P, 1964.

Camus, Albert. *Albert Camus: Lyrical and Critical Essays*. Ed. P. Thody. New York: Alfred A. Knopf, 1968.

_____. *Caligula and Three Other Plays*. Trans. S. Gilbert. New York: Vintage, 1958.

_____. *The Fall*. Trans. J. O'Brien. New York: Vintage, 1956.

_____. *The First Man*. 1994. Trans. D. Hapgood. New York: Vintage, 1995.

_____. *The Myth of Sisyphus and Other Essays*. 1942. Trans. J. O'Brien. New York: Vintage, 1955.

_____. *The Plague*. Trans. S. Gilbert. New York: Vintage, 1948.

_____. *The Rebel: An Essay on Man in Revolt*. 1951. Trans. A. Bower. New York: Vintage, 1956.

_____. *Resistance, Rebellion, and Death*. Trans. J. O'Brien. New York: Vintage, 1960.

_____. *The Stranger*. 1942. Trans. M. Ward. New York: Vintage, 1988.

Carroll, David. *Albert Camus the Algerian: Colonialism, Terrorism, Justice*. New York: Columbia UP, 2007.

_____. "Camus's Algeria: Birthrights, Colonial Injustice, and the Fiction of a French-Algerian People." *MLN* 112.4 (1997): 517-49.

Cruickshank, John. *Albert Camus and the Literature of Revolt*. New York: Oxford UP, 1960.

Djebar, Assia. *Le Blanc de L'Algérie*. Paris: Albin Michel, 1995.

Esslin, Martin. *The Theatre of the Absurd*. 1961. Third ed. New York: Vintage, 2001.

Foley, John. *Albert Camus: From the Absurd to Revolt*. Montreal: McGill-Queens UP, 2008.

Hochberg, Herbert. "Albert Camus and the Ethic of Absurdity." *Ethics* 75.2 (1965): 87-102.

Isaac, Jeffrey. *Arendt, Camus, and Modern Rebellion*. New Haven, CT: Yale UP, 1992.

Judt, Tony. *The Burden of Responsibility: Blum, Camus, Aron, and the French Twentieth Century*. Chicago: U of Chicago P, 1998.

Kelly, Debra. "*Le Premier Homme* and the Literature of Loss." *The Cambridge Companion to Camus*. Ed. E. J. Hughes. Cambridge: Cambridge UP, 2007. 191-202.

Lazere, Donald. *The Unique Creation of Albert Camus*. New Haven, CT: Yale UP, 1973.

Luppé, Robert de. *Albert Camus*. Trans. J. Cumming and J. Hargreaves. London: Merlin, 1966.

Memmi, Albert. *The Colonizer and the Colonized*. Trans. H. Greenfield. Boston: Beacon P, 1965.

Merton, Thomas. *The Literary Essays of Thomas Merton*. Ed. Patrick Hart. New York: New Directions, 1981.

Nora, Pierre. *Les Français d'Algérie*. Paris: René Julliard, 1961.

O'Brien, Conor Cruise. *Albert Camus of Europe and Africa*. New York: Viking, 1970.

Onimus, Jean. *Albert Camus and Christianity*. Trans. E. Parker. Tuscaloosa: U of Alabama P, 1965.

Quilliot, Roger. *The Sea and Prisons: A Commentary on the Life and Thought of Albert Camus*. 1956. Trans. E. Parker. Tuscaloosa: U of Alabama P, 1970.

Sagi, Avi. *Albert Camus and the Philosophy of the Absurd*. Trans. B. Stein. Amsterdam: Rodopi, 2002.

_____. "'Is the Absurd the Problem or the Solution?' *The Myth of Sisyphus* Reconsidered." *Philosophy Today* 38.3 (1994): 278-284.

Said, Edward. *Culture and Imperialism*. New York: Vintage, 1993.

Sartre, Jean Paul. "An Explication of *The Stranger*." *Camus: A Collection of Critical Essays*. Ed. G. Brée. Englewood Cliffs, NJ: Prentice-Hall, 1962. 108-21.

Scherr, Arthur. "Camus's *The Stranger*." *Explicator* 59.3 (2001): 149-53.

Todd, Olivier. *Albert Camus: A Life*. Trans. B. Ivry. New York: Carroll and Graf, 2000.

Willhoite, Fred, Jr. *Beyond Nihilism: Albert Camus's Contribution to Political Thought*. Baton Rouge: Louisiana State UP, 1968.

Zaretsky, Robert. *Albert Camus: Elements of a Life*. Ithaca: Cornell UP, 2010.

Ziolkowski, Theodore. "Camus in Germany, or the Return of the Prodigal Son." *Yale French Studies* 25 (1960): 132-37.

CRITICAL
READINGS

Camus's Hug

Philip Hallie

In front of me now is one of those French paperbacks that come covered with cellophane. The cellophane has turned speckled brown, but it has kept the cardboard cover of the book itself creamy white for more than thirty years. The little book contains two talks that Albert Camus gave in Stockholm in December of 1957 when he received the Nobel Prize for Literature. Camus gave it to me after we had been talking for almost two hours in his office on the top floor of his publisher's building in Paris. At the end of our talk, he wrote some polite words on the inside title page: "To Monsieur Philip Hallie, with all good wishes for his work and for our shared hopes, very cordially, Albert Camus." While he was writing, he said, to himself as much as to me, "Words. Well, not much, but . . . here."

Still, the words he wrote were a summary of our last two hours together and of our brief friendship. It was one of Camus's deepest convictions that language must be lean—if it would not lie. Lying for him was not so much saying what is false as it was adding to what is true. You are lying when you say you care and you do not. You are truing if you are staying close to the "*verité charnelle*," the flesh-and-bone details of how you yourself see and feel and act. He meant what he wrote.

The conversation was about our *espoirs communs*, our shared hopes; we both wanted to write and to speak truly, and lately we had been having trouble doing it. For both of us, it was hard to speak from the heart and still make sense to other people. It was late in the spring of 1959, and he was adapting novels to the stage instead of speaking straight from his own anguish and his own sensualism; I was writing about Michel de Montaigne, a sixteenth-century Frenchman who wrote personal essays that expressed his feelings and thoughts, many of them not mine. Albert Camus was a great man, I was a young philosophy student from America, but we both needed to write, and we warmed to each other.

The first time I ever laid eyes on the person of Albert Camus was over the heads of hundreds of students at a matinee in Paris's Théâtre Antoine. Camus had adapted Dostoevski's novel *The Possessed* for the stage, and at this performance of the play, the theater was full of young people who belonged to a group called *La Jeunesse Musicale*. My wife and I had joined the group so that we could go with them to see in person the leading artists of France. A few weeks before, we had seen and heard Francis Poulenc in action, looking and moving like a majestic bank president, playing some of his piano pieces, and telling us that there was no such thing as religious music: there was just music to which we attached religious words and feelings. Now Camus was going to talk with us about his stage adaptation of Dostoevski's novel about some Russian political fanatics.

The play centers around a rich, handsome, would-be revolutionary named Nicholas Stavrogin, who wants to bring a sick Russia to health by bloodletting—by killing people. In the end, he all but destroys everybody he touches and then hangs himself. In the theater when the last curtain fell on his suicide, there was silence for a few seconds, then a short burst of applause from the young audience, and finally a desultory tapering down. Apparently the long play had exhausted more than exhilarated the audience.

Before the applause ended, a lithe, dark man leaped up on the stage, without using the steps, and then he raised his arms, with a wistful smile on his face. It was Albert Camus, the man many of us thought of as one of the few good men in a broken world, a lay saint. Oh, those of us who had read everything we could get our hands on by and about him knew that he and the world around him were in agony. He was born and raised in Algeria, and he was a descendant of Europeans, both genetically and culturally. Ever since the early nineteenth century, Algeria had been a possession, even a "prolongation" (as some put it) of continental France. But now, in the middle of the twentieth century, there was a powerful drive in Algeria for independence. The Berbers and Arabs—more than nine million of them—were in the center of a struggle to achieve independence from the mainland; and the European French citizens of Algeria—more than a million of them—were involved in that struggle. His early work as a writer had been as a journalist for the *Alger-Républicain*, a daily publication that was very critical of French rule in Algeria. Camus's early writings consisted of reports on the desperate living conditions of Arabs in Algeria, and in fact he was the only French journalist ever forced to leave Algeria because he sided with the Muslims. In 1956 when the Algerian drive for independence was becoming very strong, he went back to Algeria in the hope of reconciling Muslims and Europeans; but his irenic message about "French and Arabs associating freely" sounded like the old colonialism to the Muslims and looked like surrender to the Europeans.

On a larger stage, the communist left saw him as too far right; and the right saw him as too far left. When he spoke up politically, he was attacked left and right; and when he was silent, he was accused of complicity with the rightist Europeans.

I saw him as a moralist, not a political figure, someone who was deeply suspicious of political abstractions like "right," "left," "colonialist," and "anti-colonialist." He was convinced that murder was what the bitterly contending parties were out to legitimize, whatever high-flown clichés they used. The "*verité charnelle*," the flesh-and-bone truth, was that particular people kill and suffer, and political polarities can make us cruelly indifferent to this truth.

Two years before the performance at the Antoine, he had received the Nobel Prize for Literature, the youngest Nobel laureate in literature since Rudyard Kipling. At 5:30 in the evening of December 12, 1957, in Stockholm, just after he received the prize, he participated in a painful question and answer session at Stockholm University. He told an angry Muslim interrogator that he denounced murder in all its forms and that "terrorism . . . in the streets of Algiers, for example . . . could strike my mother or my family. I believe in justice, but I shall defend my mother above justice."

Imagine how the saviors of the world took that! Suddenly the people in that university room were dealing not with saving the world from Injustice, but merely with saving a few paltry particular persons from murder!

Personal candor happens rather infrequently in political argumentation or in any other kind of abstract reasoning. When it happens, it is like having your spade suddenly turned by bedrock while you are in the process of digging a great hole for a great foundation that would support some great building. In the angry exchange with the Muslim in Stockholm, Camus is said to have turned pale, but though there was pathos in what he said about his mother and justice, there was also a simple truth: his mother was more valuable to him than any political abstractions could ever be. He was not only uttering a cry from the heart; he was also stating an un-get-over-able fact.

And it was a statement of fact that had a great tradition behind it. In the sixteenth century, during the bitterly cruel religious wars between Protestants and Catholics in France, Michel de Montaigne had made an art of avoiding abstract theological arguments and insisting on concrete, personal facts that no one could dispute. When someone asked Montaigne *why* he was a Catholic and not a Protestant, he would not spout arguable abstractions about transubstantiation or authority; he would say: "I am a Catholic because of human ties, because of how I was born and raised. I am a Catholic by the same title that I am a Frenchman." He preferred plain, ascertainable facts to great abstractions.

Sixteenth-century religious zealots hating and killing in the name of Christian love would not be moved by such facts; and twentieth-century political zealots legitimizing mass murder in the name of Justice would not be moved either. But unlike the zealots, Montaigne and Camus were not trying to coerce anybody into believing in some great cause; they were trying only to remind people that, no matter how high our abstract principles may fly, the flesh-and-bone individuals who utter these principles count, and count heavily. Human ties matter the way the heart in my body matters now. We add too much to palpable facts; we lie about them when we do not face them squarely.

Knowing all this—and especially knowing that for him legitimized murder was the great plague of mankind and his only bitterly hated enemy—people like me in the audience at the Antoine and elsewhere in the world loved and admired him in his agony. He was revolting against violence in a very violent world, and revolting against it valiantly, though pathetically. And valor and pathos were essential to what he meant by one of his key expressions: "*l'homme révolté*," "the rebel."

Anyway, he was utterly at home on the stage of the Antoine, and he seemed happy to be with all these young people. I had been told that he always became youthful with young people near him. When the applause ended, he asked for questions or statements from his audience. There was a silence that seemed to go on and on. Then to my wife's surprise, I jumped up from my seat at the back of the hall and asked: "What happens in Stavrogin's mind between the time when he hates and wants to destroy every person on earth and the time when he dreams about two islands, one full of innocent and happy people and the other full of evil? How does he move from being a nihilistic killer to being a passionate moralist?"

I thought I heard some tittering in the audience of teenagers at my American accent, but before I could get embarrassed enough to wish that I had stayed silent in my seat, Camus ran across the front of the stage in order to look straight at me, and with that long face of his that looked a little like the face of the great comedian Fernandel, he pushed his upper body over the footlights, and said, "When Stavrogin wanted to have everybody murdered, he was thinking in political abstractions. But he raped twelve-year-old little Matriocha, and then he let her hang herself so that their secret would die with her. Now he was living in the flesh-and-bone world of his own deeds. Be mortally cruel to a child, and you will learn the difference between innocence and evil. You don't find ethics in political words."

"*Ça va?*" he called out at me, still pushing his face over the footlights.

I called back, "*Oui, merci! Mais. . . .*"

Then he called out, "Come to my office at Gallimard Thursday afternoon about four o'clock, and we'll talk."

And so began my brief friendship with Albert Camus. I had read his plays, stories, and essays from beginning to end, and I had published an essay of my own on him in the early fifties; but now I was meeting him in a different world, a world of people who smell each other's breath and touch each other's flesh. I felt out of my depth, and I was trembling when I sat down, though I had not trembled while I was asking my question about Stavrogin. This man was so . . . so physical!

* * *

Thursday was a very warm, late-spring day, and by the time I had gotten to the top of the winding staircase that ended at Camus's office at Gallimard Publishing House, I was wiping sweat from my forehead. His door was wide open, but I could not see him. I called out, "Monsieur Camus?" There was a brief commotion, and suddenly he stood before me with a half-inward smile and his right hand out. Even though he was about my height, somehow I could not look straight into his eyes. I found that my attention was caught by his gray denim shirt, open at the collar with no tie. We shook hands, and then he touched my left shoulder and gently directed me to my right. I sat down in a chair next to his desk, just a few inches away from where he sat behind his desk.

On an impulse that afternoon I had brought with me an envelope full of photographs I had taken a few months before during a month in Russia. They were mainly pictures of young people in the streets of Moscow and Kiev, and I knew of his concern for children in a surly world.

As I reached into my jacket pocket to pull the envelope out, he leaned toward me with that long face and said, "What have you got there?" I told him. He leaned back in his chair, motioned me to leave the envelope in my pocket, and said, "No. Please. I do not want to look at them. The government authorizes murder there."

I must have blushed; I certainly felt ashamed: I should have known that Camus was far from being a friend of Russian communism. I should have known that for him Russian communism was propelled by what he once called "a brutal desire for justice." Communism, and every doctrine like it, put public rancor above personal love.

I let the envelope stay in my jacket and simply looked at him.

"You are an American. What kind of work do you do in America?"

I told him that I was a philosophy teacher at Vanderbilt University in Nashville, Tennessee, and that I was glad to get away for a year. I was a little tired of trying to teach adolescents about wisdom year after year. They hadn't suffered enough; they hadn't paid their dues.

He told me that writers get tired, too. Every new writing gets either praised or panned by people who claim to be objective or matter-of-fact. But both critics and writers live in abstractions. They are a little like Stavrogin when he forgets what he did to Matriocha and praises the abstract politics of mass murder.

After he said this, he became restless and started moving things around on his desk. Then he leaned back and told me that lately he had been having trouble writing because he had written too much to the nihilists, who enjoy their despair. He for one did not feel despair. He felt that there is something people can live for. Moments of experience can be illuminated and captured in art and in acts of compassion. We can live without apology and without appeal to higher authorities. And we can fight against the penchant for killing that is at work in human history. He went on to say that he was having trouble writing these things because they do not have the lean clarity he wanted his writing to have. He used to think that there is no goal, no meaning implicit in life. Now he was having second thoughts about this, but he couldn't write about goals and meanings clearly enough.

His warmth melted away my self-consciousness, and I found myself giving him advice. (I was giving *him* advice!) I suggested that he draw a sharp line in his mind between being objective and being subjective and that he write with frank subjectivity. I told him I was spending the year in Paris studying Montaigne, who wrote personally not scientifically, who offered not proofs but essays, expressions of what was in his own heart and mind.

I had my Pléiade edition of Montaigne's *Essays* with me (I carried it everywhere that year), and when I handed it to him, he immediately turned to the wonderful paragraph in Montaigne's essay "On Cruelty" that tells how Montaigne hated cruelty above all other vices and how he could not see a chicken's neck wrung without misery; nor could he bear to hear the scream of a hare in the teeth of the hunting dogs. Still, he loved to hunt.

After he read it to me, he said, "See. He is double, and he is honest about it."

Then Camus said that in his recent book, *The Fall*, he had come a long way toward writing subjectively. But even here he was trying to express the duplicity of a whole generation, rather than the doubleness of a particular fleshly man. He had not touched the carnal truth of himself, or of anybody else.

The Fall is a narrative told in the first person by a man named Jean-Baptiste Clamence. At one time Clamence had been a lawyer in Paris who served the poor without fee, never accepted a bribe, and helped blind people cross the street—in short, he found pleasure in being morally noble. After helping a blind person to cross the street, he would automatically tip his hat toward him or her and take a bow. One day he realized that the hat tipping and the bow were not for the blind person, who could not see him, but for the public. He realized that he was a play actor taking a bow, a Janus, a two-faced god—publicly caring, but privately careless.

One drizzly night in November, when there were very few people about, he was crossing the Pont Royal toward his home on the Left Bank. He found himself passing a slender young woman dressed in black, leaning on the bridge railing and staring into the water. He was moved at the sight of her neck between her dark hair and her coat collar, but he hesitated only a moment and kept on walking. Soon after he left the bridge, he heard a scream and the splash of a body striking the water. He stopped again, without turning around, and he heard the cry repeated loudly in the silent night air. Cries were going downstream; then they stopped suddenly. He stood there trembling, thinking something like "Too late, too far." Then he walked away. He told no one.

Years later he would hear laughter coming from behind him, but, when he turned around, there was nobody there laughing. He had become ridiculous; he was no longer a noble public figure. At the very end of his narrative, he wonders what he would do if he had a second chance to help the girl, but all he can come up with is, "Brr . . . ! The water's so cold! But let's not worry! It's too late now! It will always be too late. Fortunately!"

After he read the passage in Montaigne to me and mentioned *The Fall*, I took the neat little book out of his hand and turned to one of the passages I hold dearest in all of Montaigne's writings, a sentence in the essay "On the Art of Conversation": "We are always dealing with particular men, and it is a marvel how fleshly man is."

He told me he cherished it too. And there was silence. I still wonder if he was thinking of the ending of *The Fall*: "Brr . . . ! The water's so cold!"

Possibly because of the silence, I suddenly realized that we had been talking a long time, and I felt that I had imposed myself upon him, that I had intruded into his privacy by sitting there at his desk and talking as if we had all the time in the world. And so I jumped up from my chair and begged his pardon for keeping him so long. He smiled inwardly, with his head cocked to his right. Then he reached for the little paperback of his Nobel Prize speeches, wrote his comment about our common hopes, and handed the book to me. He said something about our being able to talk more some day; but I think we both had a feeling that this was not likely, since he had a trip to take, and I was sailing home with my family in a few weeks.

We shook hands, and his hand felt surprisingly small in mine, with his long face looming large a few inches away from me. Maybe his hand seemed small because we were both somewhat excitable Mediterraneans, sweating a little with our intense leaning, desk-pounding, talking, and reading, and our hands slid in each other. He walked with me to the door of his office, and I started the long descent down the wooden staircase. When I got to the bottom of the stairs there wasn't a thought in my head, just a feeling of sadness, incompleteness, passivity.

On the ground floor of Gallimard, the receptionist was rearranging some papers on her small desk. As was my habit, I started checking my pockets to be sure I hadn't forgotten anything. The Montaigne was there, and the photographs were in another pocket. I opened the little book in my hand, and suddenly I realized I had left my glasses up in Camus's office—I must have taken them off in the heat of our discussion and left them on his desk. I was walking toward the young receptionist, getting ready to ask her to get them from Camus and keep them for me until tomorrow morning. They were only reading glasses, and I could do without them overnight.

But before I got to her desk, I heard a rumble coming from atop the long staircase. Feet were pounding up there, and I heard Camus's voice calling to me, "'allie! 'allie! 'allie!" He was pounding down the stairs, and when I looked up the staircase, I saw that he was holding onto the bannister with both hands as he descended on the run. Somebody had once told me that he had a phobia against bannisters. Apparently he didn't trust them. But down he ran. He got to the bottom of the stairs so suddenly that I had to jump back in order to keep from being stepped on. He stood in front of me with my glasses in his left hand and a big happy smile on his face, "*Tes lunettes! Les voici!*" he called out as if I were on the far side of the lobby, and he handed them to me. Right after I took them he raised his open arms so that his hands fell on my shoulders, and he said, as he squeezed my shoulders, "*t'ai trouvé! t'ai trouvé!*" "I've found you! I've found you!"

Then, without another word, he turned and started the long ascent up the Gallimard staircase. I remember thinking for a moment about his poor lungs; people who knew him personally had thought that he would die while young because of them.

In a daze, I walked out into the street, and as I walked out I realized that we had been talking about important things, and his hug had warmed me to him as nothing else he had ever said or written had warmed me. And so, walking down the sidewalk I pulled a pen out of my jacket, and started outlining in the last blank pages of the Nobel book some of the things we had talked about. The words are still there, in red ink, all jumbled by my walking. I had walked a dozen or so steps when I felt that there was someone looking down on my back; I turned, and there in the window of his office that opened on rue Sebastien-Bottin stood Camus looking down at me intently.

I do not know what made me do it, but I turned my whole body toward him up there and blew him a kiss with my hand and a big smile. He pulled his head back, and I do not know if he smiled too. It was dusk, and he was far away.

Months later, in January of 1960, I was back in Nashville, Tennessee, reading a term paper for a philosophy course when my wife turned on the radio. Before I could ask her to turn the volume down, I heard that Albert Camus had just been killed in an automobile wreck south of Paris. The driver of the car was his publisher, Michel Gallimard. Camus had been sitting with him in the front seat of Gallimard's sports car, a Facel Vega, and when the car hit a tree, Camus was thrown against the rear window. He died instantly. A reporter wrote that there was a look of horror on his face.

I got up and went out to our front stoop and sat down. I was still holding the term paper I had been reading. I am almost certain that I wrote something on the back of the paper while I was sobbing with rage. I think I wrote: "Camus is dead." This was no more and no less than the truth.

For almost two decades I never published a word about Camus, though I continued to teach his writings and though my studies in the French Resistance during the 1940-1944 German occupation of France kept leading me back to him. In spite of his tuberculosis he played a very active role in the Resistance. In fact, it could be argued that as the editor of the important underground newspaper *Combat* he was part and parcel of the soul of that Resistance. But I couldn't distance myself enough from him to write about him. I felt that he was too close to discuss in print. His last slightly shy hug meant too much for me to try to convey and too much for me to ignore.

And the passing of the years did not help much. Then in 1977 I came across the story of the war years in the village of Le Chambon in south-central France. This Huguenot village of about three thousand people, perched on a plateau in a rugged mountain range, saved the lives of about five thousand refugees—most of them children—during the first four years of the forties, when the Germans occupied France. The villagers were nonviolent. I found myself studying their story as a detailed instance of hospitality to strangers in dangerous circumstances. I believed—and I still believe—that goodness has to do with saving and spreading the joy of life; and I believe that goodness happened there.

In the course of my months of living in the village and getting to know the surviving villagers, I would hear from time to time about Monsieur Camus, who lived over there in Le Panelier during much of the time when the rescue machine of Le Chambon was in full operation. Le Panelier was—and is—a gray, granite fortress-farm on the outskirts of the village of Le Chambon. Camus had gone there for the clear mountain air and the peaceful environment that his poor lungs required. Every twelve days he would go up to the city of Saint-Etienne for pneumothorax injections, but his tuberculosis did not keep him from continuing to work hard on what I believe will be his most enduring work, *The Plague*.

My friend Pierre Fayol, one of the key *responsables* of the French Resistance in the mountain Department of High Loire, told me that Camus was one of the few people empowered to hand out awards to people in the Resistance; but Fayol did not tell me more. I heard that Camus had met, at least once, the leader of the village, Pastor André Trocmé, whose aggressive nonviolence and careful planning did much to make the village the safest place in France for Jewish children. But this was all I heard.

Some of the names in Camus's novel resemble very closely the names of Chambonnais; and the symbolic meaning of the plague in Camus's novel was the same as the ideas Pastor Trocmé preached and practiced during those four dangerous and bloody years. In the novel, the plague is not only inguinal fever carried by fleas on dead rats; it symbolizes the cruel German occupation of France at the time Camus was writing; and, above all—or rather at the bottom of it all—it symbolizes the capacities of man—and indeed of the world at large—for killing and for letting killing happen. Trocmé and his villagers saved those thousands of children without hating or hurting anyone (he did not hate the Germans; he was trying to keep them from doing more evil by killing more children); and Doctor Rieux and the other workers against the plague in Camus's novel were trying to save people's lives—simply that. The novel was as much about Le Chambon during the rescue years as it was about continental Europe in the first four years of the forties. And they were both about the pathos and beauty of goodness.

During all of his mature life as a writer, the suffering and death of children were for Camus the crucial instance of evil in history and literature. I do not know whether Camus knew much about the rescue operation going on during his stay in the outskirts of Le Chambon, but the novel he was working on in Panelier fit Trocmé's Chambonnais like a glove. Trocmé did nothing to prevent the Germans from winning the war, and Rieux accomplished nothing as far as stopping the plague is concerned; but both of them resisted as best they could and diminished a little the forces in the world that kill and let kill.

Long after I wrote a book about Le Chambon in the war years, I started having dreams of Camus in Le Chambon. I saw him meeting refugee children at the little railroad station in the village in the early afternoon; and more than once I saw him hugging a few of them shyly and leading them from the station to tiny Madame Barraud's house, which is near the station, or to round-faced Madame Eyraud's house, which is farther away, where the Street of the Soul's Song meets the Street of Lambert.

Two French words summarize the mood (for it is a mood and not a philosophic system) that Camus expresses in his writings and in his life and death. The words are: *solitaire* and *solidaire*. Only one consonant separates the two words from each other, but the difference between aloneness and union is immense. We are born into separateness; then, after a while, we die into it; and, in between our birth and our death, we are strangers and afraid in a world we never made. And yet we feel solidarity with others, love, from time to time. We live out our lives apart from others and as a part of others.

The book Camus gave me is as surely out there, separate from my eyes and my fingers, separate from me, as it is rectangular and cream colored under the brown cellophane. And so every person or thing I see out there is not in me. Out-thereness is not distance. A book is as "out there" as a star or another person. We measure or guess distances with numbers; we do not measure or guess about out-thereness—we simply experience it; we know it as swiftly and as surely as we know that there are colored things in the world.

No one I have ever known has felt the anguish of out-thereness as poignantly as Camus. In the evolution of his ideas, Camus never lost the feeling that the world he moves in is not his, is not himself. There is what he called a "divorce," an abyss between our deepest, private feelings and the world out there. For Camus the richest image of that divorce is Sisyphus with his stone. Sisyphus was king of Corinth, but he was a rebel. He defied the gods, and, in punishment for this, he spent all eternity in the underworld pushing a heavy stone up a hill, only to have it totter at the top and roll down the hill again and again and again. Camus imagines Sisyphus with his cheek against that cold stone, his shoulders pushing against it, his helping foot wedged under it; but what interests Camus especially is the moment when the stone is rolling back down the hill and Sisyphus is watching it go, knowing that he is accomplishing nothing in this alien world.

Each morning is like this for each of us. I have to wake up in the morning again and again and again. I never accomplish making the world part of myself or making my self part of the world out there. But there are things I can do: I can see with utter lucidity the divorce between myself and the world; I can understand my solitude without blinking, or sadness, or despair. And I can do more. I can find peace by taking "the path of sympathy" as Camus puts it in *The Plague*. I can revolt against the ultimate separation between a self and the world—death. I can be *solidaire* with the defenseless of the earth by fighting the plague, the need in mankind to kill and to let others kill.

As he put it in his Nobel laureate speech at the City Hall of Stockholm, he wanted to put himself at the service, not of the makers of history, but rather of the victims of that history. And he would have to do this again and again and again, knowing that his revolt against death would never defeat death. He would just try to limit the harm done. The world is not benign; there will always be victims, but we can feel solidarity with the victims we can embrace; we can feel the joy of helping a few people a few times. The rock will roll down the hill again; but when we are pushing it up the hill with our cheek against it and our arms spread out on it, we can be close to that hardness and make a little difference, though only temporarily. We can have the joy of friendship, of love, even while we forget nothing, not even murder.

* * *

My dreams and my thoughts about Camus taking refugee children across the wide, gray-granite square of Le Chambon to the home of Madame Barraud or Madame Eyraud have driven me after all these years to write this remembrance of Camus. Camus is long dead, smashed by the alien rock of the world, but the somewhat shy and distant embrace he gave me at Gallimard after he handed me my reading glasses is as real to me as the most recent embrace I have had from my grandchild. The abyss of out-thereness is crossed, but it is not.

From *The American Scholar* 64.3 (Summer 1995): 428-435. Copyright © 1995 by the author. Reprinted by permission of *The American Scholar*.

Silence Follows:
Albert Camus in Algeria _____

Robert Zaretsky

On January 22, 1956, the residents of Algiers, abandoning their usual Sunday pastimes of strolling the boulevards and gathering at cafés, instead piled into the city's central square, the Place du Gouvernement. On one side stood a stormy crowd of European settlers, known as pieds-noirs, whose leader, a bar owner and brawler named Jo Ortiz, vowed that Algeria was and would always be part of France. On the other side of the square thronged thousands of Arabs and Berbers kept in check by the Front de Libération Nationale (FLN), the clandestine movement dedicated to Algeria's independence from France. Dividing the two hostile groups was a cordon of French gendarmes.

The crowd flowed against the ramparts of the plaza's Cercle du Progrès, a meeting hall straddling two worlds: behind spilled the Kasbah, the ancient Muslim district laced by alleys and passages; in front sprawled Bab el Oued, a working-class neighborhood of Spanish immigrants. Within the hall, pieds-noirs and Arabs sat in tight rows and craned their heads toward the hall's stage. On the dais sat two pieds-noirs—a Catholic priest and Protestant minister—and a local Muslim notable. But these three men were stage scenery for the man who embodied the increasingly forlorn hope that their two worlds might avoid a collision. Stubbing a Gauloise under his shoe, gripping the text of his speech that called for a civilian truce, a drawn and waxen-faced Albert Camus walked to the podium, chained to a task no less absurd than the one the gods had assigned to Sisyphus.

Still, the Greek gods had never demanded Sisyphus' head. Since his arrival in Algiers, Camus had received several death threats. Now, as he stood behind the podium, he heard calls for his death from Ortiz's red-faced mob. As the bedlam outside grew, the brawny childhood friends who formed Camus' impromptu bodyguard—he called them his "gorillas"—kept glancing at the doors. For years Camus had insisted that Algeria belonged to the Arab and Berber peoples no less than to the pieds-noirs. But as he prepared to speak, he feared each side had already concluded that Algeria belonged to them alone.

* * *

The killing began in 1945, when Arab nationalists in the town of Sétif held a demonstration marking France's liberation from Germany. Someone fired a shot; guns and knives replaced banners and flags; rampaging protesters overwhelmed the small police force and murdered more than one hundred French residents. As massacres go, this was especially horrific: women's breasts were sliced off; men's genitals were stuffed into their mouths. France's response was equally appalling: organized repression and vigilante violence seized the region for the next several days. More than fifteen thousand Arabs and Berbers were killed, often in grisly fashion.

Camus had been in Algeria shortly before these bloody events, visiting his family in Algiers, whom he had not seen since 1942. He had also planned to visit other parts of Algeria to study the conditions of the Arab and Berber populations. As a muckraking reporter for a local newspaper in 1939, Camus had filed a series of shocking articles on the abysmal condition of the Berbers. But he was no longer an obscure French-Algerian journalist: publication of *The Stranger* and *The Myth of Sisyphus* had transformed their author into a world-renowned philosopher of the absurd, just as his editorship of the newspaper *Combat* had made him the voice of the French Resistance.

These changes, however, did not efface Camus' attachment to his native Algeria—on the contrary. Surrounded by the intellectuals of Paris's Left Bank, Camus played up his origins, speaking street argot, strutting the street walk of Algiers in the company of Jean-Paul Sartre and Simone de Beauvoir. If it was an act, it was one driven by Camus' abiding sense of exile when away from Algeria. While Camus' affection remained unchanged for the Algeria from which "he had never recovered," Algeria was no longer the country of Camus' childhood. The experiences of war and liberation galvanized the political expectations of Arabs and Berbers, while hardening the resistance of European settlers. The sails of Arab nationalism were filling, and French Algerians feared the coming storm they had largely created. Having throttled interwar efforts to extend the franchise to an indigenous population that outnumbered them ten to one, the pieds-noirs continued to resist compromise after 1945.

Unlike most pieds-noirs, Camus held that the credo of French republicanism applied no less to the colonized as to the colonizers in Algeria. This conviction hardened during his travels through Algeria in 1945. Back in Paris shortly before the massacre at Sétif, Camus forecast the nationalist explosion. Little had changed in the conditions of the rural population since his earlier series of reports: too little food for too many mouths, too many republican ideals given the lie by selfish pieds-noirs and feckless French administrators. The math of rationing was simple: pieds-noirs were entitled to three hundred grams of bread per day, while Arabs and Berbers usually received less than a hundred and fifty. This staggering inequality was imposed not only on a people who were "not inferior except in regard to the conditions in which they must live," but who had "spent the past two years fighting for the liberation of France." France's duty was clear: it had to "quell the cruelest of hungers and heal inflamed hearts."

Camus reminded the readers of *Combat* that, while the crisis was most immediately economic and material, its roots were political and historical. For more than a century, France had failed to apply its democratic principles to Algeria's native peoples. For this reason, France would have to "conquer Algeria a second time." This provocative declaration underscored a prosaic truth: the French Republic's ideals reached no further than the European neighborhoods in Algeria. If Algeria were to remain part of France, France had to reconquer it by the systematic and sincere application of the rights, duties, and benefits of citizenship. Ultimately, Camus declared, "Our feverish and unbridled desire for power and expansion will never be excused unless we make up for them by unwavering attention to the pursuit of justice and the spirit of self-sacrifice. Despite the repressive actions we have just taken in North Africa, I am convinced that the era of Western imperialism is over."

Camus grasped far better than most of his contemporaries that *Combat*'s slogan, From Resistance to Revolution, had inspired not just men and women living under the Nazi occupation, but also those living under French colonial rule. The French civilizing mission could only be fulfilled, he announced, by bringing "more complete liberation to everyone it subjugates." If France failed to do so, it would "reap hatred like all vanquishers who prove themselves incapable of moving beyond victory." His warning not to recreate France's experience under the Nazi occupation was remarkable: Few on the Left, much less the Right, cast French actions in such terms. More remarkable was his call for justice *because* of the blood that had just been shed. "Unfortunate and innocent French victims have lost their lives, and this crime in itself is inexcusable. But I hope that we will respond to murder with nothing other than justice, so as to avoid doing irreparable harm." Yet irreparable harm may already have been done: by 1956, when Camus spoke at the Cercle du Progrès, French and Arabs had shackled themselves to an infernal logic—civilian casualties were not collateral damage of war, but its very goal.

* * *

In Camus' novel *The Plague*, one of the characters, Tarrou, does not distinguish among those killed by the deadly disease. "All I maintain," he tells the novel's narrator, Dr. Rieux, "is that on this earth there are pestilences and there are victims, and it's up to us, so far as possible, not to join forces with the pestilences." He quickly adds: "That may sound simple to the point of childishness; I can't judge if it's simple, but I know it's true." In the mid-1950s, Camus had used his public celebrity to apply Tarrou's ethic to Algeria's worsening situation. In an open letter to an Algerian friend, Camus acknowledged that the spiral of massacre and counter-massacre had pushed him to the "verge of despair." How could it be otherwise? "We know nothing of the human heart," he wrote, "if we imagine that the Algerian French can now forget these massacres." But he did not stop there: "And it is another form of madness to imagine that repression can make the Arab masses feel confidence and esteem for France."

Yet neither community could will the other's disappearance. The "French fact," Camus declared, "cannot be eliminated in Algeria, and the dream of a sudden disappearance of France is childish." No less puerile, though, was the hope of some French Algerians to "cancel out, silence and subjugate" nine million Muslims. French and Muslims, he insisted, were "condemned to live together." This fact, Camus felt, meant that men of good will on both sides had to risk death to secure a space where the "exchange of views is still possible."

In 1955, Camus feverishly built the case for a civilian truce in a series of editorials in the liberal French journal *L'Express*. In calling for a roundtable at which all the factions would sit, Camus showed his hand: the antagonists, sitting across from one another, would have to *attend* to one another: to see and hear their fellow human beings. This might, Camus thought, give a "meaning to the fighting—and perhaps render it vain." His onrush of editorials climaxed in early January 1956 with a proposal for a civilian truce. Deploring the deaths of French and Muslim civilians, condemning both sides' habit of holding only the other side responsible, Camus declared: "Soon only the dead will be innocent." He demanded that both sides denounce the violence aimed at civilians. Pieds-noirs had to "recognize what is just in [their] adversary's cause, as well as recognize what is not just in their own repressive measures." As for the FLN, it had to "disavow the murdering of innocent lives." Both sides had to agree to spare civilians: "We must all demand a truce—a truce that will allow us to arrive at solutions, a truce regarding the massacre of civilians by both sides."

Camus finally rallied his reader to the cause of French and Algerian moderates—"movements [are] taking shape everywhere"—dedicated to dialogue. Camus' desperation got the better of him: "everywhere" was limited to precious few places in Algeria, while "movements" was, in fact, a single and frail movement. Camus was aware of this movement's fragility for he had himself been in contact with it for several days. Its nucleus was the Association of Friends of Arabic Theater, pieds-noirs and Muslims who shared a love of theater. Among the members were several of Camus' lycée and university friends: Jean de Maisonseul, Charles Poncet, and Louis Miquel. On the Muslim side was, most importantly, Amar Ouzegane. Twenty years earlier, Ouzegane and Camus both belonged to the Algerian Communist Party, and both were eventually expelled from its ranks. But by 1955, unknown to Camus, Ouzegane had, like the other Muslim participants in the theater group, gone over to the FLN.

When the group contacted Camus with their idea of joint political action in Algiers, he agreed. But preparations for the public forum were hardly promising: at a meeting on January 19, an Arab schoolteacher blurted out: "To hell with the civil truce! What we need is absolute and unconditional independence now." Stunned, Camus turned to Miquel: "What the hell am I doing here? We're screwed. Do they really want us to drop our pants?" At the same time, a friendly police official warned the group that pied-noir extremists were busy forging tickets: they planned to mob the hall and disrupt the proceedings. The group quickly printed new tickets, while the Arab participants assured Camus that they would guarantee security. Violence seemed inevitable; more than once, Camus considered canceling the event.

Yet he persisted, despite his justified suspicions of the FLN's role in his public appearance, despite his shock upon seeing how radicalized both sides had become, despite his fear that Paris was willfully blind to the depth of the problem. True despair is not born, he believed, when facing a stubborn opponent or in the exhaustion of unequal combat. Instead, despair comes "when we no longer know why we are struggling—or, indeed, if struggle is necessary."

* * *

At the Cercle de Progrès, Camus met despair, though he refused to name it. He believed both sides were right; the problem, tragically, was that each side claimed sole possession of the truth. They had lied about themselves, lied about their opponents, and were committing real crimes, drowning Algeria in one another's blood. Outside, the chants from Ortiz's mob grew louder, while a great murmur like a basso continuo rose from the Muslims. Stones began to rattle against the windows.

Camus began to speak: "This meeting had to take place," he declared, "to show at least that an exchange of views is still possible." He asserted that he was a private, not public, figure. But with war seeping into the realm of the private, he and his colleagues had stepped forward, in the knowledge that "building, teaching, creating [are] functions of life and of generosity that could not be pursued in the realm of hatred and bloodshed." We must not deny, Camus continued, historical and demographic facts. In Algeria "there are a million Frenchmen who have been here for a century, millions of Muslims, either Arabs or Berbers, who have been here for centuries, and several rigorous religious communities." Yet extremists were trying to deny this reality by terrorizing not just the other side, but also the moderate members of their own ethnic groups. If both sides did not open a dialogue, the Frenchman will make up his mind "to know nothing of the Arab, even though he feels somewhere within him, that the Arab's claim to dignity is justified, and the Arab makes up his mind to know nothing of the Frenchman, even though he feels, somewhere within him, that the Algerian French likewise have a right to security and dignity on our common soil." If each and every Frenchman and Muslim did not make an honest "effort to think over his adversary's motives," the violence would carry Algeria away.

Camus paused as a hum rose from the audience. Looking across the hall, Camus saw that Ferhat Abbas, the last great moderate voice of Algerian nationalism, had just arrived. Like Camus, Abbas was a product of the French republican school system; like Camus, Abbas continued to believe that the principles informing this education must be applied to all men and women, Arab and pied-noir alike; like Camus, Abbas believed the two peoples had no choice but to coexist. As Abbas made his way to the stage, Camus met him halfway and the two embraced. For a moment, a blast of applause overwhelmed the gathering storm outside; for a moment, Camus' plea for a civilian truce seemed possible.

But the furies outside the hall seemed to have sensed the momentary surge of optimism. The pieds-noirs redoubled their efforts: they launched heavier volleys of stones at the building, shattering several windows, all the while cursing Camus and his associates as traitors. Camus spoke quickly, fearing the mob was about to burst into the hall. How absurd, he announced, to appear in this tumult, asking for nothing more than that "a handful of innocent victims [i.e., civilians on both sides] be spared." But his words were muffled by the uproar. Though the committee had planned a public discussion after the speech, Camus asked that it be cancelled: it seemed clear that the conference would soon give way to disorder and much worse. The visitor left the hall as he had arrived, surrounded by his cordon of "gorillas."

When Camus flew back to Paris later that day, he insisted that he would "sacrifice everything to the truce" and that the meeting was just the first step. But he also confessed he did not know what the next step could possibly be. For now, he admitted, "I have only doubts." Camus' doubts ripened into despair when, a few months after his appearance at the Cercle du Progrès, Abbas himself joined the FLN.

* * *

In his essay *The Rebel*, published in 1951, Camus discusses a group of men and women he calls the "fastidious assassins." They were early twentieth-century Russian revolutionaries who tried to overthrow the

Tsarist regime. For Camus, they were the last of their kind: never again would history see the "spirit of rebellion encountering the spirit of compassion." They were revolutionaries despite themselves, dedicated to a cause whose price left them sleepless, haunted by unforeseen consequences to the innocent. For Camus, the greatest praise to pay these men and women is "that we would not be able to ask them one question that they themselves had not already asked and that, in their life or by their death, they had not partially answered."

Camus was drawn, in particular, to Ivan Kaliayev. In 1905, Kaliayev assassinated one of the Tsar's uncles, the Grand Duke Sergei, but only on the second try. Kaliayev aborted his first attempt when he saw two children sitting next to the duke in the royal carriage. He defused the bomb he was about to throw, saving the life of the children but endangering his own and fellow conspirators' lives. When Kaliayev finally carried out his plan two days later, he allowed himself to be arrested and walked calmly to his execution.

In his 1949 play *The Just Assassins*, Camus has Kaliayev's fellow revolutionary Stepan berate him after the failed attempt. "Children!" he explodes. "There you go, always talking about children!" The utilitarian calculus is straightforward: "Not until the day comes when we stop being sentimental about children, will the revolution triumph and we be masters of the world. . . . Nothing that can serve our cause should be ruled out . . . There are no limits." Stepan's moral absolutism was echoed by apologists for the FLN: a revolutionary convinced he was on the right side of history was free to use terrorism.

For Camus, too many individuals on both sides were guilty not just of murder, but also of flattening life into abstractions or stereotypes. In particular, Camus struggled against the Left Bank's simplistic view of the pieds-noirs. The great majority of them were not *richards*: wealthy European landowners and industrialists who carry "riding crops, smoke cigars and drive Cadillacs." Most, like his family and neighbors in working-class Algiers, were from modest backgrounds. The people, Camus feared, would pay the heaviest price for the Left's "murderous frivolity [and] rethread the stitches of reasoning torn out by . . . every head that falls."

His failure as a peacemaker haunted Camus. He felt used by the FLN, whose role in organizing the event at the Cercle du Progrès he discovered only after the fact. Yet he was also estranged from Parisian friends who saw his efforts as little more than grandstanding—or, worse yet, arguing on behalf of the status quo. Beauvoir spoke for Sartre and their circle when she defended the FLN's use of terrorism— "We refused to feel indignant about [their] methods of fighting"—and denounced Camus' "hollow language." Less than a week after Camus' intervention in Algiers, Sartre spoke at a pro-FLN rally in Paris: taking aim at his former friend, he ridiculed "tender-hearted realists" who called for reforms in Algeria. The answer was revolution, not reform: "The neocolonialist is a fool who still believes that the colonial system can be overhauled."

* * *

Shortly after his return from Algeria, confronted by mounting hostility from both sides and the collapse of his proposal for a civilian truce, Camus resigned from *L'Express* and told his friends he would no longer speak or write on Algeria. The French government's serial capitulations to the pied-noir mob had smothered Camus' hope that the Republic would prove equal to its ideals. Events had also demolished his earlier conviction that neither pied-noir nor Arab truly wanted mutual destruction: the urban hell of the Battle of Algiers revealed that each side was determined to pound the other into extinction. What more could he say at this point? Nothing, he believed: silence was all he had left.

The clamor stirred by Camus' silence was deafening, particularly as the French military in Algeria institutionalized the practice of torture. The horrifying reports in conversations and journals grew so frequent that Beauvoir bitterly noted the "same boring program of electric goads, immersions, hangings, burnings, rape funnels, stakes, nails torn out, bones broken." And where was her estranged friend Camus? Beauvoir "was revolted by [his] refusal to speak." Even fellow *pieds-noirs* like Jean Daniel and Jules Roy who had come to accept the inevitability of Algerian independence were puzzled by Camus' silence.

Though he did not speak publicly about Algeria, Camus continued to act privately. He wrote more than 150 appeals for Arab prisoners facing imprisonment or death, sending his letters to government ministers or friends in the administration. He pleaded for the lives of FLN militants as well as Communists, taking care in each case to note the specific circumstances: this prisoner did not kill blindly, for example, or that prisoner did not kill anyone at all. The appeals sometimes succeeded, but more often they failed, leaving Camus with a new appreciation of the absurd. A few days after sending a letter to French President René Coty asking him to pardon several militants, he read in the newspaper that three of the condemned men had been shot. *"Fifteen days after the execution,"* he observed, the president's aide "informs me that my letter held the attention of the President and was transmitted to the higher council of the magistracy. Bureaucracy of dreamers."

* * *

A different bureaucracy of dreamers eventually forced Camus from his stubbornly held silence. In late 1957, Camus was dining with a friend in a Paris restaurant when a waiter hurried to his table: the radio had just announced that Camus had won the Nobel Prize for Literature. Upon hearing the news, Camus grew pale and agitated: Malraux, he insisted, should have received the prize. The following day, he wrote in his journal: "Nobel. Strange feeling of overwhelming pressure and melancholy."

It was natural that Camus was burdened by the news. He suspected that politics had influenced the Swedish Academy: the Battle of Algiers had captured the world's attention and Camus represented the last and best chance for reconciliation. Did not the Academy affirm that Camus' work "illuminated the problems of human conscience in our times"? The dilemma was that by breaking his silence over Algeria, Camus would betray his conscience; by maintaining it, he would betray the world's expectations. No less troubling, just as he had nothing more to say on Algeria, Camus worried he had nothing more to create. Until the publication of *The Fall* that year, Camus had not published a major work of fiction since *The Plague*. Tellingly, when Camus said Malraux should have been given the prize, many other writers and critics in Paris agreed. "No matter what," he reminded himself, "I must overcome this sort of fear, of incomprehensible panic where this unexpected news has thrown me."

When Camus arrived in Stockholm in January, his fears were partly confirmed. A local newspaper welcomed him with the question on most people's minds: Why was the conscience of his generation silent on his native Algeria? Camus' circumspection gave way when, shortly before the Nobel ceremony, he met with a large gathering of university students. Few asked about literature; current events, instead, were on their minds. The dialogue had already veered toward Algeria when a Muslim student demanded to know why Camus spoke so freely about violence in Eastern Europe, but not Algeria. Before Camus could reply, the student began to insult him. Waiting with scarcely controlled anger for the student to pause, Camus finally spoke: "I have never spoken to an Arab or to one of your militants as you have just spoken to me in public. You are for democracy in Algeria, so be democratic right now and let me speak."

The student replied with new salvos of insults. It was as if everything and nothing had changed since his public lecture nearly two years before at the Cercle du Progrès: instead of enraged pieds-noirs, it was now a representative of Muslim Algeria who refused to listen. Yet Camus insisted on being heard: "Though I have been silent for a year and eight months, that doesn't mean I have stopped acting. I've always been a supporter for a just Algeria in which two equal peoples would live peacefully. I've repeatedly demanded that justice be rendered to the Algerian people and that they be given full democratic rights." He had stopped speaking out for these rights because "the hatred on both sides is now so great that an intellectual can no longer intervene without taking the risk of making the violence worse." And so, Camus declared, he had decided to wait for a moment when he could unite rather than divide peoples. As his frustration continued to mount, he told his antagonist that some of his comrades were "alive today thanks to efforts you are not aware of." He then turned to the heart of the matter, which was the possible effect of terror on his own family: "I have always condemned terror. But I must also condemn terrorism that strikes blindly, for example in the streets of Algiers, and which might strike my mother and family. I believe in justice, but I'll defend my mother before justice."

* * *

While the audience at Stockholm applauded Camus' declaration, the Left in Paris denounced it. When *Le Monde*'s cerebral editor, Hubert Beuve-Méry, first read his correspondent's account, he rubbed his eyes and demanded reconfirmation. When his reporter confirmed the quotation, Beuve-Méry muttered: "I knew Camus would say something bloody stupid." As far as Beauvoir was concerned, Camus had finally come clean, proving he was little more than a shill for the pieds-noirs: "The fraud lay in the fact that he posed at the same time as a man above the battle, thus providing a warning for those who wanted to reconcile this war and its methods with bourgeois humanism."

The American critic Michael Walzer recently set Beauvoir's claim on its head: Camus *did* put the pieds-noirs first, but was right to do so. Objectivity, Walzer suggests, is not all that it is cracked up to be: the "critical distance" of critics like Beauvoir and Sartre empties life and makes for an "ideologically flattened world." Complexity and ambiguity, shadows and blur are all eliminated; vast canvases are turned into cartoons; political choices are made easy at the expense of different, often antagonistic truths.

Herein lies Camus' importance as an observer, Walzer argues. It is because of, not despite, his deep roots in Algeria that Camus' words, and silences, are so important. Were it not for his particular identity, Camus would have lacked credibility with his fellow pieds-noirs; were it not for his particular experiences, Camus would have lacked clarity on the tragic implications of the war. Camus believed the "values I ought to defend and illustrate today are average values. This requires a talent so spare and unadorned that I doubt I have it." These everyday values were the universal claims of French republicanism refracted through his Algerian childhood, including both pieds-noirs and Arabs, but focusing on *les siens*: one's own community. "Camus would not have said," Walzer reassures us, "that French and Arab lives were of equal importance in his eyes." This is as it should be: "Morality required the mutual acceptance, not the abolition or transcendence, of these different meanings. The Frenchmen had his own loyalties, and so did the Arab; and each had a right to his own."

Walzer's interpretation might well apply to the characters in *The Stranger*, but does it apply to Camus? Had he been incapable of taking the distance required to measure the claims of both sides, Camus would not have become silent—or, at least, not silent in the same way. From his youthful days as a reporter and PCF militant to his mature days as editor of *Combat* and advocate of a civilian truce, Camus represented Arabs and Berbers no less than the pieds-noirs. If, as Walzer writes, Camus' silence was "eloquent in its hopelessness," it is not because he refused to surrender his primal loyalties to the pied-noir community. Instead, Camus refused to surrender his loyalty to *both* communities, just as he would not surrender his lucidity in regard to the tragic character of the human condition.

The truths at play in Algeria were, for Camus, incompatible. His native land was not an abstraction, but his very life. It was, in part, precisely because he *was* a pied-noir that Camus was ideally placed to express the Algerian dilemma. In a letter Camus sent to *Le Monde* shortly after his trip to Stockholm, he wrote that he felt closer to the Muslim student at the meeting than those "Frenchmen who talk about Algeria without knowing it." His young antagonist, at least, "knew what he was talking about." His face, Camus added, was not marked by hatred, but by "despair and unhappiness. I share that unhappiness: his is the face of my country."

Camus' insistence that the young man's face was not one among many, but the sole face of his country reflects his life-long struggle to balance the two great forces in his life "even when they contradict one another." For Camus, there is beauty, but there are also the humiliated: "Whatever difficulties the enterprise may present, I would like never to be unfaithful either to one or the other." But, he continues, "this still sounds like ethics, and we live for something that transcends ethics. If we could name it, what silence would follow!"

But sometimes this silence, Camus observed in his Nobel lecture— given just two days after his encounter with the Algerian student— "takes on a terrifying sense." An admirer of Greek tragedy, Camus met this order of silence in the work of Sophocles. His gods never speak, while his heroes rarely speak once they take full measure of their impossible situations. The chorus lapses into silence, as does the audience, both echoing the silence of the cosmos. Perhaps Camus understood the Sophoclean silence. There would be no dues ex machina, no Euripidean contraption to free Algeria from its paralyzing knot of opposing claims. As for the far more modest mechanisms of human reason and compassion, they had already been found wanting. Only silence could follow, as terrifying now as it was then.

From *Virginia Quarterly Review* 86.1 (2010): 214-222. Copyright © 2010 by Robert Zaretsky. Reprinted with permission of Robert Zaretsky.

Caligula:
Camus's Anti-Shaman

Patricia Hopkins

Caligula's revolt has been interpreted by various Camus scholars as historical, philosophical, or aesthetic in nature, and a convincing case can be made for each of these approaches.[1] A careful study of the text, however, suggests another possibility that I would like to explore, that is, the notion of Caligula as an ironic shaman who, having experienced a ritual initiation through a mythic descent into hell, seeks to re-create the primordial chaos of pre-history and a lost paradise through a systematic destruction of the foundations of Western rationality and morality.

Let us recall the principal stages of Caligula's evolution. The most significant event takes place before the play begins: following the death of his sister Drusilla, Caligula disappears for three days and returns disturbingly transformed. Camus's source, Suetonius, does not elaborate upon the length of this disappearance, stating only that:

> following her death, he proclaimed a general cessation of law in all courts. During which time, a capital crime it was for any man to have laughed, bathed, or supped together with his parents, wife or children. And being impatient of this sorrow, when he was fled suddenly and by night out of the city, and had passed all over Campania, to Syracuse he went; and so from thence returned speedily again with his beard and hair overgrown. (231-32)

Camus, however, in specifying an absence of three days (the length of Christ's sojourn in hell), opens the door to the possibility of a descent followed by a profound transformation. The death of his mistress-sister is a pretext for Caligula's realization that "Ce monde, tel qu'il est fait, n'est pas supportable" [This world, as it is constituted, is unbearable] (*TRN* 15). The spectator can only surmise the depth of this transformation, but there are several allusions in the first scenes to the fact that Caligula up to this point in no way resembled the monster who will henceforth embark upon an exuberant reign of terror. The young poet Scipio declares: "Il était bon pour moi. Il m'encourageait et je sais par coeur certaines de ses paroles. Il me disait que la vie n'est pas facile, mais qu'il y avait la religion, l'art, l'amour qu'on nous porte. Il répétait souvent que faire souffrir était la seule façon de se tromper. Il voulait être un homme juste" [He has been good for me. He encouraged me, and I have memorized some of the things he said. He used to tell me that life is not easy, but that religion, art, and love enable us to bear it. A thought that he often repeated is that to cause suffering is the only way to go wrong. He wanted to be a just man] (*TRN* 19).

It will become apparent that Caligula has become the exact antithesis of the role model described by Scipio. His fanatical mission will now be to illustrate in all its horror the simple realization that "les hommes meurent et ils ne sont pas heureux" [Men die, and they are not happy] (*TRN* 16). He thus sets out to subvert and undermine the essential values that the Western world holds most dear: the family, work, patriotism, religion, literature, and art. And he does this through theatre, staging a series of spectacles to enlighten and mystify his unfortunate audience. When confronted with rational and conventionally moral resistance, he explains that he is merely imitating and intensifying the incomprehensible capriciousness of the gods. In short, he is the most pedagogical of tyrants, constantly reinforcing the lesson that men are mortal and that any notion of transcendence is rendered absurd by the inevitability of death.

The dynamics of Caligula's transformation bear a certain resemblance to the initiatic rites of shamanism elaborated by Mircea Eliade. What characterizes the shaman, Eliade believes, is not so much the possession by "spirits," but the ecstasy produced by his ascent to heaven or descent to hell. Every initiation includes a period of isolation and a certain number of trials and ordeals forcing the novice to undergo an "initiatory illness," an illness revolving about an experience of mystical death or resurrection (*Myths* 79-80). The initiation itself often follows a profound crisis bordering on madness. Madness, in fact, may appear as a form of initiation, *le mal sacré* being a means of attaining revelation. Although this is essentially a religious phenomenon, it enters into literature under a symbolic configuration and can be traced, as Léon Cellier has done in *Parcours initiatiques*, from the romantic novel of the nineteenth century through Proust. Cellier outlines the triptych of the initiatic process as separation, initiation (through symbolic death), and return, or rebirth. Initiatory rites, by which the hero undergoes a radical modification of his social or religious nature, are most often expressed through the myth of the quest (119). The goal of the quest, untranslatable in rational terms, assumes a poetic or allegorical form.

For Camus's hero, the object of the quest is the moon, which for him is the incarnation of the impossible. In the eyes of the patricians, Caligula's behavior is quite simply madness, and they are incapable of seeing it as anything but a threat to their material comfort and security. However, in a private moment with his mistress Caesonia, Caligula expresses his real ambition:

[De] quoi me sert ce pouvoir si étonnant, si je ne puis changer l'ordre des choses, si je ne puis faire que le soleil se couche à l'est, que la souffrance décroisse et que les êtres ne meurent plus. . . . Toi aussi, tu me crois fou. Et pourtant, qu'est-ce qu'un dieu pour que je désire m'égaler à lui? Ce que je désire de toutes mes forces, aujourd'hui, est au-dessus des dieux. Je prends en charge un royaume où l'impossible est roi. . . . Je veux mêler le ciel à la mer, confondre laideur et beauté, faire jaillir le rire de la souffrance. (*TRN* 27)

[What good is this astonishing power if I cannot change the order of things, if I cannot make the sun set in the East, diminish suffering, and keep mortals from dying . . . You, too, you think me crazy. And yet, what is a god that I aspire to be his equal? What I desire with all my heart today stands above the gods. I support a kingdom where impossibility is king . . . I wish to blend the sky with the sea, confound ugliness and beauty, wring laughter out of suffering.]

This last remark is especially significant: Caligula's aim goes beyond the simple desire to destroy and obliterate the existing order of things. It has a positive component, that of re-creating the world and overturning the course of nature. To do so, it is necessary to simulate a return to the amorphous state of chaos that precedes human history, to rival the Creator in the first days of creation. Having experienced an existential confrontation with the absurd, Caligula will attempt to pass on the experience to his subjects by stripping existence of the comfortable labels and categories that bourgeois thought imposes upon it. In *Le Mythe de Sisyphe*, Camus describes the sudden revelation of the "otherness" of the world in the following way:

Au fond de toute beauté gît quelque chose d'inhumain et ces collines, la douceur du ciel, ces dessins d'arbres, voici qu'à la minute même, ils perdent le sens illusoire dont nous les revêtions, désormais plus lointains qu'un paradis perdu. L'hostilité primitive du monde, à travers les millénaires, remonte vers nous. . . . Une seule chose: cette épaisseur et cette étrangeté du monde, c'est l'ab surde. (*E* 108)

[At the foundation of all beauty lies something inhuman, and these hills, the softness of the sky, these traces of trees—see how they suddenly lose the illusory sense in which we clothe them, becoming more distant than a lost paradise. The primitive hostility of the world rises up against us across the millennia . . . One single thing: this density and strangeness of the world is the absurd.]

Here Camus equates the "primitive hostility" of the world with the absurd, indicating the divorce between the world's original and fundamental significance and human consciousness. If Caligula can accomplish the impossible by obliterating contradiction (between sea/sky, beauty/ugliness, laughter/suffering), then he can make the absurd tangible to others, for the formerly reassuring mental categories will no longer suffice.

The world that Caligula seeks to represent is not unlike the primal, pre-formal chaotic state of archaic man and is suggestive of a symbolic return to chaos that may precede any new creation. According to Eliade, the "madness" of the future shamans, their "psychic chaos," is a sign that the "profane man is on the way to dissolution, and that a new personality is about to be born" (*Myths* 80). In other words, the man who lives in "time" must dissolve himself in chaos so as to be reborn through ecstasy in the primal state. Again, according to Eliade, the shaman's ecstasy reveals another world: "the world in which everything seems possible; where the dead return to life and the living die only to live again; where one can disappear instantaneously; where the 'laws of nature' are abolished; and where a certain superhuman 'freedom' is exemplified and made dazzlingly *present*" ("Recent" 186).

Caligula's intentions recall the behavior of archaic, mythical man in the world of the sacred. His new and "terrible freedom" derives from his discovery of his "man-godhood." His separation from the mundane, quotidian existence of his fellow man suggests the dichotomy between the profane world and the sacred, although in this case it would be more appropriate to speak of a demonic sacred. In fact, one could even find synonymous here the terms "sacred" and "absurd," since Caligula seeks to *deify* the absurd and since both concepts imply the opposite of the human, rational world of limits defended by Cherea and other modest rebels in the play who oppose Caligula on a purely secular level. In his philosophical works, Camus often makes use of religious language to designate any form of transcendence that surpasses the bounds of rational human action. In *Le Mythe de Sisyphe*, he analyzes various attempts, by Kierkegaard and others, to transform the absurd into religious certainty by deifying the incomprehensible: "C'est ainsi que, par un subterfuge torturé, il [Kierkegaard] donne à l'irrationnel le visage, et à son Dieu les attributs de l'absurde injuste, inconséquent et incomprehensible" [It is thus that, through a twisted subterfuge, he [Kierkegaard] provides a face for the irrational and the attributes of the unjust, inconsequent, and incomprehensible absurd for his God] (*E* 127), having already concluded that "l'absurde devient dieu (dans le sens le plus large de ce mot)" (*E* 122). Any attempt to suppress or surpass the bounds of rationality automatically leads, in Camus's eyes, to a kind of religious conversion insofar as it sacrifices reason in order to embrace the incomprehensible.

Later, in *L'Homme révolté*, his continuing preoccupation with the temptation toward transcendence is seen in his frequent use of *le sacré* to designate any betrayal of reason. The following passage, although it concerns the surrealists' revolt, could very well describe Caligula: "Il [le révolté] est à la recherche, sans le savoir, d'une morale et d'un sacré. La révolte est une ascèse, quoique aveugle. Si le révolté blasphème alors, c'est dans l'espoir d'un nouveau dieu. Il s'ébranle sous le choc du premier et du plus profond des mouvements religieux, mais il s'agit d'un mouvement religieux déçu" [He [the rebel] is, without realizing it, in search of a moral and a sanctity. The rebellion is an asceticism, albeit a blind one. So if the rebel blasphemes, it is in hope of a new god. He shakes himself up with the shock of the first and most profound of religious gestures, but it is the gesture of a disappointed believer] (*E* 509). In a sense this passage summarizes the entire argument of *L'Homme révolté*: that the loss of an absolute leads inevitably to the search for a new absolute, that all revolutions come full circle to replace the old gods with new ones. Hence the need for an "ascetic" revolt, one that stubbornly resists any effort to transcend the possible. Any absolute—be it political or philosophical—is by definition religious.

Caligula may seem hostile to the realm of the sacred, yet the very passion with which he pursues a final liberation from the human condition impels him in the direction of the sacred—which, for our purposes, we might designate as the "deified absurd." His ambition to rival the gods suggests at the very least a collusion with the sacred/deified absurd. In other words, the essence of his revolt is religious.

Caligula's passage from the concrete world of time and space to the ahistorical realm of the deified absurd occurs specifically at the end of the first act when he confronts his image in the mirror and triumphantly declares himself "Caligula!" As several commentators have pointed out,[2] Caligula exists on two levels in the play: on one level, he is the actor who performs the role of Caligula; on another level, he stands apart as the conscious witness of his tragic fate. A symbolic death occurs at this moment, in which the profane Caius is reborn as the "theatrical" Caligula.

After assuming his mythical and legendary persona before the mirror, he announces to Caesonia: ". . . c'est moi qui t'invite à une fête sans mesure, à un procès général, au plus beau des spectacles. Et il me faut du monde, des spectateurs, des victimes et des coupables" [I am the one who invites you to a boundless feast, to a public trial, to the most beautiful of spectacles. And I need a crowd, spectators, the victims and the guilty] (*TRN* 28). It is thus by means of a festival that Caligula proposes to awaken his subjects from their lethargy and force them to an awareness of the sacred horrors of existence. Roger Caillois, in *Man and the Sacred*, delineates the characteristics of the primitive festival as follows:

> It is a time of excess. . . . The holiest laws are violated, those that seem the very basis of social life. Yesterday's crime is now prescribed, and in place of customary rules, new taboos and disciplines are established, the purpose of which is not to avoid or soothe intense emotions, but rather to excite and bring them to climax. . . . Civil or administrative authorities see their powers temporarily diminish or disappear. . . . Masked actors personify the Gods or the dead. All excesses are permitted, for society expects to be regenerated as a result of excesses, waste, orgies and violence. It hopes for a new vigor to come out of explosion and exhaustion. (164)

As emperor, Caligula is able to take upon himself the collective function of festival, and despite (or perhaps because of) the outrageous absurdity of his Grand Guignol spectacles,[3] his intention is still the fundamentally sincere desire to create a new order from chaos. His impassioned outburst to Caesonia, devoid of his usual mockery, suggests an obscure hope that a new world might possibly be born from the complete leveling of this one: "Et lorsque tout sera aplani, l'impossible enfin sur terre, la lune dans mes mains, alors, peut-être, moi-même je serai transformé et le monde avec moi, alors enfin les hommes ne mourront pas et ils seront heureux" [And when everything is leveled, the impossible finally brought to earth, the moon in my hands, then maybe I will myself be transformed and the world with me, then finally the men will not die and they will be happy] (*TRN* 27). Each of his grotesque reforms is either an exaggeration or a parody of the license permitted at times of festival: he divests the patricians of their prestige and dignity by forcing them to serve as domestics; he awards a medal of honor to the most frequent visitor of the brothel; he disguises himself as Venus in a burlesque ceremony of religious worship; he masquerades as a ballerina and demands that his audience, under pain of death, participate in this "artistic emotion"; he stages a poetic competition in which the players must compose a poem on death in one minute, the most pedantic performers being promptly executed. All of these spectacles reflect to a certain degree Caillois's remarks concerning the rituals of the festival: "The festival not only involves debauches of eating and drinking and sex, but also those of expressions—words and gestures, cries, ridicule, and insults, . . . jousting tourneys between groups of men and women, . . . movements, such as erotic pantomime, violent gesticulations, and simulated and real conflict" (121). Whether or not Caligula's intentions are political or philosophical, the means that he employs—inversion of normal behavior and values—are essentially signs of the return to the primitive epoch of fluidity and confusion. Again, in the words of Caillois, "the festival, being such a paroxysm of life and cutting so violently into the anxious routine of everyday life, seems to the individual like another world in which he feels sustained and transformed by powers that are beyond him" (98).

Another aspect of Caligula's performances that should be noted is the androgynous quality of his masquerades. Eliade recalls that androgyny is the primary symbol of the primordial Totality, a merging of all contraries in order to attain a state of perfect indifference and neutrality. He states that "the divine androgyny which we find in so many myths and beliefs has its own theoretical significance. The real point of the formula is to express—in biological terms—the coexistence of contraries, of cosmological principles (male and female) within the heart of the divinity" (*Patterns* 420).

It is perhaps not by accident that Caligula's appearance as Venus is accompanied by a litany, based on a series of antitheses, in which the supplicants pray for the gift of divine indifference:

Toi qui es comme un rire et un regret/ une rancoeur et un élan/ . . . Enseigne-nous l'indifférence qui fait renaître les amours/ . . . Toi, si vide et si brûlante, inhumaine, mais si terrestre, enivre-nous du vin de ton équivalence et rassasie-nous pour toujours dans ton coeur noir et salé. (*TRN* 63-64)

[You who are like a laugh and a regret/ a rancor and a rapture/ . . . Teach us the indifference that brings love back to life / . . . You, so empty and so burning, inhuman, but so earthly, intoxicate us with the wine of your equivalence and sate us forever with your black and salty heart.]

This plea for divine impassivity and neutrality recalls Eliade's elaboration of the goal of the archaic orgy, the *coincidentia oppositorum*, whereby all contraries are merged and all attributes disappear in a reintegration of man with the cosmos (*Patterns* 29). Although the ceremony here is bawdy and burlesque, the lyrical prayer reveals a nostalgia for a lost paradise, for a primordial and mysterious state of unity in which dialectical opposites coexist without negating one another and paradox is exalted for its own sake.

Caligula's Venus masquerade entails a theatrical parody of a reli-

gious initiation of his subjects into the domain of the sacred (or the deified absurd) and thus corresponds to the practices of the archaic festival, which is a time for the "transmission of myths and rites, a time in
which spirits appear to novices and initiate them" (Caillois 100). In his
efforts to compete with the gods, Caligula seems to realize instinctively that he can do so only on the level of spectacle, by substituting
the *paraître* for the *être*. Hence the theatrical nature of his ceremonies—the Venus show, followed by the pantomime in which he appears grotesquely costumed in a tutu. Since these spectacles are
mounted with one purpose in mind—to demonstrate the absurd dramatically—they suggest a correlation between the absurd (deified) and
play, especially when we recall that Camus in his *Carnets* considered
"Le Joueur," with its multiple connotations in French, as a subtitle to
his work (1: 58).[4] This correlation between the deified absurd and play
is not unlike the one between the sacred and play which Caillois establishes in *Man and the Sacred*. Elaborating on Huizinga's study of play
and the sacred, he thus compares the dynamics of religious ritual and
play:

> An enclosed space is delimited, separated from the world and from life. In
> this enclosure, for a given time, regulated and symbolic movements are ex-
> ecuted, which represent or reincarnate mysterious realities in the course of
> the ceremonies, in which, just as in play, the opposing qualities of exuber-
> ance and regimentation, of ecstasy and prudence, and of enthusiastic delir-
> ium and minute precision, are present at the same time. At last, one
> transcends ordinary existence. (155)

And he adds that "intense religious emotion is accompanied by a performance that is known to be artificial, by a spectacle that is know-
ingly played but that is in no way meant to be a deception or a diversion" (155).

Of all of Caligula's spectacles, the one that would most appear to be
a deception or a diversion is the apparently lighthearted moment in act

4 where, in the midst of the efforts of the conspirators to regroup their forces, he appears in silhouette to perform an inane stylized dance. The befuddled spectators are invited to participate in the moment of "artistic emotion" by Caesonia, who adds matter-of-factly that those who fail to appreciate the beauty of the dance will be beheaded (*TRN* 88). Yet this brief scene serves not only to illustrate the fawning hypocrisy of the patricians, but also to evoke brilliantly the inextricable relationship between art, ritual, mystery, the absurd, danger, and death. Cherea's reluctant admission that "C'était du grand art" [It was great art] (*TRN* 88) implies that perhaps he alone has perceived the profound implications of Caligula's *danse macabre*.

By transforming the deified absurd into play, Caligula is both iconoclastic and sacrilegious in establishing new games in which the rules are a perverted distortion of those of the gods. When Scipio accuses him of blasphemy, he exclaims: "Non, Scipion, c'est l'art dramatique! L'erreur de tous ces hommes, c'est de ne pas croire assez au théâtre. Ils sauraient sans cela qu'il est permis à tout homme de jouer les tragédies celestes et de devenir dieu. Il suffit de durcir le coeur" [No, Scipio, it is dramatic art! The mistake of all these men is not believing enough in theater. Otherwise, they would know that every man is permitted to play celestial tragedies and become god. It is enough to harden the heart] (*TRN* 69). Once again, Caligula has revealed with apparent sincerity the secret of his behavior: having achieved divine indifference following the revelation that everything is equally (in)significant, he is able to emulate the supreme capriciousness and cruelty of the gods by abandoning his humanity.

Underlying all of Caligula's theatrical activities is the myth of conquering the moon. The tragic Caligula remains defenseless at the mercy of the absurd, while Caligula the player attempts to domesticate and guide it through an atavistic transformation of cruelty into dramatic ceremonies resembling those found in ancient cultures and rituals. Throughout his quest, however, he subconsciously realizes the futility of his pursuit. One commentator, David Sprintzen, remarks that "by saying his need is for the impossible, he attests from the outset to the fact that he places little or no hope in the projected transformation of the metaphysical order of things" (68).

Caligula's pursuit is doomed not only in itself, but in its radical annihilation of the profane, which, in Camus's play, is synonymous with moderation, security, and the obstinate refusal of all forms of transcendence. Its spokesman is Cherea, who understands Caligula's fascination with the absurd as the supreme temptation and the greatest of dangers. When Cherea explains to Caligula, "[J'ai] envie de vivre et d'être heureux. Je crois qu'on ne peut être ni l'un ni l'autre en poussant l'absurde dans toutes ses conséquences" [[I] want to live and to be happy. I believe that, in drawing out all the consequences of the absurd, neither is possible] (*TRN* 78), he states the basic conflict in the play between the sacred (as the deified absurd) and the profane, at least in the light of Caillois's definition of the profane as "the constant search for a balanced or just environment that permits living in fear and moderation without exceeding the limits of the allowable. . . . The departure from this tranquility, from this place of relative calm in which stability and security are greater than elsewhere, is equivalent to the entrance of the sacred into the world" (137). Unlike his bourgeois coconspirators, who fear Caligula as a threat to their physical well being, Cherea realizes instinctively that the sacred is the primary obstacle to human freedom. In opposing Caligula, he steadfastly refuses all recourse to transcendence and thus announces the emergence of modern, non-religious man who *"makes himself*, and he only makes himself completely in proportion as he desacralizes himself and the world" (Eliade, *Sacred* 203).

The final scenes of the play reinforce the dual nature of Caligula's failure: on the one hand, the triumph and the reestablishment of the profane through the assassins' knives; on the other, Caligula's symbolic self-destruction in breaking the mirror in which, after a final confrontation with himself, he sees only the image of a man. In breaking the mirror, he recognizes and destroys the sacred imposture that he has maintained, more or less consciously, throughout his reign of terror. At the same time, in this ultimate confrontation with himself, he seems to realize fully the self-destructive nature of his quest. "The world of the sacred," Caillois concludes, "appears to be that of the dangerous or the forbidden. The individual cannot approach it without unleashing forces of which he is not the master. . . . In these forces resides the source of all success, power, luck. But when invoking them, one dreads becoming their first victim" (25).

Caligula is the demonic embodiment of the impulse toward a metaphysical revolution so often found in religious and totalitarian ideologies. We might even borrow the term "negative transcendence" from Erich Heller in his essay on Kafka, in which Kafka's world is viewed as an epiphany of the demonic sacred (178). Caligula's absurd parody of the shaman's role of spiritual healer and guide culminates in the creation (and destruction) of an anti-shaman who perverts the language and the revelation of the sacred in his obsession to transform the immutable nature of things. He is, as Camus notes in a 1937 entry in the *Carnets*, both an "angel" and a "monster" that everyone carries within (1: 43). Caligula's cry, "À l'histoire, Caligula, à l'histoire!" [To history, Caligula, to history!] (*TRN* 108), implies an entrance into the world of history, which begins when the world of myth ends. This entrance into "history" suggests his symbolic role as a permanent and cyclical aspect of human evolution, that is, the temptation toward transcendental absolutism that eventually results from the destruction of the existing order and the desire to create Utopia. Camus went on to analyze and denounce this tendency in *L'Homme révolté*. Having long ago rejected Christianity as "une mythologie que demande la foi" [a mythology that faith requires] (*Carnets* 2: 155), he was equally unable to accept historical materialism, which enslaved man to the new god of history. As for Caligula, he will reappear throughout history in various shamanistic counterparts as diverse as Sade, Hegel, Nietzsche, and Marx (to name but a few of the "cases" in *L'Homme révolté*). Hence his final words, "Je suis encore vivant!" [I am still alive!] (*TRN* 108), evoking the eternal recurrence of shamans and anti-shamans who will perpetuate the deification of the absurd.

Notes

[*Editor's Note:* Translations appearing in square brackets are provided by the volume editor, unless otherwise noted.]

1. Cruickshank emphasizes the philosophical and absurd nature of Caligula's revolt (192-207); the influence of historical events on the successive revisions of the manuscript is examined by Germaine Brée (43-51) and I. H. Walker (263-77). For a variety of aesthetic approaches, see Lewis, Clayton, Arnold, Harrow, Bauer, Laillou-Savona, and Stoltzfus.

2. For a study of the mirror as a device to initiate the play within the play, see Laillou-Savona (87, 93), Bauer (39-41), and Stoltzfus (77-80).

3. See Raymond Gay-Croisier, who characterizes Caligula's dramatic spectacles as "un jeu dans le jeu grand-guignolesque d'inspiration élisabéthaine et une parodie du sacré et de sa ritualisation" (quoted in Stoltzfus 77).

4. Many commentators have "played" with the term's invitation to ambiguity. Brée (45) and Freeman both emphasize the notion of Caligula as a gambler, while Bauer (34-44) and Laillou-Savona (77-94) elaborate upon the actor/artist aspect. Stoltzfus goes beyond the context of acting or gambling in order to characterize Caligula's "gratuitous manifestation of unhampered individual " as "free play" (85). In the course of his essay, Stoltzfus frequently interprets Caligula's actions in the light of the sacred, but does not, as I have attempted here, directly relate them to shamanism.

Works Cited

Arnold, A. James. "Camus's Dionysian Hero: *Caligula* in 1938." *South Atlantic Bulletin* 38 (1973): 45-53.

Bauer, George. "*Caligula*: Portrait de l'artiste où rien." *Albert Camus, La Revue des Lettres Modernes* 419-24 (1975): 34-44.

Brée, Germaine. "Camus's *Caligula*: Evolution of a Play." *Symposium* 12 (1958): 43-51.

Caillois, Roger. *Man and the Sacred*. Trans. Meyer Barash. Glencoe, Illinois: The Free Press, 1959. Trans. of *L'Homme et le sacré*. 2nd ed. Paris: Gallimard, 1950.

Camus, Albert. *Théâtre, récits, nouvelles*. Ed. Roger Quilliot. Paris: Bibliothèque de la Pléiade, 1962. (*TRN*)

_____. *Carnets*. 2 vols. Paris: Gallimard, 1962-64.

_____. *Essais*. Ed. Roger Quilliot and Louis Faucon. Paris: Bibliothèque de la Pléiade, 1965. (*E*)

Cellier, Léon. *Parcours initiatiques*. Neuchâtel: Presses Universitaires de Grenoble, 1977.

Clayton, Alan J. "Camus, Apulée et la lune." *Romanic Review* 61 (1970): 209-18.

Cruickshank, John. *Albert Camus and the Literature of Revolt*. New York: Oxford University Press, 1960.

Eliade, Mircea. *Myths, Dreams, and Mysteries*. Trans. Philip Mairet. New York: Harper & Row, 1960. Trans. of *Mythes, rêves, et mystéres*. Paris: Gallimard, 1957.

_____. "Recent works on Shamanism." *History of Religions* 1 (Summer 1961): 152-86.

_____. *Patterns in Comparative Religion*. Trans. Rosemary Sheed. New York: Sheed and Ward, 1958. Trans. of *Traité d'histoire des religions*. Paris: Gallimard, 1966.

_____. *The Sacred and the Profane*. Trans. Willard R. Trask. New York: Harcourt, Brace and Company, 1959. Trans. of *Le Sacré et le profane*. Paris: Gallimard, 1956.

Freeman, Edward. *The Theater of Albert Camus: A Critical Study*. London: Methuen, 1971.

Harrow, Kenneth. "*Caligula*: A Study in Aesthetic Despair." *Contemporary Literature* 14 (1973): 31-48.

Heller, Erich. *The Disinherited Mind*. Cambridge: Bowes and Bowes Publishers, Ltd., 1952.

Laillou-Savona, Jeannette. "La Pièce à l'intérieur de la pièce et la notion d'art dans *Caligula*." *Albert Camus, La Revue des Lettres Modernes* 419-24 (1975): 77-94.

Lewis, R. W. B. "*Caligula*: or the Realm of the Impossible." *Yale French Studies* 25 (1960): 52-58.

Sprintzen, David. *Camus: A Critical Examination*. Philadelphia: Temple University Press, 1988.

Stoltzfus, B. F. "*Caligula*'s Mirrors: Camus's Reflexive Dramatization of Play." *French Forum* 8.1 (1983): 75-86.

Walker, I. H. "The Composition of *Caligula*." *Symposium* 20 (1966): 263-77.

A Reading of Albert Camus'
*La Mort Heureuse*_____

George Strauss

The theme of death—be it murder or suicide—plays a considerable part in modern literature. One could even go so far as to argue that several of the more philosophical authors regard the problem of death as one of the corner stones of their systems. The question of whether murder is justifiable occurs in several modern novels.

Dostoyevsky treats the problem in *Crime and Punishment*. His Raskolnikov argues already that murder is permissible, provided the ends justify the means. He already thinks in terms of an elite. This is a thought which was taken up by Gide in *Les Caves du Vatican*, the main difference between Lafcadio and Raskolnikov being that Gide's hero has freed himself from all Christian guilt feelings. Malraux also takes up the problem. He does not seem to be concerned with individual happiness so much as with the relationship between the murderer and the victim on the one hand and social evolution on the other. Sartre also treats the theme. Both Hugo and Oreste commit murder in their endeavour to achieve social integration. To some extent we shall find that *La Mort heureuse* goes beyond the works that we have mentioned, in so far as it justifies death and murder as integral parts of life.

In *La Mer et les prisons—Essai sur Albert Camus*[1] Roger Quilliot states that *La Mort heureuse* retraces a kind of spiritual itinerary—the itinerary which Camus might have followed in order to overcome his initial turmoil if he had not also been a sportsman, an actor and a journalist. This would appear to be somewhat reminiscent of the technique of André Gide who created characters out of possible developments of his own disposition. The lyrical tone and the passion and fervour of the book create a link with another aspect of Gide's work in so far as they remind us of *Les Nourritures terrestres*. Certain parts of *La Mort heureuse* are a hymn to happiness, to joy and to life. Whole passages read like prose poems.

"Dans cet épanouissement de l'air et cette fertilité du ciel, il semblait que la seule tâche des hommes fût de vivre et d'être heureux." (*La Mort heureuse* p. 29)

[In this expanse of the air and this fertility of the sky, it seemed that the sole task of men was to live and be happy.]

Elsewhere Emmanuel sings in his happiness. He explains that it is something which rises in his chest when he is happy, when he is bathing.[2] (p. 35) Camus is concerned here with rendering the pulsating quality of joyous life. He says in another passage that life is breathing in great gulps on the ocean and in the harbour. (pp. 43-44) On the morning of the murder we get a careful commentary on the same thing—

"Une grande joie glacée, des cris aigus d'oiseaux à la voix mal assurée, un débordement de lumière impitoyable donnaient à la matinée un visage d'innocence et de vérité." (*La Mort heureuse* p. 26)

[A great frozen joy, sharp cries of birds with faltering voices, a pitiless flood of light gave the morning a face of innocence and truth.]

We find here that the lyricism serves a philosophical purpose. We get the feeling that the murder is just one more expression of this overflowing life force. The reader notices that the words "innocence" and "truth" are being stressed, that the morning is suffused with light, that the air is filled with the cries of birds but that all these things are pitiless.

In the introduction, Jean Sarocchi states that the murder was inspired either by *La Condition humaine* or by *Crime and Punishment* or by both. Quilliot, on the other hand, points out that the very tone of the book would suffice to mark the enormous difference which separates the two works. He stresses that Mersault commits his murder in innocence, without regret, without remorse.[3] This is the detail which allows us to gauge the extent to which Camus' thought has progressed beyond Dostoyevsky's position at the time of *Crime and Punishment*. Dostoyevsky was a Christian and as such concerned with sin and atonement. These played no part in Camus' thought at all. There is only one criterion that concerns him and that is human happiness. Mersault has, indeed, moments of hesitation. He trembles, but one could regard this as a mere physical reaction due to the tenseness of the situation—moral doubt simply doesn't come into it. We read that millions of little white smiles descended from the blue sky as he leaves Zagreus' house (p. 29). Mersault goes home and falls asleep. In the flashbacks which give us the background to the murder, we learn that Mersault is bored. He desires to get married, to commit suicide or to subscribe to *l'Illustration*. He has to make some desperate gesture (p. 68). We can see from this that he is seeking fulfilment, a passionate and full life, a life which is beyond his reach while he is spending eight hours a day in his office. It is also apparent that all actions are regarded as equal in the face of the absurdity of the human condition.

The problem of the book, according to Jean Sarocchi, is how to die happy. That is to say—how to lead a life which is so happy that death itself becomes happy. The first part of the book shows us the dark side of this problem of living and dying happily—that is to say, lack of money, lack of leisure and lack of emotional control. The second part of the book, thanks to financial independence and to an adequate organisation of his leisure time—thanks, above all, to a certain inner peace—is the bright side of the situation. Quilliot comments that, on the whole, Mersault succeeds in obtaining without religion, what Christians normally obtain from their religion—that is to say, joy in spite of death and in death itself.[4] As we shall see, he obtains this by means of a certain asceticism, an asceticism which reminds us of Gide's Ménalque, an asceticism which will play a considerable part in Camus' later works.

The problem of the book is really the attainment of the good life. In the case of Mersault we have an almost mystical transformation which turns evil into good. Zagreus comments that the only serious topic of conversation is the justification of one's life. He points out to Mersault that all the things that one normally derives satisfaction from are really non-essentials, that they only become worthwhile if they become factors in the creation of happiness. (p. 69-70) Zagreus goes on to explain that one cannot be happy without money and tells us that by the time he had reached the age of 25 he had understood fully that all those who had the sense, the will and the desire to be happy had the right to be rich. "The demand to be happy appeared to me the noblest expression of the human heart. In my eyes everything was justified by this desire. All one needed to realise it was a pure heart." We can see echoes of Raskolnikov's philosophy in this because Zagreus seems to distinguish between those who have the endowment that entitles them to this happiness and the others. He seems to be saying, moreover, that the élite has the right to obtain riches by any means at all, provided this money were devoted to the creation of happiness. We also find overtones of Gide's *Nourritures terrestres* and of Ménalque. These depend partly on the fervent lyrical tone, partly on the basic assumption of Zagreus' philosophy which does not differ greatly from the thought of Ménalque. Furthermore, the situation seems to be the same. Zagreus is teaching his pupil, Mersault, a lesson in the same manner in which Ménalque is teaching his pupil, Nathanaël. There is also an overall resemblance that exists between Zagreus and Ménalque. They both set out to become rich in order to lead a full life. They both feel that things are only attainable if one has the necessary money. It is obvious that Mersault is an attentive pupil and applies this lesson when he kills his teacher in order to inherit from him the money which would allow him to lead a life of happiness—a life of happiness, he might well argue, which would be beyond the physical means of a cripple. Zagreus teaches us further that we must attain our happiness in spite of the stupidity and violence of the world in which we live. He insists that it is a measure of the baseness and cruelty of our civilisation that happy people have no history. It is interesting to note that at the time of *La Mort heureuse* Camus already felt that the aims of happiness and of history were incompatible. Having thus negated social canons, Zagreus goes on to deny religious canons saying that one must find one's happiness in this world rather than in the next. Zagreus does admit that it is very hard to justify his mutilated legs. He admits that he cannot possibly attain to happiness, but he is, nevertheless, convinced of the goodness and desirability of life so long as he feels its dark flame burning inside him. The reader is again struck by the passionate fervour of this love of life. (p. 70) Zagreus tells Mersault that a man who has as beautiful a body as he has, has only one duty—that is to say, the duty to love and to be happy. In a variant, this body is described as a promise of happiness. Mersault retorts bitterly:

> "Don't make me laugh. How can one be happy if one spends eight hours a day in an office?"

There is no doubt that the pupil is in complete agreement with his master. Mersault explains that what worries him is that he did not want to strive after happiness in spite of his environment—what he really wants is passive happiness—he wants to be open to everything the world has to give him, to let himself go, to absorb life through his pores. This openness to the impressions of the senses and the emphasis on sensuality as a means of attaining joy are strongly reminiscent of *Les Nourritures terrestres*.

> ... Il y a quelques années, j'avais tout devant moi, on me parlait de ma vie, de mon avenir. Je disais oui. Je faisais même ce qu'il fallait pour ça. Mais alors déjà, tout ça m'était étranger. M'appliquer a l'impersonnalité, voilà ce qui m'occupait. Ne pas être heureux, 'contre'. Je m'explique mal, mais vous comprenez, Zagreus.
> —Oui, dit l'autre.
> —Maintenant encore, si j'avais le temps ... Je n'aurais qu'à me laisser

aller. Tout ce qui m'arriverait par surcroît, eh bien, c'est comme la pluie sur un caillou. Ça le rafraîchît et c'est déjà très beau. Un autre jour, il sera brûlant de soleil. Il m'a toujours semblé que c'est exactement ça, le bonheur." (p. 71)

[Some years ago, everything loomed before me, they used to speak to me about my life, my future. I used to say yes. I even did what I had to do for it. But already even then, all that was strange to me. What occupied me was making myself impersonal. Not to be happy, "against." I am explaining myself poorly, but you understand, Zagreus.
—Yes, said the other.
—Even now, if I had the time....I would only let myself go. Everything in addition that would happen to me, well, would be like the rain on a stone. It refreshes, and it is already very beautiful. Another day, it will be burning with sunlight. It has always seemed to me exactly like that, happiness.]

Mersault tells us that each time he thinks of the progress of joy and sorrow in him, he is passionately conscious that the game he is playing is the most serious and the most exalting of them all. He knows what degree of aliveness he will attain. We see that like Ménalque he wants to experience and feel as much as possible. Needless to say, office work is a serious obstacle to his development. He says that acting, loving and suffering constitute living, which he defines as being transparent, as accepting one's destiny.[5] Like Gide's Thésée, Mersault wants to play the cards which life has dealt him. He affirms that he would not make an experiment of his life—he would *be* the experience of his life. This states Mersault's position in almost Sartrian terms.

Mersault tells us that man learns to understand man through those things which go beyond man, through his flight towards himself and towards the certitude of the greatness which sleeps in him. This is a statement that could have been made by Raskolnikov or by Gide's Prométhée, for this is after all what Gide's *Prométhée* is about, at least in part: man's endeavour to go beyond himself, to create a "man-god."

Mersault insists that the love which others bear him must not tie him down in any manner. He is afraid of all trammels. It is obvious that this refusal to be tied by love may lead to the sort of solitude that he feels when he stands on the bridge in Prague. He is conscious of the hostility of this solitude which contains neither fervour nor human kindness, but even in this solitude he is passionately alive. He will leave Prague, therefore, and return to the south because he needs to feel passionate life around him, regardless of whether this passion is an expression of joy or of sorrow. Even the sorrow of Cardona inspires him with respect:

> Comme chaque fois qu'il se trouvait devant une manifestation brutale de la vie, Mersault était sans force et plein de respect devant cette douleur de bête. (p. 87)

> [As every time he found himself confronting evidence of life's brutality, Mersault was powerless and in awe of this stupid sorrow.]

Mersault rebels against human misery. He does not rebel against human pain and sorrow however, which are expressions of life, but rather against the sort of lifelessness which is the result of routine drudgery, against the absence of passion and human kindness he felt in Prague. Right through the Prague episode Mersault is haunted by a Sartrian nausea.

> Une affreuse douceur lui venait à la bouche devant tant d'abandon et de solitude. À se sentir si loin de tout et même de sa fièvre, à éprouver si clairement ce qu'il y a d'absurde et de misérable au fond des vies les mieux préparées, dans cette chambre, se levait devant lui le visage honteux et secret d'une sorte de liberté qui naît du douteux et de l'interlope. Autour de lui des heures flasques et molles et le temps tout entier clapotait comme de la vase. (p. 97)

[His mouth was overcome by a frightful softness in the face of such abandonment and solitude. To feel so distant from everything, even his fever, to experience so clearly the absurdity and misery beneath the best prepared lives in this room, the shameful and secret visage of a sort of freedom that is born of doubt and the underworld rose up before him. Around him soft and flabby hours and the entirety of time sloshed like sludge.]

It is easy to see that Mersault shares some of Roquentin's troubles. It is interesting that nausea is connected with a feeling of freedom, which in turn seems to be based on loneliness and on being abandoned by the world. This freedom is almost complete, but it is suspect. It is the sort of freedom Tityre enjoyed. It is the freedom which comes before human commitment, whereas the freedom Mersault is trying to achieve would be freedom that comes after commitment, after the liberating act. Only after the murder will Mersault be able to attain the complete freedom of those who have made their peace with life, only then will he achieve the passivity of those who are happy in accordance with life rather than in spite of life.

During his lonely stay in Prague he feels porous—attentive to any sign the world might give him. He feels in himself a deep fissure which opens him to life. This fissure, again, has Sartrian overtones. One feels that it is at least akin to the inner division of the man who found it impossible to be in-itself and for-itself at the same time. Out of this arises Mersault's reaction to the strange cucumber odour which haunts him and awakens in him a truly existentialist anguish. Under the influence of this anguish, the fissure which separates him opens wider. He ends up physically ill and vomits. To some extent this is due to the fact that this odour brought him the feeling of an old world, of a wicked and painful world which had taken refuge in the room of the café and in the souls of the men who were there. Mersault is truly forced to face himself and each time he finds the same odour and the same anguish. At one moment he decides that at all costs he had to avoid emotional crises like the one that made him vomit. He therefore decides to make a plan and to visit methodically all the historical sites Prague has to offer. We are reminded of Roquentin who writes the history of M. de Rollebon. In both cases we find our heroes trying to hide behind a sham activity in order to avoid facing their problems. Needless to say, this doesn't work. We read that the smell and the melody had become Mersault's psychological home. Associated with this smell we find the macabre Kafkaesque death of the man in the street. Somehow this is reminiscent of the hostile visions that haunt Roquentin. It is an expression of the hostility of the world—of the existentialist fear that things are not what they seem, that sudden violence lurks around the corner. Mersault even shares the Sartrian hero's feeling that his limbs lead their own secret existence.

> De là, ses mains, bêtes vivantes et farouches sur ses genoux, appelaient ses regards. L'une, la gauche, était longue et souple, l'autre noueuse et musclée. Il les connaissait et dans le même temps les sentait distinctes, comme capables d'actions où sa volonté n'eût point pris de part. (p. 113)

> [From there, his hands, live, ferocious beasts on his knees, were attracting his attention. One, the left hand, was long and supple, the other gnarled and muscular. He knew them and at the same time felt them as distinct, capable of actions in which his will had no role.]

Another facet of the book is the strong distinction between Northern Europe and the Mediterranean regions, a distinction which Camus shares with several other authors such as Gide and Thomas Mann. The god who was being adored in Prague was the god whom one fears and honours, not the one who laughs with mankind during the warm games played in the sun and in the ocean. It is evident that we find here the comparison between the Christian North and the Pagan South, between the austerity of the cold regions and the joy of the Mediterranean basin. This is a thread which runs right through the works of Camus and which plays a very strong part in other works such as *l'Immoraliste* and *Death in Venice*. Linked to this appears the thought that man undermines man's strength. It appears that man here is to be read as man-made laws and traditions, whereas the world of nature leaves man's essential being intact (p. 132). Mersault escapes—he leaves the north and flees headlong towards Italy. The train takes him out of the old world and leads him to the threshold of a new world where desire would be king. The resemblance with Michel's similar flight imposes itself. Camus speaks of "la course folle du train" [the crazy route of the train]. This reminds us of Gide, who says:

> "Cette descente en Italie eut pour moi tous les vertiges d'une chute. . . . Il me semblait quitter l'abstraction pour la vie." (*l'Immoraliste* p. 458 (Pléiade))

> [Descending into Italy had for me all the dizziness of a fall . . . It seemed to me like abandoning abstraction for life.]

The important thing, though, is that in this train Mersault watched, tense and lucid. He was fleeing towards the south, he was fleeing towards life—but he was lucid. He used this trip in order to think. He states that one needs time in order to live. Life, like any other work of art, needs meditation. So, whereas on the one hand he was feverishly racing towards the regions of sensual existence, he was on the other hand meditating—trying to gather his strength for the supreme act. We find, therefore, that the south which offers life, in contradistinction to the dead, cold north, is at the same time the region which demands a murder as the price of that life. Mersault is driven by thirst, by hunger, by the desire to live, to enjoy, to embrace. The gods who were burning him up were also driving him into the ocean of life. He finally lands in the old quarters of the harbour of Genoa.

> Dès le premier cyprès, droit sur la terre pure, il avait cédé. Il sentait encore sa faiblesse et sa fièvre. Mais quelque chose en lui avait molli, s'était détendu. Bientôt à mesure que le soleil avançait dans la journée et

qu'approchait la mer, sous le grand ciel rutilant et bondissant d'où coulaient sur les oliviers frémissants des fleuves d'air et de lumière, l'exaltation qui remuait le monde rejoignit l'enthousiasme de son coeur. Le bruit du train, le jacassement puéril qui l'entourait dans le compartiment bondé, tout ce qui riait et chantait autour de lui rythmait et accompagnait une sorte de danse intérieure qui le projeta, pendant des heures, immobile, aux quatre coins du monde et enfin le déversa, jubilant et interdit, dans Gènes assourdissante, qui crevait de santé devant son golfe et son ciel, où luttaient jusqu'au soir le désir et la paresse. Il avait soif, faim d'aimer, de jouir et d'embrasser. Les dieux qui le brûlaient le jetèrent dans la mer, dans un petit coin du port, où il goûta le goudron et le sel mélangés et perdit ses limites à force de nager. Il s'égara ensuite dans les rues étroites et pleines d'odeurs du vieux quartier, laissa les couleurs hurler pour lui, se consumer le ciel au-dessus des maisons son poids de soleil et se reposer à sa place les chats parmi les ordures et l'été. (p. 121)

[From the first cypress, right on the pure land, he had given up. He still felt his weakness and fever. But something in him had softened, relaxed. Soon, as the sun moved through the day and the sea approached, under the big shining, leaping sky, from which rivers of air and light flowed down the rustling olive trees, the excitement that shook the world joined the enthusiasm of his heart. The noise of the train, the childish chatter surrounding him in the crowded compartment, all that laughed and sang around him accompanied rhythmically a sort of inner dance that for hours projected him, immobile, to the four corners of the world and finally poured him, jubilant and forbidden, into deafening Genoa, bursting with health before its gulf and sky, where desire and laziness fought each other until the night. He was thirsty, hungry to love, enjoy, and embrace. The gods who were burning him cast him into the sea in a small corner of the harbor, where he tasted tar and salt mixed together and swam without limit. He then wandered through the narrow streets full of smells of the old neighborhood, let the colors scream for him to burn up the weight of the sun in the sky above the houses and positioning cats within the garbage and the summer.]

That is to say, as he himself expressed it a few pages earlier, Mersault affirms his solidarity with the world in its most repulsive aspects and declares himself life's accomplice, even in its filth and its less graceful moments. This is the crucial decision Mersault has made. He has rejected the cold morality of the north—he has freed himself of the nausea that it caused in him—he has opted for life in all its forms and he has decided to pay the price which this life would exact. We are reminded here of Gide's saying that he has sympathy even for the dog who is gnawing a bone.[6] We read that in Mersault's loins "the warm curled-up beast of desire was stirring with fierce gentleness." Mersault who has been pining for a woman's love, realises at last that he is not made for it. For years, tied to an office, he had pursued a happiness for which he secretly knew he was not fitted. He had played at being happy. He had never really consciously opted for happiness; never, until the day when he committed the murder. From that moment onwards, because of one single, lucid, calculated gesture, his life had changed and everything had become possible. Although the birth of this new man had not been painless, Mersault feels that the achievement had been worth the pains it had cost. He had at least achieved a position which allowed him to be present to himself, to face himself. This situation he was going to maintain for the rest of his life, even at the cost of the kind of solitude which he had found so hard to bear in Prague. But he soon forgot the murder altogether because he felt innocent. Completely given up to joy, he at last understood that he was made for happiness. We can see that the murder was only the beginning, the beginning of freedom, the beginning of existence, of passive openness to all that life had to bring.

After the murder, Mersault moves into *La Maison devant le monde* which is not a house where one finds entertainment but a house where one finds happiness. It is a house filled with a strange, chaste kind of sensualism, where the body has a soul in which the soul has no part. (p. 142) There is an insistence on the sensual qualities of cats which reminds us of Baudelaire. Lucienne introduces a further sensual element which is quite distinct from the chaste enjoyment of *La Maison devant le monde*. Mersault feels her unbridled desire and wants to drink from her living lips the meaning of this inhuman world which lies asleep like a silence enclosed in her mouth. She perceives through her body things which her mind could not seize. It is for this reason that he decides to make her his own. He marries her but, just like the hero of *l'Étranger*, states that marriage has nothing to do with the problem. Mersault does not want to be loved, as we have already seen. In fact, we feel that this is one reason for moving out of *La Maison devant le monde*. He is afraid that Catherine may fall in love with him. It is partly for this reason that he forms his relationship with Lucienne. When the latter complains that he does not love her, he states outright that love had never been mentioned between them. As for Catherine, he tells her that she must, herself, be responsible for her life—that it would be wrong to accept her life from the hands of a man. As far as he is concerned, the secret of life is to master all the pain and sorrow which fill our heart. This secret provides us with the lesson that leads us to a happy ending. *La Maison devant le monde* provides an existence which is characterised by poetry, an existence which is based on openness to all of life's sensations.

Il s'est approché de Catherine et regarde par-dessus son épaule de chair et de soleil, dans sa rondeur de ciel. Rose s'est approchée du mur et tous les quatre sont devant le Monde. C'est comme si la rosée soudain plus fraîche de la nuit lavait sur leurs fronts les signes de leur solitude et les délivrant d'eux-mêmes, par ce baptême tremblant et fugitif les rendait au monde. A cette heure où la nuit déborde d'étoiles leurs gestes se figent sur le grand visage muet du ciel. Patrice lève le bras vers la nuit, entraîne dans son élan des gerbes d'étoiles, l'eau du ciel battue par son bras et Alger à ses pieds, autour d'eux comme un manteau étincelant et sombre de pierreries et de coquillages. (p. 148)

[He approached Catherine and looked over her shoulder of flesh and sun, in her roundness of heaven. Rose approached the wall, and all four are facing the World. It is as if the sudden cooler dew of the night bathed their foreheads with the signs of their solitude and liberated them from themselves, through this trembling and fugitive baptism returned them to the world. At that hour in which the night is filled with stars, their gestures freeze on the sky's great mute face. Patrice lifts his arm toward the night, in his excitement causing a shower of stars , water squeezed by his arm from the sky and Algiers at his feet, around them like a sparkling and dark coat of stones and shells.]

Existence itself seems to become a lyrical poem.

When Mersault leaves the house, whether for the reason stated before or for any other reason, he leaves by car. The speed of the car produces various sensations in him. The rapture of speed is one that Mersault shares with Camus, but the trip is also characterised by other sensations, by the feeling of solitude, of complete isolation, by the enjoyment of the sun and the ocean. Mersault feels that he is enjoying a privileged moment which allows him to come to grips with himself.

Seul l'avion permet une solitude plus sensible à l'homme que celle qu'il découvre dans l'auto. Tout entier présent à lui-même, consciemment satisfait de la précision de ses gestes, Mersault pouvait en même temps revenir à lui-même et à ce qui l'occupait. (p. 152)

[Only the airplane allows a solitude more remarkable for man than that which he discovers in the automobile. Entirely present to himself, consciously satisfied with the precision of his gestures, Mersault was able simultaneously to return to himself and to what occupied him.]

This coming to grips with himself has been mentioned before; it is partly meditation, partly a sense of heightened awareness. I have used the words "privileged moment" deliberately because there seems to be an echo here of the privileged moments of Anny (La Nausée). Mersault is on his way to le Chenoua, a village where he will seek the most complete isolation possible. We find here another possible reason for his leaving *La Maison devant le monde*. We feel that he oscillates between various extremes of experience in an endeavour to find complete happiness. Having tried congenial company, he will now try asceticism. The experiment ends in disappointment. He finds that he cannot really achieve complete happiness in solitude. He attributes this to a lack in himself but finally gives in, calls Lucienne and succeeds in finding his way back to the world through her. It is on this occasion that he tells her that there can be no question of love between them. One feels here that like Gide's Michel he has a certain idea of his life and that he subordinates other human beings to his desire to fashion his life according to that pattern. It is not a question of Lucienne's happiness at all. It is purely a question of Mersault's full development. Notwithstanding his failure to adapt to complete solitude, he has profited from his state, he has learned to appreciate the slow progress of time which one feels when one has nothing at all to do. He has learned to tread the painful road which leads to the supreme art of doing nothing. This, we remember, was the aim of the young man who wanted to be happy without being happy "against" his environment, who wanted to be happy by doing nothing, by absorbing sensations as they came. This is the true happiness of asceticism.[7]

Mersault, therefore, lets himself go in life as if he were sliding into water.[8] He explains this more fully when he tells Catherine that it is an error to think that one must choose, that one must do what one wants to do, that there are conditions of happiness. What really counts is the desire to be happy, a kind of enormous ever-present consciousness; the rest—women, works of art, worldly success—they are only pretexts, a canvas which is ready to be embroidered by us. It is important not to forget in this connection that this absence of deliberate effort applies only to the condition that follows the one essential act of choice, the one liberating act, that everyone of us has to commit. Another condition of this happiness is that it can only be tested fully in confrontation with its opposite. That is to say that it is death which gives its price to life. In this connection, however, one must never forget that this death which gives its price to life, must never be allowed to choke life.[9] Mersault's isolation was itself only a station on his road. He needed this solitude in order to face whatever he had to face in himself, to find out what was sun and what was tears. Now that this has been done he is sure that he is happy. He is sure now that one doesn't live more or less happily, one *is* happy and death doesn't alter this; if one is really happy, death only comes as an extension of happiness. This is the conclusion at which Mersault arrives when he has attained happiness. It is an existentialist conclusion which has already been foreshadowed by his earlier statement (p. 73) that he would be the experience of his life.

Mersault still has to justify his murder. This problem is taken up in the discussion with Dr. Bernard who states that he despises an action which is dictated by self-interest. Mersault justifies himself fully because he had, after all, only faced the essential and immoral truth that one has to conquer one's human dignity and that without money this is impossible. He had decided to fight money with money. He had rejected the sordid, revolting curse which forces the poor to live out their lives in misery. He had not wanted money for money's sake. He had, therefore, not acted out of self-interest. This gives a social dimension to Mersault's action, which seems to assume an exemplary nature. Mersault appears to reject the curse of poverty on behalf of the untold millions who suffer it. Like Prométhée he offers his fate as a sacrifice on the altar of the future of the race.

A man's destiny is always thrilling provided it is lived with fervour. He had fervently carved out his own destiny, made to measure. The words "made to measure" are important in terms of what has been said before—that is to say, that we must each live out our fate; "fate" being defined as that which is pre-ordained in terms of our own disposition. Mersault accepts his fate in the innocence of his heart.[10] He accepts this green sky and this earth which is steeped in love. He accepts them with the same shiver of passion and desire which shook him when he killed Zagreus in the innocence of his heart. (p. 186) As we pointed out earlier, the trembling that Mersault experienced is very different from the moral doubts of Raskolnikov. Mersault knows that the murder was justified in terms of his happiness. He knows this in spite of Dr. Bernard's contempt for actions which are not disinterested.

In his *Carnets* (Vol. I, p. 104), Camus already writes that Mersault catches cold on leaving Zagreus after the murder and comments that this cold is the origin of the illness which will finally kill him. Mersault's illness is mentioned twice in the novel (pp. 179, 190). We have the feeling that the whole action of the book unrolls against the background of Mersault's illness, that is to say against the sure prediction that Mersault must die. His quest for happiness has to be seen in this context, just as Michel's quest has to be seen in the context of his tuberculosis.[11] Towards the end of the book (p. 193-4) we see that Mersault enjoys the supreme delights of happiness which seem to be procured for him by the sensations caused by the sea on the one hand and by his fatal illness on the other. In a way this mixture of death and happiness is the very root of Camus' thought. One has to lose one's self in order to find one's self.[12] It is also worth noting that his realisation of the absurdity of life is based on the continual presence of death in the background of human happiness.[13] This is in fact the essential characteristic of Mersault's happiness: it embraces both absurdity and the presence of death. He had at last achieved what he had been looking for. The peace which filled him was born out of the patient abandonment of himself which he had pursued and attained with the help of this warm world which denied him without hostility. Final happiness could, therefore, only be based on the complete renunciation of self. But even the hostility of the world which is such an essential part of absurdist thought is here seen as warm, as a kind of benign indifference, rather than as unkind hostility. It would appear as unkind hostility only to those who were still incapable of renunciation. One last desire lived in Mersault's heart; he wanted to encounter death while there was still some health in his body. He did not want death to carry off a husk that was already drained of life. He did not want to die in a coma—he wanted to see clearly. We are reminded of Goethe's demand for more light. He was filled by a vast core of tenderness and hope which doubt-lessly was the basis of his fear of death, but which at the same time assured him that he would find a reason for dying in what had always been his reason for living. (p. 197)

Quilliot insists that Zagreus faced his death with his eyes open, that it was his assassin who shut them.[14] Factually this may be true, but as far as Mersault's attitude is concerned, it may be truer to ascribe this shutting of the eyes not to a shirking of the responsibilities but rather to the kind of momentary reflex of excitement which had caused his tem-porary trembling. A more interesting comparison between Zagreus and Mersault may lie in the fact that Zagreus has tears in his eyes at the mo-ment of death, whereas Mersault dies happy. This may well be due to the fact that Zagreus, although he had managed to make the essential decision and to free himself, was then prevented from living by his in-firmity, whereas Mersault dies satisfied and fulfilled. An important as-pect of Mersault's death is that it somehow closes the cycle—that is to say, that the death which he suffers corresponds to the death he has in-flicted. This is a view which appears also in *Les Justes* where there is considerable emphasis on the fact that those who have inflicted death must face death in their turn.

> . . . Il y parvient par une sorte d'ascèse nietzschéenne qui, du plus profond de l'inquiétude, le ramène à la sérénité par la lente conquête d'une indifférence spontanée. Il y parvient par la conscience de soi, qui naît de la mort donnée et de la mort reçue. Patrice Mersault comme Meursault ne se connaissent que du jour où ils ont tué et se voient à leur tour condamnés. Le choc de la mort donnée est révélateur, purificateur pour l'un comme pour l'autre. Quant à la mort reçue, n'est-elle pas aussi source d'apaisement? La communauté, la fraternité des défunts prend ici le caractère d'un échange quasi mystique, mais d'une mystique tout humaine, dont *Les Justes* nous fourniront un nouvel exemple. "Celui qui avait donné la mort allait mourir." (*La Mer et les prisons* p. 90)

[...He arrived at it by a sort of Nietzschean asceticism that, from the depths of anxiety, brought him back to serenity through a slow victory over a spontaneous indifference. He arrived at it by a consciousness of the self, born of the given death and the received death. Patrice Mersault, like Meursault, lacks self-knowledge except for the day in which he killed and found himself condemned. The shock of the given death is revealing, purifying for each of them. As for the received death, is it not also a source of healing? The community, the fraternity of the dead here assumes the character of a quasi-mystical exchange, but of a mysticism completely human, of which *The Just Assassins* will furnish us with a new example. "He who imposed death was going to die."]

If we look at this in another way, we find that Zagreus reaps what he has sown. Quilliot comments that by his own cynicism, the cynicism of a pure heart, he incites Mersault to murder. We have already mentioned that there is a didactic element in Zagreus' conversation with Mersault. Zagreus tells us that everything was strange to him, that he tried to become impersonal. Later we find that Mersault seeks to attain the same impersonality. It is Zagreus who first gave Mersault the idea of asceticism. At the end of the book the delirious Mersault speaks of Zagreus' face which rose before him in its blood-stained brotherhood. The term "blood-stained brotherhood" shows us that the parallelism of their two fates had not escaped Mersault either. It is interesting to note that emphasis is placed on the fact that Mersault, just like Zagreus, looked life in the face at the moment of death. In a way, therefore, we have a situation which is parallel to that in *Crime and Punishment*, for the killer dies. But, although he dies, there could be no question of Christian expiation. It is shown to be a fact of life that only those who are prepared to die have the right to kill. It is life itself which justifies the killing; there is no sense of crime. It is for that reason that Zagreus' face is a brother's face, which does not frighten Mersault. Mersault has a vision of brotherhood; Raskolnikov, under similar circumstances, had nightmares. (p. 199)

Worn out and at the end of his tether, Mersault rejoins his victim, Zagreus; like Zagreus, he thanks life for permitting him to feel to the last the burning warmth of its flame. (p. 201) He, therefore, feels violent brotherly love for this man from whom he felt so separate and he understands that in killing him he had consummated with him a marriage which would live for ever. Of all the possible existences that it could have been given to him to live, he understands now which had been his. "He had met in all awareness and courage the choice which destiny creates inside a man. Therein lay his happiness in living and in dying. He understood now that to have been afraid of the death which he formerly regarded with the fear of a dumb animal, would have meant fearing life too." We see thus that death means different things for different people. Whereas it renders all life absurd and makes wretched the existence of the bulk of humanity, it becomes part of life and happiness in the case of the few who are capable of acting, of making the great gesture which helps them attain true freedom,[15] the freedom without which life is not possible.

Mersault is fully conscious, face to face with his body—his open eyes contemplating death. In an infinite desert of solitude and of happiness Mersault is playing his last cards.[16] Even at the last moment he is capable of sensual enjoyment and he looks at the swollen lips of Lucienne and sees behind her the smile of the entire earth. He is looking at her lips with the same eyes and with the same desire with which he contemplates death and, a stone amongst stones, he returns in the joy of his heart to the truth of emotionless worlds.

Ultimate happiness appears to be an odd mixture of sensual enjoyment and ascetic passivity, available only to those who have obtained true freedom from the laws of an absurd world by their willingness to give and receive death without flinching.

With kind permission from Springer Science+Business Media: *Neophilogus*, "A Reading of Albert Camus' *La Mort Heureuse*," 59.2, 1975, 199-212, George Strauss. Copyright © 1975 by Springer Science+Business Media B.V.

Notes

[*Editor's Note:* Translations appearing in square brackets are provided by the volume editor, unless otherwise noted.]

1. p. 91.

2. It is interesting to note this love of bathing; it is a trait which is common to most of Camus' heroes and to Camus himself. Gide's Michel also obtained spiritual satisfaction from bathing.

3. op. cit. p. 87.

4. op. cit. p. 90.

5. This choosing one's fate in accordance with one's natural endowment is a characteristic which is common to many characters of Gide, Sartre and Camus.

6. "Même le chien qui dévore un os trouve en moi quelque assentiment bestial." *Si le grain ne meurt* . . . p. 595 (Pléiade II).

7. This may also help us to understand the old man in *La Peste* who transfers peas from one pot to another.

8. The expression is characteristic of Camus' love of the sea. It helps us to see that for him water provides a caress which generates sensual enjoyment.

9. This is very well worked out by Thomas Mann in a scene in *The Magic Mountain* where Castorp is driven to this realisation during a vision he has when overcome by exhaustion during a snow storm.

10. The word "innocence" recurs sufficiently often in the novel to be significant in terms of the author's intention.

11. The whole of Thomas Mann's *The Magic Mountain* unrolls in a sanatorium for tubercular patients. Mann and Gide both appear to attach considerable importance to the role illness plays in the development of their protagonists.

12. This is reminiscent of the "Stirb und Werde" of Goethe's *Faust*. The idea also occurs frequently in the works of André Gide, who seems to use it in order to emphasize that the sensualism of the Immoraliste needs to be transcended by ascetic renunciation.

13. pp. 191-192

> . . . A cette heure, où sa vie lui paraissait si loin, seul, indifférent à tout et à lui-même, il parut à Mersault qu'il avait atteint enfin ce qu'il cherchait et que cette paix qui l'emplissait était née du patient abandon de lui-même qu'il avait poursuivi et atteint avec l'aide de ce monde chaleureux qui le niait sans colère. Il marchait légèrement et le bruit de ses pas lui paraissait étranger, familier sans doute, mais au même titre que les froissements de bêtes dans les buissons de lentisques, les coups de la mer ou les battements de la nuit dans la profondeur du ciel. Et aussi bien il sentait son corps, mais avec la même conscience extérieure que le souffle chaud de cette nuit de printemps et l'odeur de sel et de pourri qui montait de la mer. Ses courses dans le monde, son exigence du bonheur, l'affreuse plaie de Zagreus, pleine de cervelle et d'os, les heures douces et retenues de la Maison devant le Monde, sa femme, ses espoirs et ses dieux, tout cela était devant lui, mais comme une histoire préférée entre toutes, sans raison

valable, étrangère à la fois et secrètement familière, livre favori qui flatte et confirme le plus profond du coeur, mais qu'un autre a écrit. Pour la première fois, il ne se sentait pas d'autre réalité que celle d'une passion à l'aventure, d'un désir de sève, d'un instinct intelligent et cordial de la parenté du monde. Sans colère et sans haine, il ne connaissait pas de regret. Et assis sur un rocher dont il sentait le visage grêlé sous ses doigts, il regardait la mer se gonfler silencieusement sous la lumière de la lune. Il pensait à ce visage de Lucienne qu'il avait caressé et à la tiédeur de ses lèvres. Sur la surface unie de l'eau, la lune, comme une huile, mettait de longs sourires errants. L'eau devait être tiède comme une bouche et molle et prête à s'enfoncer sous un homme. Mersault, toujours assis, sentit alors combien le bonheur est près des larmes, tout entier dans cette silencieuse exaltation où se tissent l'espoir et le désespoir mêlés d'une vie d'homme. Conscient et pourtant étranger, dévoré de passion et désintéressé, Mersault comprenait que sa vie même et son destin s'achevaient là et que tout son effort serait désormais de s'arranger de ce bonheur et de faire face à sa terrible vérité.

Il lui fallait maintenant s'enfoncer dans la mer chaude, se perdre pour se retrouver, nager dans la lune et la tiédeur pour que se taise ce qui en lui restait du passé et que naisse le chant profond de son bonheur, Il se dévêtit, descendit quelques rochers et entra dans la mer.

[At that hour, in which his life appeared so distant, alone, indifferent to everything and to himself, it appeared to Mersault that he had finally attained what he had sought and that this peace that was suffusing him was born out of the patient abandonment of himself that he had pursued and attained with the help of this warm world that negated him without anger. He walked lightly, and the sound of his steps appeared strange to him, familiar without doubt but just like the rustling of animals in the the mastic bushes, the pounding of the sea, or the beating of the night in the depths of the sky. And he also felt his body, but with the same outer awareness as the hot breath of the spring night and the odor of salt and rot rising from the sea. His movements in the world, his need for happiness, the terrible plague of Zagreus, full of brains and bones, the sweet and restrained hours in the House Before the World, his wife, his hopes and his gods, all that was before him, but like a story preferred above all the others, without valid reason, strange at the time and secretly familiar, a favorite book that flatters and confirms what is deepest in his heart, but that was written by someone else. For the first time, he felt no reality other than the passion for adventure, a desire to sap, a friendly and intelligent instinct of kinship with the world. Without anger or hatred, he knew no regrets. And sitting on a rock whose pockmarks he felt beneath his fingers, he watched the sea rise silently in the moonlight. He thought about Lucienne's face that he had caressed and the warmth of her lips. On the smooth surface of the water, the moon cast long, wandering smiles. The water should be as warm and soft as a mouth and ready to sink under a man. Mersault, still seated, then felt how close happiness is to tears, whole in this silent exaltation in which hope and despair are woven together within a man's life. Conscious and yet estranged, consumed with passion yet disinterested, Mersault understood that his life and his fate concluded there and that all his effort would henceforth be oriented toward that happiness and toward coming to terms with its terrible truth.

He now had to sink into the warm sea, lose himself to find himself, swim in the warmth and the moon to silence in him what was left of the past and allow the deep song of his happiness to be born. He undressed, climbed down some rocks, and went into the sea.]

14. Op. cit. p. 87.
15. p. 200

. . . Cette mort qu'il avait regardée avec l'affolement d'une bête, il comprenait qu'en avoir peur signifiait avoir peur de la vie. La peur de mourir justifiait un attachement sans bornes à ce qui est vivant dans l'homme. Et tous ceux qui n'avaient pas fait les gestes décisifs pour élever leur vie, tous ceux qui craignaient et exaltaient l'impuissance, tous ceux-là avaient peur de la mort, à cause de la sanction qu'elle apportait à une vie où ils n'avaient pas été mêlés. Ils n'avaient pas assez vécu, n'ayant jamais vécu. Et la mort était comme un geste privant à jamais d'eau le voyageur ayant cherché vainement à calmer sa soif. Mais pour les autres, elle était le geste fatal et tendre qui efface et qui nie, souriant à la reconnaissance comme à la révolte.

[. . . This death that he had looked at with the panic of a beast, he understood that being afraid of it meant being afraid of life. Fear of death justified an unlimited attachment to what is alive in man. And all those who had not made decisive gestures to raise their lives, all those who were consumed by fear and magnified impotence—all those feared death, because of the sanction it brought against a life in which they had not participated. They had not lived sufficiently, had never lived. And death was like an action that forever deprived the traveler who had sought in vain to quench his thirst. But for others, it was the fatal and tender gesture that effaces and negates, smiling at the recognition as at rebellion.]

16. We have already mentioned that in common with Gide's Thésée, Mersault believes that one has to play the cards which life has chosen to deal one.

Richard Wright's *The Outsider* and Albert Camus's *The Stranger*_____

Yoshinobu Hakutani

Although the likeness in theme, character, and event between *The Outsider* and *The Stranger* has been pointed out, it has not been studied in any detail. In general, critics have regarded Wright's philosophy in *The Outsider* as nihilistic. Charles I. Glicksberg, in "Existentialism in *The Outsider*" and "The God of Fiction," saw parallels between Wright and Camus in the treatment of the metaphysical rebel, calling Cross Damon's philosophy most consistently nihilistic.[1] More recently, critics have demonstrated Camus's influences on Wright in his conception of Cross Damon.[2] Edward Margolies in his comparison of Damon and Meursault pointed out that "both men kill without passion, both men appear unmoved by the death of their mothers; both men apparently are intended to represent the moral and emotional failure of the age."[3]

It would be quite tempting to compare the two works if they were the products of the same age and the particular philosophy they dealt with was in vogue. It is a well-established fact that Wright lived and wrote *The Outsider* in France, where he maintained a close contact with such influential writers as Camus, Sartre, and de Beauvoir. Moreover, Camus's indifferent philosopher can conveniently be placed side by side with Wright's protagonist, who contemplates human existence through his exhaustive reading of Nietzsche, Hegel, Kierkegaard, and Dostoevski. One suspects, however, that the comparison of the two novels would never have been made unless the two novelists were both caught up in the philosophical context of existentialism. This meant that the literary likeness was taken for granted. Meursault kills a man; he is charged with a murder, tried, and convicted in a world of court, jury, and judge. Damon, on the other hand, kills more than one man, not only an enemy but a friend, a mentor, and an ally, and is responsible for the suicide of a woman he loves. But he is never charged with a crime, brought to a trial, or convicted. Unlike Meursault, who encounters his death in the world of daylight in Algiers, Damon is himself murdered by two men, the agents of the Communist Party, on a dimly lit street in New York. *The Outsider*, therefore, is fiction of a different order, brought together with *The Stranger* in an assumed definition of human existence in the modern world. Although the two novels are regarded largely as existentialist, giving attention to the crucial details that differentiate the narratives makes Meursault and Damon radically different in their ideology and action.

It is time to reexamine *The Outsider* and the black tradition and experience that underlies it. Comparing this novel with an avowedly existentialist novel like Camus's *The Stranger* will reveal that Wright's novel is not what critics have characterized. Contrary to disclaimers, Cross Damon is not a black man in name only. Not only is his plight real, but all the incidents and characters he is involved with, which at times appear to be clumsily constructed symbols, nonetheless convey well-digested ideas. He is not "pathetically insane" as a reviewer described him.[4] The book bewildered black reviewers as well, not because of Wright's novel philosophy, but because Wright seemed to have lost contact with his native soil.[5] But a detailed comparison of this novel with *The Stranger*, a novel of another culture and another tradition, will show not only that Wright's hero is not simply an embodiment of a half-baked philosophy, but that he is a genuine product of the African-American experience. Such a reevaluation of the book will also clarify misconceptions about Wright's other books as well.

The disparity between the two books becomes even more apparent if it is seen in the light of the less fashionable literary philosophy, naturalism. To some American writers, such as Stephen Crane and Theodore Dreiser, naturalism is a doctrine that asserts the indifference of the universe to the will of man.[6] Camus, though his naturalistic vision is not conveyed with Dreiser's massive detail or analyzed by Zola's experimental method, nevertheless constructs his novel to dramatize a climactic assertion of universal indifference. Wright's novel, on the other hand, is filled with the events and actions that exhibit the world's concerns with the affairs of man. The outside world is indeed hostile to Damon, a man of great will and passion. Refusing to be dominated by it, he challenges its forces. But Meursault, remaining much of a pawn, is not willing to exert himself against the forces which to him have no relation to existence.

Heredity and environment, the twin elements in naturalistic fiction, are more influential on human action in *The Stranger* than they are in *The Outsider*. Though heredity has little effect on Meursault's behavior, environment does play a crucial role. Meursault is consistently shown as indifferent to any of society's interests and desires: love of God, marriage, friendship, social status. He is averse to financial success or political power; he receives only what is given or acts when acted upon. He is, like Dreiser's Sister Carrie, "a wisp in the wind"; he is more drawn than he draws.[7] This explains his passivity. Camus painstakingly accounts for human action just as Zola or Dreiser demonstrates the circumstances under which it occurs.

Camus shows that Meursault, who had no desire to kill the Arab, merely responded to pressures applied by natural forces. The blinding sun and the glittering knife held by the Arab caused Meursault to fear and forced him to pull the trigger. If the man with the knife had been a Frenchman, Meursault would not have acted with such rashness. Given the history of Arab-French colonial relations, Meursault's antagonism toward the Arabs might have subconsciously triggered his action. Camus's emphasis in this narrative, however, is placed on the elements of chance, that is, the blinding sun and the glittering knife, rather than on the social elements such as the disharmony between the French and the Arabs.

This idea of chance and determinism is absent in Wright's concept of human action exhibited in *The Outsider*. Each of the four murders committed by Damon is premeditated, the suicide of a woman is directly related to his actions, and his own murder is a reprisal for the actions he could have avoided. In each case it is made clear that Damon had control over his action; in each murder he was capable of exerting his will or satisfying his desire. In marked contrast to Meursault, Damon exerts himself to attain the essences of his own existence. They are the very embodiments of the abstract words of society—friendship, love, marriage, success, equality, and freedom—to which he cannot remain indifferent. Wright takes pains to show that they are not empty dreams. The fact that Damon has been deprived of them at one time or another proves that they constitute his existence.

The Outsider represents a version of existentialism in which human action is viewed as the result of an individual's choice and will. To Wright, the individual's action must be assertive and, if need be, aggressive. This is perhaps why he was more attracted to Sartre and de Beauvoir than to Camus. In an unpublished journal Wright wrote:

> Sartre is quite of my opinion regarding the possibility of human action today, that it is up to the individual to do what he can to uphold the concept of what it means to be human. The great danger, I told him, in the world today is the very feeling and conception of what is a human might well be lost. He agreed. I feel very close to Sartre and Simone de Beauvoir.[8]

If Wright's protagonist is considered an existentialist actively in search of an essence in the meaningless existence, Meursault seems a passive existentialist compelled to do nothing in the face of the void and meaningless universe. Focused on the definition of existence, their views are alike: Damon at one time says, perhaps uncharacteristically, "Maybe man is nothing in particular."[9] The point of disparity in their world view, however, is the philosophy of the absurd. While Meursault is convinced of the essential absurdity of existence, Damon is not. If one judges life inherently meaningful as does Damon, then it follows that his action to seek love, power, and freedom on earth is also meaningful. Conversely, however, if one judges life absurd as does Meursault, then it follows that his action is also absurd.

What is absurd is this dilemma of Meursault between his recognition of chaos and his search for order. It is the conflict between his awareness of death and his dream of eternity. It is the disparity between the essential mystery of all existence and one's demand for explanation. The fundamental difference in attitude between Meursault and Damon is that Meursault seeks neither order, nor a dream of eternity, nor explanation, while Damon is passionately in search of such an essence. Meursault's passivity, moreover, stems from Camus's attitude toward his art. Camus tries to solve the existentialist dilemma by arguing that an artist is not concerned to find order, to have a dream of eternity, or to demand explanation, but to experience all things given. The artist describes; he does not solve the mystery of the universe that is both infinite and inexplicable.

Whereas Camus's hero resists action, Wright's is compelled to act. Wright endows his hero with the freedom to create an essence. Damon's revolt is not so much against the nothingness and meaninglessness of existence as it is against the futility of man's attempt to make illogical phenomena logical. In the eyes of the public, Damon is as guilty of his murder of the fascist as Raskolnikov is guilty of his murder of the pawnbroker in *Crime and Punishment*.[10] Both crimes result from premeditated actions; Meursault's killing of the Arab is accidental.

Some critics find a contradiction in Damon's view of the world. Earlier in the story, Damon considers man "nothing in particular" (p. 135), but at the end of his life he asserts, "We must find some way of being good to ourselves. . . . Man is all we've got. . . . I wish I could ask men to meet themselves" (p. 439). Likewise his inaction initially makes him see nothingness and meaninglessness in human existence but in the end his action results in his realization of loneliness and "horror" on earth (p. 440). In short, what appears to be a contradiction in Damon's view of existence is rather a reflection of activeness and aggressiveness in his character.

The chief difference in philosophy between the two books derives from the differing philosophies of the two novelists, Wright and

Camus. Though both men are regarded as rebels against society, their motives for rebellion differ. Damon rebels against society because it oppresses him by depriving him of the values he and society share, such as freedom in association and opportunity for success. Meursault is aloof from society because he does not believe in such values. Moreover, he does not believe in marriage or family loyalty. His obdurate attitude toward society is clearly stated in Camus's preface to the American edition of *The Stranger*:

> I summarized *The Stranger*—a long time ago, with a remark that I admit was highly paradoxical: "In our society any man who does not weep at his mother's funeral runs the risk of being sentenced to death." I only meant that the hero of my book is condemned because he does not play the game. In this respect, he is foreign to the society in which he lives; he wanders, on the fringe, in the suburbs of private, solitary, sensual life. And this is why some readers have been tempted to look upon him as a piece of social wreckage. A much more accurate idea of the character, at least one much closer to the author's intentions, will emerge if one asks just how Meursault doesn't play the game. The reply is a simple one: he refuses to lie. To lie is not only to say *more* than is true, and, as far as the human heart is concerned, to express more than one feels. This is what we all do, every day, to simplify life. He says what he is, he refuses to hide his feelings, and immediately society feels threatened.[11]

If Meursault is characterized by his refusal to play society's game, Damon is a type of person who cannot resist playing such a game. If society is threatened by Meursault's indifference to it, it is Damon rather than society that feels threatened.

This estranged personality of Meursault is reflected in his relationship with his mother. Some critics have used his calm acceptance of the bereavement as evidence for his callousness.[12] But the fact that he does not cry at his mother's funeral would not necessarily suggest that he is devoid of emotions. Had Meursault thought her death would have spared her the misery of her life or that death would be a happier state for man, he should not have been aggrieved by the passing away of his mother. What makes him a peculiar character, however, is the fact that an experience which would be a traumatic one for others is for him devoid of any meaning. *The Stranger* thus opens with the protagonist's unconcerned reaction to his mother's death: "Mother died today. Or, maybe, yesterday; I can't be sure."[13] But as the story progresses he becomes a more sensitive individual. He is indeed disturbed during the vigil by the weeping of his mother's friend. And every detail, whether it is the driving home of the screws in the coffin lid or the starting of the prayers by the priest, is minutely described. Throughout the story there is no mention of Meursault's disliking his mother. He fondly reflects on her habits and personality; he affectionately calls her *Maman*.

By contrast Damon's relationship with his mother betrays not only the estrangement between them but also his hostility to the racist society that had reared her. His mother, the product of the traditional Christianity in the South that taught black children subservient ethics, tries to mold her son's character accordingly. It is only natural that Damon should rebel against such a mother, who moans, "To think I named you Cross after the Cross of Jesus" (p. 23). He rejects his mother not only because she reminds him of Southern Negro piety but because she is an epitome of racial and sexual repression:

> He was conscious of himself as a frail object which had to protect itself against a pending threat of annihilation. This frigid world was suggestively like the one which his mother, without knowing it, had created for him to live in when he had been a child. . . . This God's NO-face had evoked in his pliable boy's body an aching sense of pleasure by admonishing him to shun pleasure as the tempting doorway opening blackly onto hell; had too early awakened in him a sharp sense of sex by thunderingly denouncing sex as the sin leading to eternal damnation. . . . Mother love had cleaved him: a wayward sensibility that distrusted itself, a consciousness that was conscious of itself. Despite this, his sensibilities had not been repressed by

God's fearful negations as represented by his mother; indeed, his sense of life had been so heightened that desire boiled in him to a degree that made him afraid. (pp. 17-18)

The young Damon's desire to free himself from such a bondage is closely related to his inability to love any black woman, as shown by his relationship with Gladys, his estranged wife, or Dot, his pregnant mistress. The only woman he loves is the white woman Eva, the wife of his Communist friend Gil Blount. Damon falls in love with Eva despite, and partly because of, the fact that a black man's desire for a white woman is taboo. He feels an affinity to her, for he discovers that she, too, is a fearful individual and that she had been deceived into marrying her husband because of a political intrigue. Damon is tormented by the envenomed abstraction of racial and political myths. Unlike the white phonograph salesman, who seduces the wife of a black man in "Long Black Song," he is permanently frustrated. Since *The Outsider* portrays a rich variety of racial and political animosities, his love life is defined in terms of the forces beyond his control. To him the consummation of his love for Eva means the ultimate purpose of his new existence. It is understandable that when that goal appears within reach and yet is taken away from him, he finds only "the horror" that he has dreaded all his life (p. 440).

Meursault's relationship with women, on the contrary, is totally uninhibited socially and psychologically. His relationship with Marie is free from the kinds of racial and political entanglements which smother Damon's relationship with Eva. Meursault, the perfectly adjusted man, does not suffer from any kind of repression. His action for love is motivated from within according to logic rather than convention or sentiment. In his life, love of woman is as natural an instinct as is eating or resting; love is more akin to friendship than marriage. He helps Raymond, for he says, "I wanted to satisfy Raymond, as I'd no reasons not to satisfy him" (p. 41). Meursault is kind and benevolent as Damon is not; he is relaxed and content as Damon is tense and frustrated.

Meursault's indifference to existence is epitomized by his love life. His attitude toward Marie bears a sort of impersonal, superhuman mode of thought. To the public such an attitude is inhuman, unconventional, and unethical. His view of love is no different from that of death; interestingly enough, his sexual relations with Marie begin immediately after his mother's death. If death occurs beyond man's control, so does love. His meeting with her takes place by mere coincidence and the relationship that develops is casual and appears quite innocent:

> When I was helping her to climb on a raft, I let my hand stray over her breasts. Then she lay flat on the raft, while I trod water. After a moment she turned and looked at me. Her hair was over her eyes and she was laughing. I clambered up on to the raft, beside her. The air was pleasantly warm, and, half jokingly, I let my head sink back upon her lap. She didn't seem to mind, so I let it stay there. I had the sky full in my eyes, all blue and gold, and I could feel Marie's stomach rising and falling gently under my head. We must have stayed a good half-hour on the raft, both of us half asleep. When the sun got too hot she dived off and I followed. I caught up with her, put my arm round her waist, and we swam side by side. She was still laughing. (pp. 23-24)

Even when a marriage proposal is made by Marie, his indifference remains intact: "Marie came that evening and asked me if I'd marry her. I said I didn't mind; if she was keen on it, we'd get married" (p. 52).

Meursault's indifference is also reflected in his reaction to the crime of which he is accused. Partly as a corollary to the nature of the crime, he is passive rather than active. Unlike Damon, he commits a crime without malice or intention. He kills the Arab not because he hates the victim but partly because he sympathizes with his friend Raymond, whose life has been threatened. Given this situation, it would be more natural for him to defend his friend than the hostile stranger. Meursault's crime is a crime of logic; it is not a murder. Camus's purpose for using crime in *The Stranger* is to prove that society, rather than the criminal, is in the wrong. Camus's intention is to prove that his hero is innocent, as well as to show that Meursault's logic is far superior to society's. When crime appears innocent, it is innocence that is called upon to justify itself. In *The Stranger*, then, it is society, not the criminal, that is on trial.

Because Meursault is convinced of his innocence, he attains at the end of his life his peace of mind, a kind of nirvana:

> With death so near, Mother must have felt like someone on the brink of freedom, ready to start life all over again. No one, no one in the world had any right to weep for her. And I, too, felt ready to start life all over again. It was as if that great rush of anger had washed me clean, emptied me of hope, and, gazing up at the dark sky spangled with its signs and stars, for the first time, the first, I laid my heart open to the benign indifference of the universe. (p. 154)

Damon is also convinced of his innocence at the end of his life. What the two novels share is not only that the hero is prosecuted by society, but that society—the prosecutor, jurors, and judge—seems to him to be always in the wrong. Camus's hero refuses to play society's game; as a result he is sentenced to death by society. Society expects him to grieve over his mother's death and refrain from having a casual affair with a woman during the mourning. But Wright's hero, induced to play society's game, loses in the end. He is tempted to participate in the normal activities of society such as a love affair and a political association. Tasting his agonizing defeat and dying, he utters:

> I wish I had some way to give the meaning of my life to others. . . . To make a bridge from man to man . . . Starting from scratch every time is . . . is no good. Tell them not to come down this road . . . We must find some way of being good to ourselves . . . We're different from what we seem. . . . Maybe worse, maybe better . . . But certainly different . . . We're strangers to ourselves. (p. 439)

The confession at the end of his life suggests that he, unlike Meursault, has always felt obliged to justify his actions. He has finally realized that they always collided with society's interests and values. As an outsider, he trusted no one, not even himself, nor did society trust him. While maintaining in his last breath that "in my heart . . . I'm . . . innocent" (p. 440), he is judging society guilty. While Meursault is a victim of his own crime, Damon is a victim not only of his own crime but of society's. Meursault, who refuses to justify his actions, always feels innocent: "I wasn't conscious of any 'sin'; all I knew was that I'd been guilty of a criminal offense" (p. 148).

Although both novels employ crime as a thematic device, the focus of the author's idea differs. Camus's center of interest is not crime but its consequences—its psychological effect on his hero. Before committing his crime Meursault is presented as a stranger who finds no meaning in life. After he is sentenced to death he realizes for the first time that his life has been enveloped in the elusive beauty of the world. "To feel it so like myself, indeed, so brotherly," he says, "made me realize that I'd been happy, and that I was happy still" (p. 154). In *The Outsider* crime is used, like accidental death or suicide, to create a new life for the hero. He murders the fascist Herndon as a reprisal; he intentionally kills the Communist Blount out of his desire for a white woman. In stark contrast to Camus's hero, to whom death has brought life and happiness, Wright's hero in the end is once more reminded of his own estrangement and horror.[14]

The two novelists' divergent attitudes toward the problems of crime and guilt are also reflected in the style and structure of their works. *The Stranger* is swift in pace and dramatic in tone, and displays considerable subjectivity, involving the reader in the consciousness of the hero. The reader's involvement in the hero's dialectics is intensified because the book consists of two parts dealing with the same issue. The first part involves the reader in a few days of Meursault's life, ending with his crime; the second re-involves the reader in the same experiences through the trial in court. Since the hero's experiences are viewed from different angles, they never strike one as monotonous or repetitious. The chief reason for the juxtaposition is for the hero, and for Camus, to convince the reader that what appears to society to be a crime is not at all a crime in the eyes of an existentialist.

This juxtaposition also elucidates the discontinuity and unrelatedness of Meursault's experiences in the first half of the story despite the reordering and construing of those experiences in the second half. As the incidents and actions in the first half are discontinuous, so is time. No days are referred to in Meursault's life except for Saturday and Sunday, his days off. Of the months only August is mentioned since Meursault, Mason, and Raymond plan to have their vacation together; of the seasons only summer. By the same token, there is no mention of the day of the month. And Meursault's age is unknown; he is merely "young."[15] As there is nothing unique about his concept of time, there is nothing unique about his experience. As points in time are discontinuous, so are the experiences. At his trial the prosecutor accuses him of moral turpitude, for Meursault shed no tears at his mother's funeral and casually started an affair with Marie immediately after. To Meursault, his mother's death, his behavior at the funeral, and his love affair are not only devoid of meaning in themselves, but discontinuous, unrelated incidents.

Similarly, the threatening gesture of the Arab, the sweating in Meursault's eyebrows, the flashing of the sun against his eyes, and the firing of his revolver occur independently of one another. If his eyes were blinded by the sun and the sweating of his eyebrows, his pulling the trigger on the revolver would not have been a logical reaction. When he is later asked by the prosecutor why he took a revolver with him and went back to the place where the Arab reappeared, he replies that "it was a matter of pure chance" (p. 110). If he does not believe that he is "morally guilty of his mother's death" (p. 128), as charged by the prosecutor, it would be impossible for him to admit that he is morally guilty of the Arab's death. This is precisely the reason why he tells the priest, "I wasn't conscious of any 'sin'; all I knew was that I'd been guilty of a criminal offense" (p. 148).

Swift and intensive though Camus's probing of Meursault's character is, the reader is deliberately kept from coming to an easy conclusion about Meursault's guilt. By contrast, the reader is instantly made aware of Damon's guilt in unambiguous terms. In *The Outsider* truly heinous crimes are constructed in advance with all the plausible justifications. Before the reader is made aware of Damon's guilt, the author has defined in unequivocal terms the particular traits in Damon's character and the particular forces in society that had led to his crimes. In so doing Wright creates a clear pattern by which Damon's motives for crime are shown. Whereas there is no such relatedness in Meursault's motives for action, there emerges in *The Outsider* a chain of events that can scarcely be misinterpreted. The murder of the fascist is committed side by side with that of the Communist.[16] Damon kills both men with malice: he murders Herndon because of his hatred for the racist as he does Blount because of his passion for the white woman. Unlike Meursault, Damon is conscious of his guilt in the instant of committing crime.

Since Damon's actions are predetermined and interrelated, Damon is constantly made conscious of the passage of time. The problems in his manhood and marriage, for example, are related to those of his childhood. His desertion of his wife is analogous to his rejection of his mother just as the Communists' rule over workers in modern times is akin to slavery in the past. *The Outsider* opens with a scene at dawn in which Damon and his friends "moved slowly forward shoulder to shoulder and the sound of their feet tramping and sloshing in the melting snow echoed loudly" (p. 1). Like Jake Jackson in *Lawd Today*, Damon, bored with his routine work, finds the passage of time unendurable. In *The Stranger*, Meursault is least concerned with time; he never complains about the monotony of his work. In fact, he dislikes Sundays because he is not doing his routine job. Damon, on the contrary, wishes every day were Sunday, or reminisces about Christmastime in a certain year.[17] More importantly, Meursault says whether he dies at thirty or at seventy it doesn't matter. For him life has no more significance than death.

For Damon life is all that matters. If his earlier life is not worth living, a new one must be created. Therefore, a freak subway accident, in which he is assumed dead, offers him another life and another identity. All his life he plans his action with hope for the future and with denial of the past. Such attitude is emblematic of the African-American tradition, the deep-seated black experience, as expressed in the spirituals. While Edgar Allan Poe's writings sometimes smack of morbid romanticism, that erotic longing for death, the spirituals reverberate with energy and vitality and convey the sense of rejuvenation. However violent and destructive Damon may appear, he inherently emerges from this tradition. Meursault, on the other hand, is the very product of the nihilistic spirit that hovered over Europe, particularly France, after World War II.

Despite Wright's effort to relate Damon's actions to his social and psychological backgrounds, *The Outsider* remains an imperfect work. Some of its faults are structural rather than philosophical. Given the kind of life Damon has lived, it is not difficult to understand his nihilistic view of the world stated earlier in the book that "man is nothing in particular" (p. 135), or his conciliatory vision that man "is all we've got. . . . I wish I could ask men to meet themselves" (p 439). But, as some critics have pointed out, it is difficult to believe that a young man with such mundane problems, renewing his life through a subway accident, suddenly emerges as a philosopher discussing Nietzsche, Heidegger, and Kierkegaard.[18] While in *The Stranger* the two parts of the story are so structured that each enlightens the other, those in *The Outsider*, the hero's life before and after the accident, are constructed as though they were two tales.

This weakness notwithstanding, *The Outsider* is unquestionably a powerful statement made by an outsider who refuses to surrender his will to live. One can scarcely find among black heroes in American fiction such a courageous and tenacious, albeit violent, man. As compared to Bigger Thomas, Wright's celebrated hero, Damon stands taller and poles apart simply because Damon is endowed with an intellectual capacity seldom seen in Afro-American fiction. Small wonder that when the novel came out, critics in general, both white and black, who were unfamiliar with such a character, failed to appreciate Wright's intention and execution in the book.[19]

The strengths of *The Outsider* become even clearer as this novel is compared with *The Stranger*. Although Damon professes to be a nihilist, as does Meursault, he is never indifferent to human existence as is Meursault. Camus's hero is called a stranger to society as well as to himself; he is indifferent to friendship, marriage, love, success, freedom. Ironically, Damon, who seeks them in life, fails to obtain them. It is ironic, too, that Meursault, to whom they are at his disposal, is indifferent to them. Wright's hero, an outsider racially as well as intellectually, struggles to get inside. Damon wants to be treated as an individual, not as a second-class citizen or a person whose intellectual ability is not recognized. On the other hand, Camus's hero, an insider but a stranger, strives to get outside.

It is hardly coincidental, then, that both novels are eloquent social criticisms in our times. *The Outsider* is an indictment against American society, for not only does Wright maintain Damon's innocence but he shows most convincingly that men in America "hate themselves and it makes them hate others" (p. 439). *The Stranger*, on the other hand, is an indictment against French society, for Camus proves that while the criminal is innocent, his judges are guilty. More significantly, however, comparison of the two novels of differing characters and traditions reveals that both Wright and Camus are writing ultimately about a universal human condition.

From *Mississippi Quarterly* 42.4 (1989): 365-378. Copyright © 1989 by Mississippi State University. Reprinted with permission of Mississippi State University.

Notes

1. Charles I. Glicksberg, "Existentialism in *The Outsider*," *Four Quarters*, 7 (January 1958), 17-26; "The God of Fiction," *Colorado Quarterly*, 7 (Autumn 1958), 207-220.

2. Michel Fabre specifically indicates that Wright's composition of *The Outsider* "was influenced in subtle ways by his reading of *The Stranger* in August 1947. He read the book in the American edition at a very slow pace, 'weighing each sentence,' admiring 'its damn good narrative prose,'" and commented:

> It is a neat job but devoid of passion. He makes his point with dispatch and his prose is solid and good. In America a book like this would not attract much attention for it would be said that he lacks feeling. He does however draw his character very well. What is of course really interesting in this book is the use of fiction to express a philosophical point of view. That he does with ease. I now want to read his other stuff.

See Michel Fabre, "Richard Wright, French Existentialism, and *The Outsider*," in Yoshinobu Hakutani, ed., *Critical Essays on Richard Wright* (Boston: G. K. Hall, 1982), p. 191.

3. Edward Margolies, *The Art of Richard Wright* (Carbondale: Southern Illinois University Press, 1969), p. 135.

4. James N. Rhea, *Providence Sunday Journal*, March 22, 1953.

5. See Saunders Redding, *Baltimore Afro-American*, May 19, 1953; Arna Bontemps, *Saturday Review*, 36 (March 28, 1953), 5-16; Lloyd L. Brown, "Outside and Low," *Masses and Mainstream*, 6 (May 1953), 62-64.

6. The indifference of the universe is most poignantly described by Stephen Crane in "The Open Boat":

> When it occurs to a man that nature does not regard him as important, and that she feels she would not maim the universe by disposing of him, he at first wishes to throw bricks at the temple, and he hates deeply the fact that there are no bricks and no temples. Any visible expression of nature would surely be pelleted with his jeers.

See *Great Short Works of Stephen Crane* (New York: Harper & Row, 1958), p. 294. Dreiser describes the forces of nature in *Sister Carrie*:

> Among the forces which sweep and play throughout the universe, untutored man is but a wisp in the wind. Our civilisation is still in a middle stage, scarcely beast, in that it is no longer wholly guided by instinct: scarcely human, in that it is not yet wholly guided by reason . . . As a beast, the forces of life aligned him with them; as a man, he has not yet wholly learned to align himself with the forces. In this intermediate stage he wavers—neither drawn in harmony with nature by his instincts nor yet wisely putting himself into harmony by his own free-will.

See *Sister Carrie* (New York: Doubleday, Page & Co., 1900), p. 83.

---

7. Cf. *Sister Carrie*, pp. 83-84.

8. See Fabre, p. 186.

9. Richard Wright, *The Outsider* (New York: Harper & Row, 1953), p. 135. Later page references to this edition are indicated in parentheses.

10. As Damon's murder of the fascist Herndon is analogous to Raskolnikov's murder of the pawnbroker, Damon's killing of his friend Joe is similar to Raskolnikov's killing of the pawnbroker's sister, Lizaveta. In the case of Joe or Lizaveta, the murderer has no malice toward the victim but intentionally kills the victim to protect himself from prosecution.

11. Albert Camus, *Lyrical and Critical Essays*, ed. with notes Philip Thody, trans. Ellen C. Kennedy (New York: Knopf 1968), pp. 335-337.

12. See, for instance, Robert de Luppe, *Albert Camus* (Paris: Temps present, 1951), pp. 46-47.

13. Albert Camus, *The Stranger*, trans. Stuart Gilbert (New York: Vintage Books, 1942), p. 1. Later page references to this edition are indicated in parentheses.

14. The kind of fear Damon suffers at the end of his struggle is clearly absent in Meursault's life. A critic, in comparing Meursault to Clyde Griffiths, the hero of Theodore Dreiser's *An American Tragedy*, comments: "Passivity in *L'Étranger* is strength, and only the strong can be indifferent. When Meursault receives this almost Buddhist illumination, he loses the two great distractions from life: hope and fear. He becomes happy, rather than terrified, in the face of his expected execution; he no longer hopes for some wild chance to deliver him from it. This prisoner is alone and freed, from within." See Stropher B. Purdy, "*An American Tragedy* and *L'Étranger*," *Comparative Literature*, 19 (Summer 1967), 261.

15. The most precise analysis of Camus's concept of time is presented in Ignace Feurlicht, "Camus's *L'Étranger* Reconsidered," *PMLA*, 78 (December 1963), 606-621.

16. Another example of this relatedness in Damon's actions is, as Margolies observes, the pattern in which Damon rejects the black women as he destroys the Communists and fascist: "When Cross murders two Communists and a fascist, his motives seem to derive more from what he regards as his victims' desire to enslave him psychologically, rather than from any detached, intellectualized, conscienceless 'compulsion' on his part. What the Communists and fascist would do to Cross if they had him in their power is precisely what his mother, wife, and mistress had already done to him. In a sense, Cross murders his women when he crushes his enemies" (Margolies, p. 133).

17. Damon's friend Joe Thomas reminds Damon of their happy days in the past. Joe speaks, "Remember that wild gag he pulled at Christmastime in 19 . . . ? . . . When the hell was that now? Oh, yes! It was in 1945. I'll never forget it. Cross bought a batch of magazines, *Harper's*, *Atlantic Monthly*, *Collier's*, *Ladies' Home Journal*, and clipped out those ads that say you can send your friends a year's subscription as a Christmas gift" (p. 5).

18. Saunders Redding, a distinguished black critic, considers *The Outsider* "often labored, frequently naive, and generally incredible." See his review in *Baltimore Afro-American* (May 19, 1953), in John M. Reilly, ed. *Richard Wright: The Critical Reception* (New York: Burt Franklin, 1978), pp. 225-227. Another reviewer finds it impossible to relate Wright's "passionless slayer" to the Cross Damon of Book I, and says,

"We can identify with the first Cross Damon, but not the later one. Wright goes out of his way to make this identification impossible." See Melvin Altshuler, "An Important, but Exasperating Book," *Washington Post* (May 22, 1953) in Reilly, pp. 203-04.

19. Orville Prescott's *New York Times* review was a typical white critic's reaction to *The Outsider*. With due respect for Wright's previous successes, Prescott politely insisted that Wright must have deplored Damon's moral weakness and irrational behavior at the end of the book, and further remarked, "That men as brilliant as Richard Wright feel this way is one of the symptoms of the intellectual and moral crises of our times" (*New York Times*, March 10, 1953). Saunders Redding, quoted earlier, noted that Wright's brand of existentialism, instead of being a device for the representation of truth, "leads away from rather than toward reality" (*Baltimore Afro-American*, May 19, 1953). Arna Bontemps was even sarcastic: "The black boy from Mississippi is still exploring. He has had a roll in the hay with the existentialism of Sartre, and apparently he liked it" (*Saturday Review*, 36 [March 28, 1953]. 15-16).

Is the Absurd the Problem or the Solution?
The Myth of Sisyphus Reconsidered _____

Avi Sagi

The approach to the absurd emerging from Albert Camus' *The Myth of Sisyphus* leaves the reader deeply troubled: having begun by claiming that the absurd is a problem to be contended with, Camus suggests an answer that "transforms the tragedy and malediction of the absurd into something with which compromise is not only possible but desirable. A sudden twist in the argument changes the absurd into a solution, a rule of life, a kind of salvation."[1]

What is the process whereby a tragic datum is transformed into a value? This question is linked to the more fundamental issue of inferring "ought" from "is"; whilst the absurd is a fact, embracing it is an ethical decision. One of Camus' critics, H. Hochberg, thus argues:

> Camus has leaped from the factual premise that the juxtaposition of man and the universe is absurd, to the evaluative conclusion that this state ought to be preserved. . . . For this transition we have no justification. Without such justification, Camus has not, in the least way, made his point. He has simply begged the question.[2]

Hochberg believes that it is not merely fortuitous that Camus finds himself thrust into this paradox; without God, values must somehow flow from ordinary human experience. This digression onto the factual-immanent world could, according to Hochberg, lead to the conclusion that values must "emerge" from facts, and what could be more natural than to have one's values emerge from what, for Camus, is one of the most fundamental facts of all—man's absurd condition?

Hochberg is certainly right in his opening premise—Camus does not acknowledge that values have a transcendental source. Does embracing the absurd, then, entail an ethical inference from fact to value?

When grappling with the problem of the absurd, is Camus attempting to formulate an ethical claim?

In an attempt to rescue Camus' move from these fallacies and paradoxes, it might be suggested that the first premise in this claim is an ethical one, whilst the second contains the factual datum of the absurd. Camus' argument is then correct, since his ethical conclusion derives from an ethical rather than from a factual premise. The basic ethical premise in this argument is the recognition of fundamental values such as honesty and integrity. R. A. Duff and S. E. Marshall claim that these values are unquestionably presumed in *The Myth of Sisyphus*. These values "first generate the idea of the Absurd, since this arises from a clear stubborn understanding of the nature of the world and the limits of human reason; it is honesty which forbids us, having recognized the Absurd, to evade it by false hope or philosophical suicide."[3]

Hence, the fact of the absurd is not derived from the factual premise of the absurd but from the ethical premise of honesty and integrity. Camus thus follows a logical course, from an ethical premise to an ethical conclusion.

In *The Myth*, Camus indeed points out that decency and integrity compel certain conclusions:

> If I become thoroughly imbued . . . with that lucidity imposed on me by the pursuit of a science, I must sacrifice everything to these certainties and I must see them squarely. . . . Above all, I must adapt my behaviour to them and pursue them in all their consequences. I am speaking here of decency.[4]

Two objections, however, could be raised against this reading of Camus' approach. First, as Duff and Marshall themselves point out, in the Sisyphian world described in *The Myth* there is no room for values. This, after all, is the very meaning of the absurd—a confrontation between the yearning for clarity and the "unreasonable silence of the world" (*Myth*, p. 32). A silent, irrational world finds no place for decency and integrity, and these values seem more suited to Camus' claim in *The Rebel*, where he argues that rebellion presumes human solidarity as the foundation of ethics. Aware of the distinction between the absurd in *The Myth* and the revolt of *The Rebel*, Camus claims: "Absurdism, like methodical doubt, has wiped the slate clean. It leaves us in a blind alley." In his later writings, he sees this as the end of *The Myth*, although he then goes on to say: "But, like methodical doubt, it can, by returning upon itself, open up a new field of investigation."[5] Defeating the absurd by protesting and rebelling against it presumes, according to Camus, a set of values and ideas deeper and more basic than the absurd; this is the message in Camus' later thought, which begins to take shape in literary works like *The Plague*, and reaches crisp formulation in *The Rebel*. *The Myth* itself, however, ends in a blind alley, unable to save such values as decency, honesty and integrity.

Second, note that, in the passage quoted from *The Myth*, decency does not function as the supreme ethical premise. The absurd does not derive from a previous value; rather, it is imposed on human beings— "lucidity imposed on me by the pursuit of a science." In other words, it does not follow from a preexisting ethical system but constitutes an ontological or anthropological premise that forces human beings to reach clarity—"What I know, what is certain, what I cannot deny, what I cannot reject—this is what counts" (p. 51). Decency is only relevant in the context of adapting one's practical behavior to one's consciousness and, according to Camus, is nothing more than logical consistency. Clearly then, the attempt to save Camus' move by turning it into an ethical argument appears implausible.

The critics as well as the apologists of this move share the assumption that Camus' argument is part of an "ethics of duty," in which the adoption of the absurd emerges as a logical conclusion. While the critics, however, see this conclusion as invalid because it rests on a factual premise, the apologists claim it is valid because it rests on an ethical premise. This thesis has obviously reached an impasse, and I wish to offer an alternative approach instead, claiming that Camus is not seeking ethical justifications for choosing the absurd. According to Camus, an immanent yearning for conscious lucidity is present in human life. When striving to understand the basic structure of human existence, human beings discover the absurd, but this conscious datum is not a premise from which Camus wishes to infer a set of duties. Rather, if the absurd is the basic datum of existence, human beings face a question: do they wish to embrace what has been revealed as the basic mode of human life, or do they wish to reject it by committing physical or metaphysical suicide? The decision to embrace the absurd is not reached through a process of logical inference; rather, it becomes a test for human beings asking whether they really wish to lead a life of conscious clarity.

As we shall see, Camus' approach combines the Aristotelian view that values reflect an immanent human yearning, with a phenomenological-existentialist method. This combination is typical of existentialist tradition, from Kierkegaard to Heidegger;[6] Camus' contribution is his portrayal of human reality as absurd, while relying on Aristotelian and phenomenological elements.

Let us turn to a more detailed analysis of this thesis. In several of his writings, Camus voices the notion that the yearning for consciousness is a basic fact of human existence. In "Pessimism and Tyranny" he argues: "We all have a dreadful need to reflect."[7] From an ontological point of view then, conscious activity embodies a basic immanent impulse. Camus speaks of a deep immanent passion for clarity in consciousness:

> The mind's deepest desire, even in its most elaborate operations, parallels man's unconscious feelings in the face of his universe: it is an insistence upon familiarity, an appetite for clarity ... the mind that aims to understand reality can consider itself satisfied only by reducing it to terms of thought.[8]

In the passage I quoted above Camus speaks of the "lucidity imposed on me by the pursuit of a science" (p. 26), and elsewhere in *The Myth* he writes: "human will had no other purpose than to maintain awareness" (p. 104).

This view of the mind as longing for a life of consciousness raises a question: How is consciousness awakened? What launches it on its course? Camus' answer is that it is the sense of the absurd that "inaugurates the impulse of consciousness. It awakens consciousness and provokes what follows" (*Myth*, p. 19). In its original state then, consciousness is best characterized as unaware of human reality and its structure; it is then set on a course resulting in its transformation and self-realization through its own sense of the absurd. This sense, which is described in *The Myth* (pp. 19-21), is the basic datum that awakens the individual to his or her own self.

The sense of the absurd thus plays a role similar to that of conscience in Heidegger's *Being and Time*. As conscience awakens and directs the *dasein* to the possibility of authentic existence manifest in the transparence of the ontological-existential structure,[9] so does the sense of the absurd direct consciousness toward itself and kindle the process of self-explication. Camus uses the term "awakens" as Heidegger uses "summoned" when referring to conscience:

> What does the conscience call to him to whom it appeals? . . . "Nothing" gets called to this Self, but it has been summoned to itself—that is, to its own most potentiality of Being its Self.[10]

Furthermore, just as conscience is usually perceived as an outside imposition (ibid., p. 320), so is the sense of the absurd perceived as entrapping human beings against their better interest; it is not by choice that human beings do not embrace the manifestations of the absurd—the meaninglessness of everyday life, alienation, or death. Finally, in Heideggerian phenomenology, conscience is the *existentiell attestation* of the possibility of authentic existence. In other words, conscience is a kind of mediating phenomenon between concrete empirical existence and the existential ontological structure, showing that the drive for an authentic existence is indeed immanent. Similarly, the sense of the absurd mediates between an inauthentic existence that has failed to acknowledge the absurd as its basic structure on the one hand, and absurd existence on the other.

Just as conscience does not create the possibility of authenticity but merely pushes toward its actualization, so does the sense of the absurd merely serve to awaken the explication process. Neither, however, creates consciousness, and were human beings bereft of consciousness, they could not sense the absurd:

> If I were a tree among trees, a cat among animals, this life would have a meaning or rather this problem would not arise, for I should belong to this world. . . . And what constitutes the basis of that conflict, of that break between the world and my mind, but the awareness of it? (*Myth*, pp. 51-52)

Indeed, the mind is unaware of this at the outset, and only at the end of the process is it able to grasp that the sense of the absurd rests on the structure of an absurd human existence. In the course of this process, the structure of the absurd is revealed as the principle containing and framing the sense of the absurd. In Camus' words: "In his recovered and now studied lucidity, the feeling of the absurd becomes clear and definite" (*Myth*, p. 26). At the beginning of the process, consciousness appears to be constituted by the sense of the absurd although, in truth, it is merely awakened by it. We are thus led to conclude that the revelation of the structure or the conception of the absurd is a process of explication which, according to Camus, is identical to the process of self-explication taking place within consciousness. In many of his writings, Camus refers to this process as one in which "the mind studies itself" (*Myth*, p. 22), and speaks of "the end of the difficult path" taken by the absurd person (*Myth*, p. 49). This is then an extended process of self inquiry, culminating in the exposure of the absurd as a reflection of the very structure of human existence.

Indeed, Camus' analysis of the absurd includes features typical of explication. Beginning with a blurred datum—the sense of the absurd—he explicitly refers to the vagueness of the absurd:

Like great works, deep feelings always mean more than they are conscious of saying. The regularity of an impulse or a repulsion in a soul is encountered again in habits of doing or thinking, is reproduced in consequences of which the soul itself knows nothing. Great feelings take with them their own universe, splendid or abject. There is a universe of jealousy, of ambition, of selfishness, or of generosity. A universe—in other words a metaphysic and an attitude of mind. What is true of already specialized feelings will be even more so of emotions basically as indeterminate, simultaneously as vague and as "definite," as remote and as "present" as those furnished us by beauty or aroused by absurdity. (*Myth*, p. 17)

This original vagueness is the first and even exclusive datum available to the mind and, in Camus' words, a beginning that culminates in "the absurd universe and that attitude of mind which lights the world with its true colours" (*Myth*, p. 18). The explication leads to clarity, once the full significance of the absurd is exposed.

Explication proceeds within the lines drawn by Husserl, and is guided by this datum. Not only does the sense of the absurd propel the wheels of the explication process, but it also remains within its own limits—"My reasoning wants to be faithful to the evidence that aroused it. That evidence is the absurd." (*Myth*, p. 50). The explication process, rather than transcending the limits of the absurd, probes it and faces it directly in an attempt to clarify it:

Up to now we have managed to circumscribe the absurd from the outside. One can, however, wonder how much is clear in that notion and by direct analysis try to discover its meaning on the one hand and, on the other, the consequences it involves. (*Myth*, p. 33)

Probing entails a complex process of description and analysis, as explication scrutinizes the basic elements at the core of human existence. Without resorting to theories, the process of explication frees the mind, in the Heideggerian sense of freedom, meaning that the mind is revealed to itself:

> The only thought to liberate the mind is that which leaves it alone, certain of its limits and of its impending end. No doctrine tempts it. It awaits the ripening of the work and of life. (*Myth*, p. 105)

Aware of the links between his own approach and Husserl's explication, Camus claims that thought "can still take delight in describing and understanding every aspect of experience" (*Myth*, p. 45).

It appears, then, that Camus is best understood when viewed through the prism of the ontology and epistemology of Husserl and Heidegger.[11] Although he disagrees with Husserl regarding several basic issues, Camus adopts the phenomenological method, which "declines to explain the world, it wants to be merely a description of actual experience" (*Myth*, p. 44). For Camus then, in its phenomenology as well as in its epistemology, the absurd aims "to enumerate what it cannot transcend" (p. 50); this focus on the empirical world and the renunciation of the one absolute truth is, in his eyes, phenomenology's greatest contribution. Relying on Husserlian formulations, Camus now claims a "profound enrichment of experience and the rebirth of the world in its prolixy" (p. 46): transcendental dimensions are set aside, and consciousness comes to be seen as one possible approach to a complex whole of experiences, releasing the world from the shallowness and the uniformity that classic rationalism had branded it with.

The integration of Aristotelian and phenomenological elements within Camus' thought can now be appreciated clearly. The Aristotelian component of consciousness' immanent yearning for self-realization is embodied in the phenomenological explication which, more than any other method, enables it to explore and explain itself without transcending the basic datum of human existence. Since Husserl and Heidegger, phenomenology has been presented as a method concretizing the transition of consciousness from potentiality to actuality. Rather than a theory, this is a pure method of the mind itself, in the flow of its immanent movement.[12]

Note that Camus approaches ethics in two ways. In one place he claims:

> We know that the system, when it is worthwhile, cannot be separated from its author. The *Ethics* itself, in one of its aspects, is but a long and reasoned personal confession. Abstract thought at last returns to its prop of flesh. (*Myth*, p. 92)

In this context, ethics implies an approach to the self, a confession revealed as a long process which, in fact, is the explication itself:

> What distinguishes modern sensibility from classical sensibility is that the latter thrives on moral problems and the former on metaphysical problems. (*Myth*, p. 95)

Absurd sensibility is part of modern consciousness and, therefore, this thinking is primarily the expression of a metaphysical concern. The meaning of this metaphysics, however, is ethical, in the sense of a return to concrete existence moulded by acquaintance with its foundations. The ethics embedded in the text is thus not a theory but a process of self-revelation leading to practical conclusions.

In this sense, *The Myth of Sisyphus* is a kind of voyage, the actualization of a process of self-knowledge, conveying the individual's "self-concern." Camus explicitly refers to the process aspects of the text:

> Is there a logic to the point of death? I cannot know unless I pursue, without reckless passion, in the sole light of evidence, the reasoning of which I am here suggesting the source. (*Myth*, p. 16)

At the end of this explication, we reach a lucid understanding and a clear perception of human reality as split between a yearning for the absolute and a longing for transcendent unity on the one hand, and an awareness of the limitations and finality of human ability on the other. This, precisely, is the concept of the absurd.

The explication indeed ends here, but not the process; the question individuals now face is what to do after discovering consciousness. When reaching the end of a process which, in the final analysis, leads them to a confrontation with their own selves, individuals must decide: Should they affirm human existence?

The decision to affirm existence does not necessarily follow from the assumption that existence is an obligation imposed on human beings, nor is it a conclusion based on a specific fact. Rather, it implies a readiness to accept the basic facts of existence as revealed through the process of explication, reflecting the notion of *amor fati*, which Camus explicitly relies on:

> Living an experience, a particular fate, is accepting it fully. Now, no one will live this fate, knowing it to be absurd, unless he does everything to keep before him that absurd brought to light by consciousness. (*Myth*, p. 53)

Elsewhere he says: "What matters is coherence. We start out here from acceptance of the world" (*Myth*, p. 69, note).

Camus' approach will be better understood if we return to the comparison between the conscience and the absurd. In Heideggerian phenomenology, "to the call of conscience there corresponds a possible hearing. Our understanding of the appeal unveils itself as our wanting to have conscience."[13] Heidegger stresses that the choice cannot refer to conscience itself, since its call is not conditioned by human beings but rather imposed on them. Human beings, however, may long for the call of conscience and welcome it, as it turns them toward themselves.[14] The decision to opt for conscience is not derived from an ethical system, but from the individual's readiness to live within conscious transparence. First and foremost, this decision is imbued with ontological-existential meaning—reflecting the human readiness to explicitly actualize the ontological structure typical of *dasein*. Similarly, Camus argues that the decision to affirm the absurd is merely the readiness to express, in explicit terms, the meaning of basic human existence. The dynamic of the immanent conscious process leads human beings to self-awareness, which, in turn, results in the need to choose whether to accept or reject the absurd. The decision to accept the absurd reflects the immanent human penchant for clarity, as well as the readiness to give it constant expression. Paradoxically, the decision to affirm the absurd allows human beings to live in harmony with the basic datum of their existence.

Ontologically, human beings can either affirm or reject this datum, and the ability to do so attests to their freedom. According to Camus, however, who continues an existentialist tradition stretching from Kierkegaard to Heidegger, the return to factuality is the authentic decision, the culmination of human existence. Hence, the authentic decision implies affirming the absurd.

Nagel, who categorically rejects Camus' interpretation of the absurd and even characterizes it as "romantic and slightly self-pitying,"[15] reaches a similar conclusion:

> Absurdity is one of the most human things about us: a manifestation of our most advanced and interesting characteristics . . . then what reason do we have to resent or escape it. (Ibid.)

Contrary to his interpretation of Camus, Nagel resembles him in his perception of absurdity as having a bearing, first and foremost, on self-understanding rather than on ethical issues. Human beings can reject absurdity and refuse to accept that their existence is absurd, but the decision to affirm absurdity does not thereby become an ethical issue. For both Camus and Nagel this is, in the final analysis, a matter of self awareness, a lucid admittance of the human condition.

The decision to affirm the absurd does entail a return to the problem; the solution, however, is not in a logical inference that derives the affirmation of the absurd from a higher ethical system. Rather, the solution is found in a process of explication through which individuals learn that the absurd is an essential aspect of human existence, and choosing it as an option actualizes the inner yearning for conscious transparence. Camus' position appears paradoxical when *The Myth* is read as an ethical rather than as an ontological existential text. In Camus' terms, the paradox reflects a misunderstanding, as it fails to take into account the fact that ethics is sustained by metaphysical rather than by ethical considerations.

From *Philosophy Today* 38 (Fall 1994): 278-284. Copyright © 1994 by DePaul University. Reprinted with permission of DePaul University.

Notes

1. J. Cruickshank, *Albert Camus and the Literature of Revolt* (New York: Oxford University Press, 1960), p. 63.

2. H. Hochberg, "Albert Camus and the Ethics of Absurdity," *Ethics* 75 (1965): 92.

3. R. A. Duff and S. E. Marshall, "Camus and Rebellion: From Solipsism to Morality," *Philosophical Investigations* 5 (1982): 122.

4. A. Camus, *The Myth of Sisyphus*, trans. J. O'Brien (Penguin Books, 1984), p. 26.

5. A. Camus, *The Rebel: An Essay on Man in Revolt*, trans. Anthony Bower (New York: Alfred A. Knopf, 1957), p. 10.

6. For an interesting analysis of the Aristotelian elements in Kierkegaard's and Heidegger's thought see G. J. Stack, *Kierkegaard's Existential Ethics* (Alabama: The University of Alabama Press, 1977), ch. 2.

7. A. Camus, *Resistance, Rebellion, and Death*, trans. J. O'Brien (New York: Alfred A. Knopf, 1966), p. 60.

8. *The Myth*, pp. 22-23. Similarly, "The will is only the agent here: it tends to maintain consciousness" (ibid., p. 61, note).

9. See M. Heidegger, *Being and Time*, trans. J. Macquarrie and E. Robinson (New York: Harper and Row, 1962), pp. 312 ff.

10. Ibid., p. 318.

11. Compare T. Hanna, *The Thought and Art of Albert Camus* (New York: Henry Regnery, 1958), p. 214.

12. Camus could plausibly have had in mind Husserl's quote from Augustine: "Do

not wish to go out, go back into yourself. Truth dwells in the inner man." *Cartesian Meditations*, trans. D. Cairns (The Hague: Martinus Nijhoff, 1977), p. 157, §64.

13. *Being and Time*, p. 314.

14. Ibid., p. 334.

15. T. Nagel, "The Absurd," in E. D. Klemke, ed., *The Meaning of Life* (New York: Oxford University Press, 1981), p. 161.

Space/Place and Home:
Prefiguring Contemporary
Political and Religious Discourse
in Albert Camus's *The Plague*_____

John Randolph LeBlanc and Carolyn M. Jones

Introduction

If we assume nothing has any meaning, then we must conclude that the
world is absurd. But does nothing have any meaning? I have never believed
that we could remain at this point. (Camus, 1970, 356)

In this 1951 statement to interviewer Gabriel d'Aubarède, Albert
Camus attempted to distinguish his work from that of his existentialist
colleagues like Jean-Paul Sartre and Simone de Beauvoir. For Camus,
the absurd provides a mere starting point: the silence of the gods on
questions of human justice is the point at which there begins a revolt
that can be productive of, for, and in community. Camus's focus on
community and his, at times, painful movement away from existentialist assumptions about the absurd prefigured important trends in contemporary political thought. While his statement seems to make a critique of the extreme understandings of postmodernism, in it, Camus
actually situates himself as an early and, perhaps, misunderstood voice
in a conversation undertaken among leading postmodern thinkers like
Jacques Derrida and Jean-François Lyotard as well as among postcolonial thinkers like Ashis Nandy and Homi Bhabha. As an Algerian
of French descent and as both participant in and critic of the Western
intellectual tradition, we argue, Camus was framing, before one was
recognized, a postcolonial discourse with the requisite postmodern
concerns about language, power, and meaning. There is always the res-
idue of an existentialist discourse in Camus, grounded as it is in the
plight of the alienated individual. But beginning in *The Rebel* and particularly in the novel *The Plague*, the clarity he experienced as partici-

pant in the Resistance brought to the fore a concern with the more overtly political problem of community-formation in a context of revolt. In this phase of his work, Camus attempts to break down the postcolonial dualities of colonized and colonizer (lest he be both) in order to find a space between them in which to articulate new forms of politics and religion through art.

Postcolonial critics from Fanon to Said roundly criticize Camus for being a voice of the colonizing west denying decolonized voices their place. For example, Camus's depictions, Said writes in *Culture and Imperialism*, 'draw on and in fact revive the history of French domination in Algeria, with a circumspect precision and a remarkable lack of remorse or compassion' (Said, 1994, 181). These readings implicate Camus in the project of blocking those who have been understood as 'other' from their place in discussions necessary for the negotiation of a new freedom and a new form of society. We challenge this latter suggestion, finding that Camus interrogates this desire for opening up dialogue on two levels. First, he broaches (after Nietzsche) the question of language and power later so elegantly pursued by fellow French-Algerian Derrida (1978), Lyotard (1988), and others. Once at the table where negotiation takes place, where discourse is developed and challenged, Camus's work asks, what language do we speak? The indigenous language often has been erased. What remains and, therefore, dominates is the language of the oppressor, in Camus's case the French with its apparent commitment to universalized revolutionary ideals (i.e. liberty, equality, fraternity). Camus interrogates our discursive reliance on these ideals: do these revolutionary ideals symbolize basic human impulses and aspirations or are they specific manifestations of a Western worldview seeking global autonomy? If they do symbolize basic human impulses, are these understood the same way in both the cultures of the oppressor and the oppressed? If not, and Camus's analysis in *The Rebel* (1991) suggests this is the proper response, are we faced with the task of creating a new language, and how? Second, Camus's work raises the question of the efficacy of the very idea of a discourse born of negotiation between or among cultures. Can the Western model of political negotiation lead to community when hierarchies are already in place? Camus argues that we need, as Toni Morrison puts it, altered/altared[1] spaces, safe spaces within which the once marginalized voice can speak and be heard. These might not be, as Camus's reputation for being 'unpolitical' (Judt, 1998, 104) suggests, the political structures to which we are accustomed. Instead, they might be spaces of communication that are illegitimate or displaced in the terms of political power, for example, intimate spaces like 'home.'

Using contemporary theories of space/place and home, we interrogate these issues in Camus's novel, *The Plague* (1972). This novel is Camus's meditation on the severest form of oppression; it is often read as a novel of the Holocaust, or at least of the German occupation of France/Western Europe. We will embrace but move beyond these readings to consider the novel's implications for the creation of community in what would emerge as a postcolonial world. Of the novel, Camus reminded Roland Barthes that, compared to *The Stranger*, *The Plague* represented 'the transition from an attitude of solitary revolt to the recognition of a community whose struggles must be shared' (Camus, 1970, 339). Community, we argue picking up Camus's assertion, is formed in the novel in the creation of necessary, but also free, spaces for actions that redefine social relationships, especially relationships of power. Camus's work here prefigures postmodern concerns in that community must also be formed in the search for a discourse that can articulate the meaning of the plague. Our central focus, therefore, will be the character of Joseph Grand, a colonial presence, who manages to resist the plague. He struggles throughout the novel to 'find his words,' especially as he tries to write the perfect first sentence of the perfect novel. Like Camus's own work, Grand's words and images are familiar, but, upon the closer examination we undertake here, their meaning, their place, is obscure. Interrogating the linkage of language and meaning to power, this essay examines Grand's 'heroic' attempt to communicate in a familiar but suddenly problematic language and what

Camus's depiction tells us about the difficulty of using an 'old' language, run through with those established meanings linked to social, cultural, and political power, in a new or fundamentally altered space.

Grand's sentence is an offering that problematizes the dominant discourse and becomes the occasion for refiguring the community. As a gesture in and for community, Grand's sentence becomes an act suggesting Derrida's later notion of hospitality (Caputo, 1997) and brings us to the metaphor of the table. The metaphor suggests the multiple levels of complication in the postcolonial situation. First, it suggests the negotiating table, the place of political interaction that in Grand's act also becomes a potential space of negotiated public and cultural meanings. Second, the metaphor also suggests the table of household, of private, interpersonal relationships, and the creolization of identities. The table of household admits the levels of intimacy on which postcolonial relationality truly takes place accounting for both the virulence of decolonization and the possibilities of postcolonial community.

Bound up as it is in insoluble intimacies and transitive meanings, the postcolonial world complicates the notion of hospitality. The question of who is guest and who is host is a shifting one, suggested in the terms *colon* (the name given Algerians of French ancestry) and native and in the difficulty Camus had negotiating his own origins. What is not different, however, is the presence of power (i.e., Grand's colonial presence). Derrida is correct when he says that the host has power—that is, the colonial language—but we argue that Grand's offering marks not only his own vulnerability (the connection of the sentence to his unresolved feelings for his ex-wife) but also the vulnerability of the very language in which he writes (a fire destroys the words, but the possibility of new meanings survives). He demonstrates a willingness to yield the self and maintain power at the same time, which is key to Derrida's understanding of the role of host: Grand is the most hospitable character in the novel.

Camus's contribution is that he concedes that power is present in all human relationships, and that power is most present in language, as we demonstrate in the analysis of Grand's initial sentence with its Parisian colonial imagery. The postcolonial situation, which Camus's work anticipates, means that there is a language in place that is 'authorized' for speaking, and, more important, for negotiation. Camus need not be a voice of colonialism—Fanon too writes in French—in order to acknowledge the pervasiveness of the colonizer's language. We all speak that language, although, as Chinua Achebe suggests, the native speaker may do 'unheard of things' (Achebe, 1988, 74) with it, stretching and changing its meaning. The language of politics becomes our common language. Freedom and change come in, as Grand's willingness to make his sentence a community project suggests, the willingness to put, truly, the language up for grabs, to listen to the voice of the other, and maybe, as Grand does to shift the focus from the language ('burn it!' Grand tells Rieux) to the level of relationship (his marriage with Jeanne). Such a display of hospitality may change both guest and host, for the guest, the stranger, in Greek thought anyway, brings change: the unexpected, danger, and the divine. Such a shift may not 'fix' anything immediately—for example, Grand does not recover his marriage, and he restarts his sentence—but it may offer a new ground of conversation, making the negotiating table a place of communion.

Plague: A Space Transformed

Contemporary thought on intermediate, transient, or what we used to call liminal spaces has focused on the freedom in those spaces. The kind of freedom available bears a relationship to the character of the space in which one moves. For example, Michel de Certeau makes the critical distinction between space and place, arguing that:

A place is the order in accord with which elements are distributed in relationships of coexistence. It thus excludes the possibility of two things being in the same location. The law of the 'proper' rules in the place: the elements taken into consideration are beside one another, each situated in its own 'proper' and distinct location, a location that it defines. A place is thus an instantaneous configuration of positions . . . A space exists when one takes into consideration vectors of direction, velocities, and time variables. Thus space is composed in intersections of mobile elements. It is in a sense actuated by the ensemble of movements deployed within it. Space occurs as the effect produced by the operations that orient it, situate it, temporalize it, and make it function in the polyvalent unity of conflictual programs or contractual proximities. (de Certeau, 1988, 117)

Places are fixed, more or less defined (i.e., political) spaces. As such, they are often hierarchical in order, modes in which meaning is authoritative. Space, in contrast, is fluid, polyvalent, full of movement and, therefore, of possibilities of change and new configurations of community. It is in these in-between spaces, as postcolonial theorist Homi Bhabha (1994) argues, that the nation is situated. There, between authoritative meanings and pure openness, combining the two in a signifying relation, the people exist and speak in their own voices. That is to say, when situated between such public structures as citizenship and private structures as kinship, the nation emerges as creative and fluid. Bhabha's 'nation', then, is not so much a political as a communal conception of space (Bhabha, 1997, 1998). To speak of space as simply political too readily draws us into conflict; political space, as Lyotard and Thebaud (1985) remind us, is always contested. The political, like the spiritual, is certainly a constitutive dimension of space, but only in part lest there be no ethical possibility beyond the outcome of the zero-sum conflict. In the fluid space suggested here, creation occurs in the presence of conflict: sometimes in spite of it, sometimes because of it, but often merely in its presence.

Camus's *The Plague* makes us think critically about how communities are formed in free spaces. Plague, indeed, creates a liminal, transitory, intermediate space, but not, initially or perhaps ever, one of pure freedom. This is a space under pressure of a definition, of violence that seems extraordinary but is in the nature of the world itself. Everyone in power is reluctant even to say the word 'plague'. While those on the Prefect's health committee, for example, know that the disease is plague, they define the situation obliquely: 'We are to take the responsibility of acting as though the epidemic were plague' (Camus, 1972, 49). As the days go on in their ordinary way, the death toll rises, until finally, the situation cannot be ignored. Dr Rieux is handed a telegram: 'Proclaim a state of plague stop close the town' (Camus, 1972, 61). Plague, initially, decreates and de-stories place. It establishes a sameness symbolized by a nearly existential isolation. 'Now we're like everybody else' (Camus, 1972, 27); it establishes a situation in which memory has no purpose. 'Hostile to the past, impatient of the present, and cheated of the future, we were much like those whom men's justice, or hatred, forces to live behind prison bars'; and, finally plague creates a need for an isolating form of imagination (Camus, 1972, 69). What everyone misses is love, the commitment to the other that is the very stuff of community; indeed, the narrator records story after story of love interrupted, love lost, love longed for. In this space there seems to be no freedom. 'Plague,' once started, silences memory and hope, isolates individuals, and empties discourse. The categories of ordinary politics, the Prefect's hesitance to call the outbreak 'plague' and take appropriate action, no longer apply and a fruitful response will have to be generated from communities political neither in origin nor purpose. For this space, with its fluidity, new configurations of community, and, possibly, new meanings to be created, all these—memory, identity, and discourse—must be re-imagined in the creative, Coleridgean sense: destroyed in order to be recreated in a space of action. What is needed, Dr Rieux says, is not orders or rules, but imagination (Camus, 1972, 60).

The Plague, although written relatively early in his career, is perhaps Camus's most mature consideration of community and, particularly, of the problematics of community-formation in a fundamentally transformed social and political environment. We argue, however, that his work is also inevitably informed by his difficult positionality as *colon* with the consequence that the novel can be read as addressing itself to the difficulties of decolonization. In our reading, Camus uses the plague to demonstrate not the oppressive colonial power of language, but rather the actual fragility of what we take for granted, including that language. Plague seems a peculiarly dated (Medieval) phenomenon, nonetheless capable, despite our 'enlightened' way of being in the world, of isolating modern, commercial citizens from each other, their own lives, and from the rest of the world. Hence the contemporary response to the 'plague' of, for example, AIDS. The assault on the ordinary that is Camus's *The Plague* has been read as a metaphor for the Holocaust, for the Nazi occupation that Camus himself resisted, and as a more general metaphor for the human confrontation with 'evil', recurrent and natural in addition to being malevolent. Each of these readings confronts the novel with questions posed and answered from a primarily European perspective. The apparent Eurocentrism of these analytical perspectives lends credence to the arguments of postcolonial critics like Conor Cruise O'Brien (1970) and Edward Said (1994). For example, Said argues that Camus is 'interesting' as both a product of and an accomplice in the 'French imperial project' (Said, 1994, 177). In general, the postcolonial criticisms hold that Camus is uncomfortably silent about the injustices and implications of colonialism (Rizzuto, 1981). Not only is there no blanket condemnation of the practice, but there are no real others in the novels.

Camus's apparent Eurocentrism, however, may well be as much a product of his critics as of his texts (LeBlanc, 2001). Camus's concerns were primarily ethical; his real foci are the individual's confrontation with the absurd, with what Arendt (1964) calls the 'banality of evil', and with other human presences. The themes Camus explores in the novel, particularly those of exile, isolation, and abstraction, suggest his interest in ethical responses to alien yet familiar circumstances. The plague, as a fictional device, rewrites the landscape of Oran much as the Holocaust, the 'end' of colonialism, or the splitting of the atom rewrite the landscape of contemporary politics. Each of these events, in their power to undermine both ontologies and epistemologies, force us to reconsider the way we think about power, about ethics, and about politics in general. In the novel, the outbreak gradually redefines a formerly familiar, modern, casual, and vacuous place as a fluid, potentially deadly, but also potentially creative space. No movement is free; encounters with others, whether routine, innocent, or purposeful may be fatal. This formerly modern commercial city, this Western construct in the north of Africa, is a place without passion where love is sterile and death is a violation of the ethic of busyness. While comprised of the same people, the same streets, and the same buildings, Oran is now a fundamentally different and alien space. As the French colonial presence erased and rewrote Oran, plague erases the place that was French colonial Oran, replacing it with a space yet to be described.

The dual effects of the plague in the novel are to render political power problematic even when properly exercised (e.g. making it illegal, for reasons of public health, to attend the burial of a loved one; quarantining the living in large camps) and to throw the character and dynamic of human relationships into sharp relief. Camus, we suggest, forces an interrogation of the way we respond to these transformed conditions, including not only the way we handle isolation and illness, but the way we handle the presence of the 'other'.[2] What language do we use when socially ingrained platitudes like 'I'm sorry to hear about the death of your beloved' have been so overused as to have lost their ability to communicate fellow-feeling? From these questions, it is a short step to wondering what language we use when our political platitudes, like 'liberty, fraternity, and equality', have been stripped of their meanings by overuse or abuse and our transformed conditions. We are clearly inadequate to the Nietzschean challenge of creating an entirely new language, so we must use the one we have. But how?

Camus suggests that the space created for us by transformative contingency, by necessity, by plague, is not a 'human' space. The plague represents the evil in nature, in the human sphere, and in the nature of creation that we confront and deal with only when it manifests itself, although it is, as the Spaniard in the novel tells us, 'they are coming out' (Camus, 1972, 9), always there. Humanizing it is the challenge confronting the characters in the novel and, Camus suggests, all human beings all the time whether we realize it or not. The reclamation of physical space is difficult, but conditions suggest directions and methods (e.g., the sanitation squads). These efforts, however, also suggest methods to reclaim social, political, and spiritual space. Humanizing the environment of Oran will require coordinated effort, the recognition of the sameness of both the condition and task of its citizenry despite otherness, despite formerly decisive and divisive differences. In other words, reclaiming the space that was Oran is a matter of being able to articulate both the problems and workable responses to the transformed conditions of plague-time. We argue that this need to communicate is the precise problem raised by Camus's depictions in *The Plague*. It is his insight that our old language is no longer applicable to these new conditions.

The character of Cottard suggests the difficulty. At the beginning of the novel he tries to hang himself, so despondent is he over his life. As the plague worsens, the aspirations of Cottard's persona turn our understanding of terms like 'respectability', 'testimony', and being a 'good sort of fellow' inside-out. Once plague breaks out, to want these things for ourselves is to want to be Cottard, the criminal, the outcast, the profoundly unstable and violent. Plague conditions create Cottard's new amiable, social personality and suggest the delicacy of our valuation of those things. Indeed, Cottard can be human only in extremity; he goes mad once the plague ends. We will argue that this vulnerability of that which we value is constituent of Camus's recognition of the still-to-come postcolonial *and* postmodern dilemmas: our language is so fragile, so well-worn, we must work out 'who speaks, how, and what language is to be used'. In the character of Joseph Grand, particularly his struggles with compatibility of the old language and new 'plague' conditions, Camus the *colon* suggests a response.

Joseph Grand: The Significant 'Insignificance' of the Human Presence

If the Oran of plague-time is a place hardly fit for human habitation, its previous incarnation was hardly more so. The opening pages of *The Plague* (Camus, 1972, 1-6), where Oran is described as a modern environment of busyness without meaning, suggests that Camus understands that 'modern' means business, competition, and quantity rather than love, community, and quality. Pre-plague Oran hardly seems inhabited by human beings at all. Camus's depiction of the modern, upon which he elaborates in *The Rebel*, is a shot across the bow of the language soon to be victorious in the Second World War: that of a classical liberalism linked to capitalism. The war in which he was a participant while composing *The Plague* is one in which the choice of sides seemed clear to him. In this sense, his work in the Resistance was a moment of great clarity. Yet to choose to oppose Hitler's National Socialism was to choose negation, a necessary 'no.' This 'no,' however, is not a 'yes' to the liberal capitalist paradigm. A more creative response would be more difficult. Consequently, in this novel, in this context, Camus, we argue, begins challenging the assumptions for which he presumably fights.

A liberalism linked with capitalism, Camus knows, values the integrity of every individual as the bearer of rights which include, and for some depend upon, the possession of property. It is to preserve this property and thus this crucial source of our identity that governing institutions are established. Classical liberal theory assumes *individual* possession of these rights before the political structures of society are established. Liberal theory then spends an inordinate amount of time, not interrogating these assumptions, but attempting to set up structures that will preserve us in these rights. Liberal theory's emphasis on the structures of political society has the effect of neglecting the real meaning of politics: negotiating interactions among authentic human presences. Liberal theory begins with the discrete individual who wishes to protect his stuff from other discrete individuals. The political order fills in the spaces between individuals by ensuring these protections. The resulting overemphasis on the forms of politics neglects consideration of the human presences of which the political must consist. The later work of John Rawls (1999) tries to save this liberalism from itself by forcing us to obscure our specific interests behind a 'veil of ignorance'. We still choose minimum conditions and the structures best to ensure them, calculating minimum requirements of the self rather than considering the other as real human presence. We then have the need for Michael Sandel to remind Rawls in particular and classical liberals in general that the unencumbered self can be a counterproductive fiction (Sandel, 1994). Camus understands this well; *The Plague* is an acknowledgement that no self is unencumbered, however alone the existential self may feel in particular circumstances.

Camus asserts a form of love to counterbalance the tendency to see modern individuals as the kind of commerce-driven automatons he depicts in the opening pages of *The Plague*. In the novel, as in Camus's work in general, love is intimately connected to imagination, to action, and to discourse. This is particularly true of the figure of the civil servant Joseph Grand. Grand tells Dr Rieux that when he and his wife 'loved each other we didn't need words to make ourselves understood' (Camus, 1972, 78). In love, action and silence take on full expressive meaning. Now with love lost, words—that is, speaking and writing—become Grand's problems. Grand is a French official, a clerk in the Municipal Office (Camus, 1972, 40), and therefore part of the colonial structure. He is a statistician (Camus, 1972, 40), one appointed during the plague to count the deaths. He seems to be an 'insignificant' person (Camus, 1972, 42), an underpaid clerk who lives a quiet, austere life. Yet, the narrator decides, Grand is, in his small way, a mystery man (Camus, 1972, 42). His mysterious qualities inform the narrative and transform those who fight the plague. First, Grand, who works with numbers, is someone who has trouble finding his words, and he expresses himself in the simplest way possible (Camus, 1972, 18). It is he who first realizes that saying 'plague' does not tell one anything: 'You see,' he tells Rieux, 'It's not so easy after all!' (Camus, 1972, 40). His focus on discourse and truth—an Enlightenment preoccupation with how to say something accurately coupled with the artist's concern to say it perfectly—marks the progress of the plague and, therefore, undergirds the narrative. Second, Grand is a rare man in his great capacity for love and compassion. When we meet him, he is with Cottard who has tried to commit suicide. Only Grand seems to care for the difficult, unstable, and vaguely criminal Cottard. In similar fashion, it is Grand who will extend his love and compassion to plague victims and to Dr Rieux, Tarrou, and the others, reminding all of their humanness, and becoming the center, in many ways, of a reconstituted community.

The characters in the novel, each very different people, provide the 'mobile elements' and varied positionalities on plague. Each represents a distinct approach to the narrative. For example, Dr Rieux, we ultimately find, is our narrator: he pulls all the discourses into one, although his own methodology is caught between that of historian and chronicler (Camus, 1972, 3, 6-7). The distinction, even movement, between historian and chronicler is significant, as is the recurring confusion over that distinction. Recall that besides Rieux, Tarrou is also labeled an historian but is really a chronicler of the obscure, of seemingly trivial but utterly necessary detail (Camus, 1972, 23) that yields insight into unique human personalities. The historian, who usually lives after or at least outside of the event, aspires to the objectivity of the social scientist. He wishes to present a dispassionate account of events, so his disposition is not unlike that of Dr Rieux when we first meet him in the novel: cool, detached, matter-of-fact. The chronicler, on the other hand, lives through the event, describing it as he goes, is transformed by the event, and his, often, unstructured and immediate impressions make up the substance of the chronicle. In a situation like plague, the chronicle itself is also potentially open-ended; the chronicler could himself be a victim whose death would not draw to a close that which is being chronicled, only the narrative itself. In these terms, the novel is much more chronicle than history; Camus ends the narrative with an assertion of just this kind of open-endedness: 'the plague bacillus never dies or disappears for good . . . perhaps the day would come when, for the bane and the enlightenment of men, it would rouse up its rats again and send them forth to die in a happy city' (Camus, 1972, 287).

Homi Bhabha's analysis of the modern nation (1994) suggests that politics errs when it tries to foreclose on the fundamental open-endedness of human experience. More than either historian or chronicler, Grand's literary sensibility teaches us that we too must learn how to live with open-endedness. To this end, he offers us his single, seemingly silly and unimportant utterance, his sentence which is his 'private work' (Camus, 1972, 32) and his own account of the 'growth of a personality' (Camus, 1972, 41). What Grand faces (and, we argue, helps others face) is that pain which, as Elaine Scarry (1987) tells us, de-stories: once expressed, it silences language and what plague comes to demand of the multiple narrators is that they face, in such discontinuity and pain, that 'there are no acceptable words, no socially sanctioned words, with which to describe the experience . . . If it can be spoken, the experience itself may already have ceded to genteel ambiguity. If the experience is spoken without compromise, every effort is often made to suppress it' (Collins, 1990). Truthful discourse cannot minimize or dramatize. Even the discourse of the historian or chronicler, therefore, cannot be made up of new words; it must take the words that are and use them to create a voice that forcefully and clearly expresses the situation and that can accept and resist silencing. That voice, in *The Plague*, is multiple and polyphonic. That is why, we think, the narrator does not reveal who he is until the end of the narrative: he does not want his voice to become authoritative. He recognizes the need to use the 'old' language to describe conditions that are profoundly 'different.'

The problem of the novel, and in this it is profoundly political, is how to create an ethic of language and an ethic of truth that can inform action in both the present moment and in the future. Telling the truth may combat the problem next time—let us see it at the center in its full complexity, at Aristotle's mean, rather than 'out there' or obscure it with a set of ideological certainties. The novel demonstrates that the problem of language and truth-telling essential to a functional political order is also related to the path of compassion, to love. The path of compassion, as articulated by Tarrou and as exemplified in Grand, involves both the capacity to feel with the 'other' and the capacity for clarity, the use of plain, clear-cut language. This path is not overtly political because it considers the human first, before order, power, property, etc. For Camus, however, it is a demand to be made of the political if a politics is to be called human. If one attends properly, sees clearly the self, the 'other', and the situation, both immediate and human, one is still part of the social, cultural, political world, the world of death, and one can still be, as Tarrou desires to be, an 'innocent murderer' (Camus, 1972, 236). Tarrou desires to be a saint, but he realizes that to be a man and a healer, as both Grand and Rieux are, is to be the best of men, for that is the most difficult task (Camus, 1972, 238). It is to love, to suffer, to survive, and also to be witness: to carry and articulate the pain of others as well as, and perhaps above, that of the self. Rieux and Grand, walking this 'path of sympathy' (Camus, 1972, 237) to peace, is a recognition that they do all of these.

Joseph Grand embodies the struggle between newly reconfigured conditions and the old authoritative language, between excess and what Derrida calls erasure (Derrida, 1978). As a low-level civil servant, he is clearly the 'colonial presence', officially documenting the effects of the outbreak and making the disaster intelligible in terms with which the governing presence will be comfortable. But Grand is also a gentle soul whose real investment is in the survival of the community. He is the only character described by the narrator as 'heroic', largely due to the way he conducts himself: he does his job during the day, volunteers in the sanitation squads afterwards, and, always in the evenings, remains committed to his 'ridiculous ideal', that is, his art.

Initially, his art, one sentence, is his solitary struggle, but as time passes it becomes an object of communal interest, even community-formation. The sentence gives Grand, and then the others, a focus beyond the press of their immediate circumstances and, more significantly, a sense of the limits of their old language. Through his art, Grand attempts to assert beauty in the midst of the horror; through his actions as both a public servant and as a volunteer on the sanitation squads, Grand is a figure in productive rebellion. His struggle with the language of the sentence mirrors that of the struggle of the authorities with the plague: both tell of the difficulty of using outmoded categories to find what is familiar or, perhaps, epiphanic in newly transformed conditions.

Grand is a man who has 'trouble finding his words' (Camus, 1972, 18). His status as a colonial presence makes this difficulty telling in two respects. First, he embodies what will be the futility of the colonial attempt to use its categories to manage the relative chaos of decolonization. Second, as the struggling artist, Grand is making the courageous attempt to adapt that language to these new conditions. However, rather than read his attachment to the language as a fetishism for the power that the language possesses, we would argue that it is, like Camus's own embrace of the French, a clinging to the known and familiar. Through the character of Grand, Camus recognizes both the futility and necessity of creating a new language. The forms of language are home in the same way a physical space is home. In this instance, the physical space as home has been erased and it falls to the language to render it as a new old home; it is the content of language that must be communal and, in terms of plague, communicable. In his depictions of Grand's labors, Camus reiterates what he suggested in the conversation over what to 'call' the outbreak: that the struggle with language is only futile when it distracts us from what must be done. Grand asserts his humanity by making the effort while continuing to do his job and serve in the squads. When the sanitation squads are created, Grand's response reveals his character:

Grand was the true embodiment of the quiet courage that inspired the sanitary groups. He had said yes without a moment's hesitation and with the large-heartedness that was a second nature with him. All he had asked was to be allotted light duties: he was too old for anything else . . . Rieux thanked him with some warmth, he seemed surprised. 'Why that's not difficult! Plague is here and we've got to make a stand, that's obvious. Ah, I only wish everything were as simple!' (Camus, 1972, 126-127)

In spite of the futility of his artistic efforts, therefore, Grand becomes for Camus 'the type who always escapes' calamities like the plague (Camus, 1972, 42). There is a timelessness to Grand's character and to his struggle, and it is this timelessness that makes his a heroic, even exemplary life (Camus, 1972, 44-45).

Grand's artistic efforts sustain his other work and the text of Grand's sentence, to the degree that in it we can trace the development of the struggle, is of particular concern. At first, the sentence and his work on the squads seem compartmentalized and separate. We come to see them, however, as integrated into Grand's whole character and into the community itself. In its initial form, the sentence reads: 'One fine morning in the month of May an elegant young horsewoman might have been seen riding a handsome sorrel mare along the flowery avenues of the Bois de Boulogne' (Camus, 1972, 99). He concerns himself with the rhythm of the wording, wanting the reader to get the feel of the young woman's ride. Adjusting oneself to new conditions means attending to rhythms. As the pressures of plague increase, Grand's colleagues take an interest in the sentence, trying to help him with his words. At first, Grand wants to keep his sentence private. He tells Dr Rieux, 'No, don't look' (Camus, 1972, 98). His hesitation is overcome, however, by his desire for community. Rieux declines to read the sentence himself; he has Grand, in his own voice, read it to him. To that Grand consents: 'Yes'. There was a timid gratitude in Grand's eyes and smile. 'I think I'd like you to hear it' (Camus, 1972, 98). Rieux first hears the sentence in the context of 'the curious buzzing sound' of the town, a 'victim world, secluded and apart' (Camus, 1972, 99) filled with 'the groans of agony stifled in its darkness' (Camus, 1972, 99). At first, Grand's sentence lies over that misery, but eventually comes to express it. The changing environment (the level of misery, the depth of plague, the energy of resistance) is reflected in the changes Grand makes in the sentence and here, as we will argue, Camus has his literary creation reflect the changing energy of the political. Initially, Grand cuts 'the month of' and changes 'elegant' to 'slim' (Camus, 1972, 127). Later, he adds 'glossy' to the description of the horse and changes flowery to 'flower strewn' (Camus, 1972, 128). The last version of the sentence that the reader sees, revealed when Grand is diagnosed with plague, has been rearranged to accentuate the pleasing environment, but now the sentence itself is left open-ended: 'One fine morning in the month of May, a slim young horsewoman might have been riding a glossy sorrel mare along the avenues of the Bois, among the flowers . . .' (Camus, 1972, 245). This is the version that Grand, when he thinks he will die, has Rieux destroy. Let us look, first, at the sentence as the reflection of a culture suddenly out of place and, therefore, politically problematic, and, second, at the new form of community it, despite its displacement, generates.

The sentence, in its various permutations, is critical in several respects. First, its content suggests an attempt by Grand to articulate a yearned for and lost ideal of European elegance, a Renoiresque landscape of European gentry. The image is, in many ways, a purely aesthetic one, suggesting springtime, fecundity, and renewal (May). That this is a female presence on a female horse riding in the 'Bois', woods, suggests something other than Paris the urban colonial center and other than the male-dominated sanitation squads and the extremely urban Oran, which is a mirror/creation of Paris. Yet the '*bois*' is in (the center of) the urban Paris and the woman is an anachronism by the mid-20th century (see, for instance, the work of Simone de Beauvoir): her riding is an image of leisure, provided by the colonial enterprise not necessity. She is an image of the colonial on the horse, separate from and above the people (and scene) she dominates, but still the center of focus and discourse. This feminine presence suggests a kind of desired or willed innocence in colonialism, much like the fiancé in Joseph Conrad's *Heart of Darkness* (Conrad, 1988). When Marlowe tells her that the last word Kurtz speaks is her name, he is telling the truth. She is 'the horror' in that lies have to be told to her to protect her, and we recognize that those lies are the 'horror' that keep the colonial system in place.

The political dimensions of these depictions are important. The very real European presence is a phantom that, even when withdrawn, dominates indirectly what it once controlled overtly. It does so through the alteration of social interactions and of space itself through renaming and refiguring, and, most important, perhaps, through ideology. Colonialism ingrains modes of thinking the world in the consciousness of both the colonizer and the colonized that are difficult to resist and almost impossible to eradicate (Fanon, 1963; Said, 1994). It cannot do so without some control of the language. As Ashis Nandy suggests in *The Intimate Enemy: Loss and Recovery of Self Under Colonialism*, the ultimate violence in colonialism is that 'it creates a culture in which the ruled are constantly tempted to fight their rulers within the psychological', and, we would add, the ideological, 'limits set by the latter' (Nandy, 1983, 3). At the same time, colonialism appropriates the 'language of defiance' of its victims (Nandy, 1983, 73). Nothing can be said, therefore, that is not instantly translated by the oppressor and rendered harmless, or the same things are said over and over—like Grand's sentence—without any impact. The question becomes how to incorporate the language of the colonial power while remaining outside of it (Nandy, 1983, 73), to be able to use and, at the same time, to critique it. This requires transforming the double-consciousness from a psychological state of silenced oppression into a recognition of fragmentation that can counter and undo the fragmentation. Chinua Achebe argues in 'Colonialist Criticism' that the colonialist critic may write in English—here, French—but 'intends to do unheard of things with it' (Achebe, 1988, 74). Grand's sentence does unheard of things. Achebe argues that 'One of the most critical consequences of the transition from oral traditions to written forms of literature is the emergence of individual authorship' (Achebe, 1988, 47). While we do not want to claim for Grand's absurd sentence the status of anti-colonial literature, we can argue that out of its absurdity revolution happens: it begins as a solitary project about identity and becomes a communal enterprise. Such a movement marks a break with classical existentialism and with Western historical linearity. The absurd sentence returns, in a way, to the oral, as a community debates its content, its meaning, and its structure. This return to the oral, we argue, subverts the authority of the language as written (e.g., the permanence of law) by opening its accepted meanings up to negotiation.

The bourgeois European ideal of Grand's vision is intelligible in these terms, and his inability to pin it down raises the necessary questions about the appropriateness and desirability of the ideal itself. Has this European presence a place in Oran in this form, or must it be rewritten or abandoned? Grand and the others are clearly not going to abandon it for to do so would be to abandon what is familiar, the colonially constructed home. However, and this is our second point, they recognize that desiring the realization of this ideal has limitations and deeper implications which are borne out in Grand's conversation with Rieux over the meaning of 'sorrel'. Grand works under the impression that sorrel is a type of horse. Rieux corrects him that it is, in fact, a color and *not a type* (Camus, 1972, 135). The old colonial assumption that a difference in appearance (here, color) marks a difference in type (colonial dualities: white/black; superiority/inferiority; human/sub-human, etc.) breaks down in the context of an attempted articulation of the European ideal. Grand's assumption, Camus suggests, while perhaps innocent, is also wrong. As a result of this conversation, Grand abandons considerations of type, taking on another adjective, 'glossy'. The inability of Grand and his compatriots to find the right adjectives suggests that efforts at description are perhaps premature, excessive and divisive, or even wrong in this reconfigured environment.

There are, as Lyotard (1988) (Lyotard and Thebaud, 1985) suggests, political implications to sentence structure. Camus's depiction of Grand's struggle with the sentence marks his concern with this idea. A sentence is a compilation of meanings, that is, assumed meanings, melded into a more authoritative meaning. Assumptions piled upon assumptions culminate in power. Nouns suggest objects, verbs action, but adjectives suggest—beyond physical descriptions—character. Grand is preoccupied with descriptive adjectives and ignores the excessively passive verb structure of his sentence. His own 'heroic' life suggests that character is revealed in action. The real problem in the sentence is the verb structure 'might have been seen', which obscures the meaning and concreteness of the sentence. It reduces the image itself to the obscurity of a dream-state. That the very real European presence 'might have been seen' (was it?, by whom?, when?) suggests, at least, that the presence has substance but the continuation of that presence in these new conditions is very much an open question. The principal difficulty in Grand's artistic enterprise is really the verb structure, taking us back in the novel to the Prefect's efforts to render an oblique early reading of the plague and, more generally, to Camus's concern with ethics. To decide upon a name defines and delimits a mode of action. The real questions to be asked in this transformed environment are about action and the form it should take. Out of these actions character will be revealed. Description in a language yet unrealized, and especially any final reading of its meaning, will have to wait.

Grand's preoccupation with the adjectives suggests that he seeks, through his art, to humanize an environment that is intrinsically hostile to the human. Rieux, Tarrou, and Rambert all realize the significance of Grand's efforts and by participating in them are drawn into a community of action bound by a shared struggle. While a postcolonial reading might argue that the European ideal that Grand seeks to express is an attempt to continue the abusive colonial presence, another reading, our reading, is that Grand speaks of the human in the language and imagery that *he* associates with the human. We inevitably speak out of what Homi Bhabha calls our 'location' and Grand's 'elegant' or 'slim' young horsewoman is an expression of his positionality, his home. It is a language, a position that the others recognize and embrace. Dr Rieux articulates Grand's role in the creation of this shared understanding as he considers the hollowness of expressions of sympathy during plague-time:

> Needless to say, he [Rieux] knew the sympathy was genuine enough. But it could be expressed only in the conventional language with which men try to express what unites them with mankind in general; a vocabulary quite unsuited, for example, to Grand's small daily effort, and incapable of describing what Grand stood for under plague conditions. (Camus, 1972, 130-131)

Grand's is not a political statement of the appropriateness or inappropriateness of the colonial presence. Rather, it is a more general statement about the nature of political order, one in which the human need to share experiences, expertise, and insights through language is recognized and negotiated. The adequacy of that language requires constant re-examination. This re-examination, Camus suggests, can become the occasion for the construction of human community. When Grand stands before the window at Christmas, looking at the toys and weeping, he becomes the embodiment of all humanity, desiring the past but trying to have some relationship to it without nostalgia or self-deception. The toys are not beautiful, but 'crudely carved wooden toys' (Camus, 1972, 243). Such crudity is all that is available in plague-time and very unlike his lovely woman on a horse. What he really yearns for is Jeanne, his wife. Rieux, watching him, expresses what Grand, Tarrou, and he have come to know without speaking of it in their work on the sentence:

that a loveless world is a dead world, and always there comes an hour when one is weary of prisons, of one's work, and of devotion to duty, and all one craves for is a loved face, the warmth and wonder of a loving heart. (Camus, 1972, 243)

The desire for love and a need for a new relation to the past—elegantly set off against more overtly political concerns about security ('prisons'), economy ('work'), and duty—seem to open Grand to plague: he feels that he cannot write to Jeanne. In that moment of paralysis but, significantly, in the presence of the loving heart of Rieux, Grand falls ill. Grand has written, at this point, almost 50 pages of manuscript (Camus, 1972, 245), all of the same sentence in different versions. This is what plague is, telling the same story over and over, in different variations. At the bottom of the manuscript, however, is one disjunctive sentence, written in 'a studiously clear hand': 'My dearest Jeanne, Today is Christmas Day and . . .' (Camus, 1972, 245), a sentence as open-ended as the last version of his sentence. Love and connection and the colonial collide on the page. When Grand demands Rieux read 'it', Rieux chooses to read the much worked-over sentence and not the beginning of the letter. Grand cries, 'Is that *it*?' (Camus, 1972, 245) and breaks his paralysis by demanding that Rieux burn the manuscript. The inability to speak love in this moment supersedes the inability to write his sentence. He does not want to die with love unspoken. To burn the letter is to burn the sentence as well, to destroy the imperfect colonial representation. In this moment, love, work (action), art and identity so long struggled over, are given up, let go, in the presence of the loving heart of Dr Rieux, who is at once witness and actor in the struggle against plague.

Here Dr Rieux narrates and acts something that he seems not to understand fully, at least in the time of Grand's illness. Narration becomes necessary action groping toward understanding. He thinks Grand refers to the sentence when he refers to the letter to Jeanne. This moment is crucial. In both religion (e.g., in the repetition of word and action in liturgy) and politics (e.g., in the repetition of word and action in the taking of oaths or in various other forms of political participation) we often narrate and enact what we do not fully understand. Dr Rieux's record allows for a reconsideration, a chance to tell over and to come (in that repetition) to a deeper understanding. Here Camus demonstrates the power of narrative as memory which we have at hand. We can go back to it at different times and with different questions and with different levels of understanding. These returns add dimension to understanding; they do not replace them or render them merely historical artifacts. These repetitions do not stagnate (like plague death), but demand and deepen interpretation, authorizing the narrative, yes, but also problematizing it while renewing our relationship to that which is narrated.

While Arendt (1958) stresses the importance of the story that issues from action, Camus suggests the importance of action that issues from story. The burning sets Grand free from the plague. Plague and love and work seem irreconcilable compartments in Grand's life, but he offers up all in the burning and his subsequent recovery is the first sign of the disappearance of the plague. The burning of the sentence/letter seems to be a kind of purification for the whole town. Grand seems to end his work, like a plague death. However, he reconsiders. The recovered Grand says that he will begin again, but not from text, from memory—and, we would add, from what he has learned as a plague-fighter: 'Yes Doctor', Grand said. 'I was overhasty. But I'll make another start. You'll see. I can remember every word' (Camus, 1972, 246). Out of action, a rewriting of narrative emerges—the same, but now at once able to bridge difference, otherness, and separation. When we last see Grand, he has both written to Jeanne and made a new start on his sentence: 'I've cut out all the adjectives' (Camus, 1972, 284), he tells Dr Rieux. Taking out all the adjectives is a linguistic metaphor for the unadorned ethic of truth-telling. It may take one all one's life to realize that one does not need adjectives.[3] Only when he can get to the unadorned truth can Grand write to Jeanne and, let go: 'let her be happy without remorse' (Camus, 1972, 244). Through his efforts, Grand asserts, in a new environment composed of the same general ingredients, the ethical value, indeed the ethical requirement, of struggling with our old language to make it articulate what should not change: our sense of, our exploration of the human.

Grand's story does not end in reunion with Jeanne; his is not the 'proud egotism' of reunion, the 'injustice of happy people', as Rieux expresses it. Rieux, the narrator of the story, takes up what Grand teaches: making another start and remembering every word. He, too, lets go of the adjectives and tries to tell the story in a language of the 'honest witness' (Camus, 1972, 281) who speaks for all, living and dead. This requires backgrounding his own suffering into a communal sense of suffering. Rieux takes on a kind of silence, becoming a kind of 'Everyman', the common voice of what he sees, not as heroism, but as men acting when necessary in the face of a common foe. To be a true healer and an ordinary man, a more difficult task than being a saint, is to speak for the victims, on their behalf and, as much as possible, in their words, to carry on in the face of plague, to admire what is best in human beings, and to love. Dr Rieux's asthma patient makes the first question of the novel, 'what is plague?', the last and gives a response: 'All these folks are saying: 'It was plague. We've had the plague here.' You'd almost think they expected to be given medals for it. But what does that mean 'plague' Just life and no more than that' (Camus, 1972, 285).

Conclusion

Postcolonialism informs political discourse in upsetting hegemonic understandings of terms like 'liberty, equality, and fraternity'. It also insists on focusing on the middle, intermediate, and transitive space between our comfortable binary oppositions. Since politics values order as mediated conflict, this transitive space—the table for instance—has not been the space of a developing political discourse. Governing is about order (see the real concern of the officials of Oran: public safety, that is, preventing panic). Governing relies upon stable, more or less agreed-upon understandings and so necessarily works against the fluidity of discourse suggested here. It is Camus's value as a political thinker that he suggests that we should either re-conceive political space as a more transitive space or abandon the idea that political space is adequate to make up community. The kind of space he suggests is the space reflective of religious meaning: faith, ritual, myth, and other religious modes are tentative structures between binaries of truth and belief, history and memory. In plague, political meanings are upset and reconceived: liberty is only action against the plague; equality emerges from common suffering and common action; and fraternity is made between people who might never otherwise meet. In the in-between, intermediate space, all elements, and all definitions are present but fluid, open for reinterpretation. Plague places the people of Oran in a liminal state between who they were and, if they really face what it means, between a new life or death. In the limen, there is new community—perhaps, a *communitas* (Turner, 1969, 96-97, 131-165) formed in the moment. It is contingent, bringing together unlikely persons, from across community lines, in a common effort.

Such a space and such a contingency reform discourse: Grand's sentence is the symbol of how the common language moves from an interior and private meaning that is nostalgic, backward-looking, and purely aesthetic to a communal, public meaning itself unsettled by the voices of others in the community. Like ritual, as Clifford Geertz (1977) describes it, Grand's sentence is a repetition that comes to originate. For Camus, in the artistic process, you recover your art by laying down your brushes like Jonas in 'The Artist at Work' (Camus, 1991b) and, in a more extreme form, like Grand. Art is the process, not the product. This is the ethical dimension of Camus's notion of art: a life lived well is a process, at best its product assumes secondary importance. That is what Grand realizes as he engages in the seemingly radical act of destroying the sentence and, then, starts over with the same material. Process keeps the space of politics, religion, and art from becoming static, hierarchical, and fixed. It also undercuts binary opposites moving towards the usual western mode of one triumphing over the other. Process means that the settling of place is never settled. If process means only contest without negotiating meaning, then the space is destroyed. This is Camus's response to Hegel's sense that there is no identity, no progress, and no civilization without the *agon*. It is also a response to those who desire a movement back, perhaps in a cyclical way, to a mode that is pre-history or a-history, like that suggested by Fukuyama's 'end of history' (Fukuyama, 1993).

In a process in which meanings can be negotiated, binaries meet, reach a moment of stability, and are then transformed. Between *agon* and murder, between exile and the desire for reunion, Camus suggests through his depiction of Joseph Grand, is a love that keeps us reworking the space without trashing it. Such an idea is an ideal, of course. It is, as we said at the beginning of this essay, a process of making altared space (sacred, communal, and transformative) out of altered space (colonized, bloody, and oppressive). When we leave Grand, we know that the sentence will be, essentially, the same, but now informed by memory and by a kind of detachment, a letting go that comes from writing, finally, to Jeanne. That detachment, combined with Grand's innate compassion, provides the balance that allows true love to be, true speaking to take place, and that constructs home. For Camus, then, home is a place of speaking that must not be abandoned. It is where disparate and, often, silenced voices can participate in the discourse safely. Detachment gives a critical edge to the speaker and the listener; compassion acknowledges the common human situation and respects pain and its authority.

Seeing Camus in *The Plague* as prefiguring postcolonial and postmodern discourse may be complicated by his avowed and unapologetic 'humanism', that is, his concern for the preservation of a necessarily universalized 'human' before all else. However, this valuation serves as a reminder that, as he argued in *The Rebel* (Camus, 1991a), revolt begins with action, a 'no' that—like Grand's 'burn it!'—may lack philosophical nicety or precision or even artistic expression. This 'no' necessarily comes from the depths of what it means to be a human amongst other human beings. To articulate that experience is the function of art, but the articulation is never final. Following fundamentally Nietzschean impulses, both postcolonial and postmodern discourses say 'no' to the fundamental assumptions of the West, of modernity, but they must be revolts in the name of something beyond discourse lest they be simple negations. Camus tries to avoid resting on a simple negation that would render us solitary: 'Far from feeling installed in a career of solitude', he wrote to Barthes in 1955, 'I have, on the contrary, the feeling that I am living by and for a community that nothing in history has so far been able to touch' (Camus, 1970, 341). This is the lesson of Joseph Grand. His revolt against the world as he finds it points to a world not yet—and perhaps never—created. However, his devotion to the human and that which makes us human—to his art, to his work, to his wife, and to his fellows living and dead—is the beginning of an articulation, the beginning of a process that politics must recognize and incorporate or cease being human.

From *Contemporary Political Theory* 2.2 (2003): 209-230. Copyright © 2003 by Palgrave Macmillan Ltd. Reproduced with permission of Palgrave Macmillan Ltd.

Notes

1. Carolyn M. Jones, *The Fiction and Criticism of Toni Morrison*, unpublished manuscript, develops the distinction between altared/altered spaces.
2. We choose to use quotation marks around the term 'other' because we believe that to say 'other' immediately problematizes 'self', keeping the space between—that intermediate space—fluid, open to both and not simply controlled by self, as in hermeneutics.
3. We are grateful to Professor Ruel Tyson for this insight.

References

Achebe, C. (1988) *Hopes and Impediments: Selected Essays*, New York: Anchor/ Doubleday.

Arendt, H. (1958) *The Human Condition*, Chicago: University of Chicago Press.

Arendt, H. (1964) *Eichmann in Jerusalem: A Report on the Banality of Evil*, New York: Penguin Books.

Bhabha, H.K. (1994) *Location of Culture*, New York: Routledge.

Bhabha, H.K. (1997) 'Editor's introduction: minority maneuvers and unsettled negotiations', *Critical Inquiry* 23(3): 431-459.

Bhabha, H.K. (1998) 'On the irremovable strangeness of being different', *Publications of the Modern Language Association of America* 113(1): 34-39.

Camus, A. (1970) 'Encounter with Albert Camus,' in P. Thody (ed.), E.C. Kennedy (trans.) *Lyrical and Critical Essays*, New York: Vintage Books.

Camus, A. (1972) *The Plague*, in S. Gilbert (trans.) New York: Vintage Books.

Camus, A. (1991a) in A. Bower (trans.) *The Rebel: An Essay on Man in Revolt*, New York: Vintage Books.

Camus, A. (1991b) 'The Artist at Work', in A. Camus (ed.), J. O'Brien (trans.) *Exile and the Kingdom*, New York: Vintage, pp. 110-158.

Caputo, J.D. (1997) *Deconstruction in a Nutshell*, New York: Fordham University Press.

Collins, G.M. (1990) 'The Color Purple: What Feminism Can Learn from a Southern Tradition', In J. Humphries (ed.) *Southern Literature and Literary Theory*, Athens, GA: University of Georgia Press.

Conrad, J. (1988) *The Heart of Darkness* (3rd edn). Norton: New York.

de Certeau, M. (1988) in S. Rendell (trans.) *Practices of Everyday Life*, Berkeley, CA: University of California Press.

Derrida, J. (1978) in A. Bass (trans.) *Writing and Difference*, London: Routledge & Kegan Paul.

Fanon, F. (1963) *Wretched of the Earth*, New York: Grove Press.

Fukuyama, F. (1993) *The End of History and the Last Man*, New York: Morrow, William, and Company.

Geertz, C. (1977) *Interpretation of Cultures*, New York: Basic Books.

Judt, T. (1998) *The Burden of Responsibility: Blum, Camus, Aron, and the French Twentieth Century*, Chicago: University of Chicago Press.

LeBlanc, J.R. (2001) 'Camus, Said, and the dilemma of home: space, identity, and the limits of postcolonial political theory'. *Strategies* 15(2): 239-258.

Lyotard, J.-F. and Thebaud, J.-L. (1985) *Just Gaming*, Minneapolis, MN: University of Minnesota Press.

Lyotard, J.-F. (1988), G. Van Den Abbeele (trans.) *The Differend: Phrases in Dispute*, Minneapolis, MN: University of Minnesota Press.

Nandy, A. (1983) *The Intimate Enemy: Loss and Recovery of Self Under Colonialism*, Delhi: Oxford University Press.

O'Brien, C.C. (1970) *Albert Camus of Europe and North Africa*, New York: Viking Press.

Rawls, J. (1999) *A Theory of Justice* (revised edn). Cambridge, MA: Harvard University Press.

Rizzuto, A. (1981) *Albert Camus's Imperial Vision*, Carbondale, IL: Southern Illinois University Press.

Said, E.W. (1994) *Culture and Imperialism*, New York: Vintage Books.

Sandel, M. (1994) 'The procedural republic and the unencumbered self'. *Political Theory* 12: 81-96.

Scarry, E. (1987) *The Body in Pain: The Making and Unmaking of the World*, Oxford and New York: Oxford University Press.

Turner, V. (1969) *The Ritual Process*, Chicago: Aldine Publishing Company.

Camus's *The Fall*:
The Dynamics of Narrative Unreliability _____

Amit Marcus

When Wayne Booth coined the term *unreliable narration*, he deemed the reader's role in identifying an unreliable narrator unproblematic (esp. 158-59). For him, the implied reader shared with the implied author an ironic distance from the norms of the unreliable narrator. Narratologists after Booth who have dealt with unreliable narration have contended that the role of the reader is not as trivial as Booth thought and hence should be thoroughly explored. For example, Tamar Yacobi uncovers the difficulties that face the reader who tries to decipher the system of norms of the implied author and offers solutions to these difficulties. She also explains the reasons that actual readers misinterpret the implied author's perspective ("Reader"). Ansgar Nünning, who rejects the term *implied author* as vague, incoherent, and anthropomorphic, relies on cognitive theories of the reading process (both "bottom-up" and "top-down" processes) to describe the ways in which the reader labels a narrator unreliable. Kathleen Wall, conversely, remarks that changes in the notion of subjectivity are reflected in the way unreliability is both presented by the author and perceived by the readers.

These scholars hold different views concerning the essence of fictional unreliability, the principles that should be employed in the classification of unreliable narrators, and the status of the reader with relation to the text in identifying this type of narrator. Nevertheless, it seems that they all assume a cognitive and/or ethical gap between the narrator and the readers, who treat this type of narrator as inferior to them in either knowledge or morality. The readers hold themselves capable of exposing the flaws of the narrator, since they themselves are immune, or at any rate less susceptible, to these flaws; and even if in certain other situations they do succumb to them, their uninvolved position vis-à-vis the fictional world enables them to judge the behavior of the unreliable narrator as irrational or immoral.[1] Accordingly, the terminology that is most frequently used with regard to the relations between the reader and the unreliable narrator emphasizes the former's role as a detached and neutral observer, researcher, detective, and judge. The reader must follow the implied author "in judging the narrator" (Booth 158), "recognize an unreliable narrator when he or she sees one" (Nünning 54), examine whether or not he or she "has reasons to suspect" the narrator (Nünning 57),[2] establish "a secret communication" with the implied author (Chatman 233), and construct the cultural or textual norms of the text (Yacobi, "Fictional" 121).

The uninvolved position of the readers leads them to the (not explicitly formulated) conclusion that they are in no way affected by the recognition of a certain narrator's unreliability. It is implied that the readers themselves are more reliable than the unreliable narrator and, thanks to this difference, capable of identifying unreliability. This difference between, and in certain cases even incommensurability of, the narrator and the readers leads the latter to believe that unreliability is merely one of the criteria in the typology of narrators, with no consequences or ramifications for the readers themselves. To make things clear, I do not deem this view to be utterly mistaken. It is indispensable for readers to feel, at least to a certain extent, and in a certain phase of the reading, that they indeed are superior to the unreliable narrator in order to classify him or her as such.[3] However, this feeling does not necessarily persist. It may change if the readers either find out new details about the narrator that urge them to reevaluate their classification or discover something new about themselves that encourages them to reconsider their superiority to the narrator. An interesting combination of these two possibilities is found in Camus's novella *The Fall* (*La Chute*). I believe that an interpretation of *The Fall* focusing on the triad narrator-narratee-reader is significant for a work whose unreliable narration both undermines the binary opposition between "unreliable narrator" and "reliable reader" and has some general implications on the position of the reader towards fiction.

The narrator of *The Fall*, who introduces himself under the pseud-onym of Jean-Baptiste Clamence, begins his account with an appeal to his anonymous narratee to accept his services (5). This appeal estab-lishes the situation of a monological dialogue,[4] which persists through-out the text. In the course of five days Clamence tells the narratee his story, which is centered on a traumatic event (mentioned only in the third day of the narration): the fall of an unknown woman into the water. The same event, to which I shall refer further on, gradually shat-ters the self-image of the narrator and evokes in him the need to reex-amine his life.[5] But this does not suffice for Clamence, who, using dif-ferent rhetorical devices, attempts to convince his narratee to make his own confession and reexamine his own life. The self-image of the narratee, contends Clamence, is—as his own self-image used to be—fundamentally mistaken and based on the perpetual self-deception that characterizes human existence. The generalizations of the narra-tor, the intimacy that he tries to foster between himself and his fic-tional narratee, and the analogies between this narratee and the readers are meant to encourage the latter to embark on a soul-search of their own.

The act of narration in *The Fall* depends as much on the willingness of the narratee to listen as on the motivation of the narrator to relate his account. This willingness requires efforts from the narratee, who fol-lows Clamence wherever he leads him. The narratee is characterized by ostensibly individual qualities: he is a French speaker in his middle age, well educated, and, in Clamence's words, "un bourgeois, à peu près" [a bourgeois, somewhat] (11). The astounding (and suspicious) similarities between the "individual" qualities of the narratee and those of the narrator are already prominent at the beginning of the novella and become even more acute when the narratee turns out to be a Pari-sian lawyer, just as the narrator used to be.[6] The reader may conclude from this similarity that it is not in vain that Clamence prefers this ad-dressee to other potential ones. Clamence tells the story of his life in a manner that seems to the reader (and probably also to the narratee) unique, and it suggests at first that the narrator wishes to create a close connection with his interlocutor. In this way the narrator achieves his need for power and control, which he openly states in the last chapter of the novella and which turns out to be one of the motivations for his narration.[7]

The narrator achieves his goal by two principal means. The first is the manner of addressing the narratee: he who is named at the beginning of the conversation politely but anonymously "monsieur" later becomes the more intimate "mon cher compatriote" [my dear compatriot] and, afterwards, the most intimate "cher ami" [dear friend] (5, 46, 80).[8] Clamence emphasizes the similarities between himself and his addressee, so that his account may seem to the latter not only as the story of another but also as his own, thus reinforcing his curiosity to continue listening. The other principal means of the narrator to attract the attention of his narratee is the digressions from his traumatic account: the narrator admits this tendency already in the opening pages ("Mais je me laisse aller, je plaide!" [But I am getting carried away, I swear!] [17]), and his words indeed seem associative and unprepared. He oscillates between past and present as well as between his personal story and his general statements regarding humanity, the narrative situation, and the places to which he leads his narratee. For example, when Clamence and his narratee wander about the streets of Amsterdam, both of them pass, perhaps unintentionally, by a house that was owned, according to the narrator, by a slave merchant. The sight of the house evokes in Clamence thoughts concerning the importance and function of slavery, and these thoughts make him consider his arrogance (48-53). Moreover, the goal of Clamence's account remains unclear almost to the end of the novella, before which it seems that he is little more than an uncontrollable chatterbox with no ability to distinguish the principal from the subsidiary.

Conversely, there are textual signs that may indicate an opposite tendency on the part of the narrator, that is, a tendency to distance himself from the narratee. For example, he never addresses the narratee by his first name (for which he does not ask); on the contrary, he persists in addressing the narratee in the second-person plural *vous*, which is characteristic of formal acquaintanceship; he makes frequent reference to historical events and to several landmarks of Western culture, especially Western literature;[9] his speech tends to an ornate and conceited style characterized by the relatively frequent use of the imperfect subjunctive, a tense rarely used in contemporary spoken French.[10] The florid style of the narrator conceals his suffering and his intention to afflict his addressee and shake his soul, yet from the beginning of his account he hints at the existence of a secret wound: "Le style, comme la popeline, dissimule trop souvent de l'eczéma" [Style, like sheer silk, too often covers up eczema] (8).

Thus the narrator plays an intricate and delicate game between drawing the narratee closer to him and distancing him, between emphasizing their common features and maintaining their discreteness and differences.[11] Moreover, it gradually becomes clear that even if a large portion of what Clamence says is indeed a consequence of the concrete and unique acquaintance with his narratee, the general framework of the account has been predetermined. The narrative structure initially gives the impression of being singular and spontaneous, but it is eventually revealed as a rhetorical device that is meant to lure the narratee, to stimulate his curiosity, and thus to cultivate his (perhaps temporary) dependence on the narrator.[12] I will now examine in greater detail the narrator's attempt to create the desired effect.

In the first two parts of the novella (5-45), which are parallel to the first two days of the narration, Clamence conceitedly presents the story of his professional success as a highly esteemed Parisian lawyer. The narcissistic portrait of the narrator is clearly articulated in his Nietzschean language: "je me trouvais un peu surhomme" [I considered myself a bit of a superman] (33). Clamence considers himself at the time in which his story took place as someone who had already arrived at the peak of his achievements, a perfect man both intellectually and morally. His life crisis (which is depicted from the end of the second part of the novella) begins with a deep and unrelenting feeling of unease incurred by a laughter that he hears behind his back on a bridge above the Seine, whose source, although not mysterious, is not entirely clear (43-44). This laughter later proves to be both internal and external (85), thus seemingly transgressing the border that separates the outside from the inside. Whatever its source, Clamence perceives it as a crying evidence for the false appearances of his life, its void pretence, and its decay concealed by arrogance. Slowly penetrating the soul of the narrator, the awareness of all of these flaws makes him remember everything that he has preferred to forget or, in his own metaphorical language (which once more evokes water and flowing), everything that has slipped above him.[13] His success story necessitates the constant and willful forgetfulness of everything that is incompatible with it, whereas remembering makes him reconstruct his life story from the beginning as a story of permanent failure and fall (53-54).

Hence Clamence has discovered motives for his behavior of which he had been unaware: how he abused his glory and the respect people felt for him in order to use them like objects; how he treated his female lovers too as means to an end, and how all his seemingly altruistic feats were based on egoistic motives.[14] The reader gets the impression that Clamence's renewed examination of his life released him from his former self-deception and that the shame Clamence feels is a sign that he has reformed his ways and experienced deep repentance. The reference he makes to his internal burning, which is the physical equivalent of shame ("La honte, dites-moi, mon cher compatriote, ne brûle-t-elle pas un peu?" [To tell the truth, doesn't shame, my dear compatriot, burn a little?] [74-75]), intensifies the impression that he is now willing to bear full responsibility for his deeds, in contrast with his past behavior. Similarly, the narrator's "digressions et . . . efforts d'une invention" (75) might be comprehended as an expression of a real and sincere mental difficulty in coping with his former self-deception and narrating it, not necessarily as a rhetorical device whose aim is to mislead the narratee. In Clamence's view, the starting point of his fall is the fall of the anonymous woman into the river Seine, whereas the reminiscence of this fall hurls him into the abyss with dizzying swiftness.[15] Whether by consequence of a conscious decision (taken hastily and under pressure) or of an instinctive reaction to a state of distress, Clamence avoided jumping into the water to save the woman. He did not even inform anybody of this occurrence and made no effort to figure out the identity of the drowned woman. But the attempt to treat as a nonevent such a dramatic event that put his system of values to the test fails when Clamence reexperiences the event, years later, as a trauma.[16]

During the period in between the fall of the woman and the hearing of the laughter, Clamence made supreme efforts to preserve his self-image as well as his image in the eyes of others; in the words of the narrator, he tried to endure his punishment but avoid a trial: ". . . la question est d'éviter le jugement. Je ne dis pas d'éviter le châtiment" [...it is a matter of avoiding judgment. I do not mean of avoiding punishment] (83). At this point, the reader is not yet informed of the exact nature of Clamence's punishment, but it is plausible to assume that it is not a punishment imposed on him by society but an internal mechanism: the feeling of guilt for failing to aid another at the time of her distress urges him to narrate his account to someone who is a total stranger to him, and guilt also makes him fall lower and lower from the Olympus of self-satisfaction.[17] As for his statement that he wishes to avoid a trial, Clamence means that he seeks to keep away from the shameful scene in which certain others (the judge or the jury) demonstrate their superiority to the defendant. They claim that they have not sinned but he has and that therefore they should not be punished, whereas he should.

Clamence anticipates the proclamation that is clearly expressed towards the end of the novel: turning his personal guilt into collective guilt releases him from the need to judge himself. Clamence stresses that for him these survival tactics transcend the boundaries of logic, because the other is perceived as a potential predator that lies in wait for every expression of weakness on his part (84). In his narration, the narrator expects the objection of the well-educated and rational narratee (or one who at least purports to have these qualities) and tries to frame a sufficient reply to it. At this phase it is enough for him to confound the narratee, make it difficult for the latter to decipher the meaning of his motives, and reinforce in him the will to fathom him. The direct address to the narratee, the questions that the narrator asks him, and the astonishing mixture of self-irony, self-pity, sarcasm, and the search for empathy achieve the desirable effect in his interlocutor: raising his curiosity so that he will continue listening to Clamence's chatter (82-83).

The narrator's attempt to rid himself of all blame and responsibility is expressed in his long-lasting hedonism. In retrospect, Clamence admits that he found shelter in debauchery to forget the laughter that defied him and threatened the ostensible security and stability of his life. Debauchery served him as a kind of sedative that makes the debaucher forget everything that exceeds immediate pleasure and the means to achieve it. In Clamence's metaphorical language, his life was shrouded in fog: "Je vivais dans une sorte de brouillard où le rire se faisait assourdi, au point que je finissais par ne plus le percevoir" [I was living in a sort of fog in which laughter was muted, so much so that I ended up no longer perceiving it] (115). The fog symbolizes an existential state in which one banishes the past and the future to the margins of one's consciousness, thus narrowing one's field of vision and deferring an account of his deeds, a comprehension of his feelings, and an analysis of his motives. Clamence's selfhood shrank, for his "forgetfulness" was not a consequence of external and uncontrollable forces, but of his chosen stage of existence.[18] This choice, Clamence emphasizes in response to the potential disapproval of his narratee, is fraught with advantages whose significance should not be underestimated.

Yet the narrator has discovered that his hedonistic way of living was founded on an internal contradiction, not in the field of logics, but in the existential sphere.[19] This way of living had instilled in him the illusion that he would live forever. It took into account neither aging nor death, which bring an end to all pleasures of the moment and render them meaningless.[20] Clamence's body eventually revolted against his insouciance, and he became ill (113). Probably for the same reason, the attempt of the narrator to forget the laughter succeeded merely for a short period. One day, at the time of a cruise initiated in order to celebrate his seeming recovery from his mental and physical crisis, Clamence notices a black point in the ocean, which immediately reminds him of the drowning woman (116-17). On the same day, he realizes that the outcry of that woman and the laughter that ensued would never leave him, that he would never again be able to immerse himself in self-forgetfulness. Clamence, therefore, feels extremely vulnerable. All of a sudden, his internal defense layers collapse like a stack of cards, his deceitful self-image cracks, and his life is about to become intolerable.

Clamence regards the same evening on which he heard the laughter for the second time as a kind of religious portent. Like some of the Biblical prophets, he has seen the light, and, like them, he too is governed by an almost uncontrollable internal impulse to tell others what they prefer not to hear. However, in contrast with these prophets, the light that has been revealed to the narrator does not show him God's will or essence but his own subjectivity: first and foremost the gap between his ostensibly altruistic existence and his deep and previously unacknowledged egoistic motives. Only by admitting his self-deception may he, so he says, find the proper reply to the laughter and the laughing people, whose nature probably remains unclear both to the narratee and to the reader. Clamence bids his interlocutor not to smile when discovering this supposedly primal and trivial truth: "Ne souriez pas, cette vérité n'est pas aussi première qu'elle paraît. On appelle vérités premières celles qu'on découvre après toutes les autres, voilà tout" [Do not smile; that truth is not as primary as it appears. What we call primary truths are those that we discover after all the others, in fact] (92). At this point of the narration, the reader and the narratee might assume that the narrator is merely asking to defend himself against the conceited and disrespectful attitude shown towards him: he is the one who has erred, who has learned a lesson from his mistakes, and now merely solicits the sympathy of someone else who has not experienced the same mistakes.

A hedonistic existence can no longer shelter the narrator from his tormented conscience. He expresses his feeling that he has to live as if he were in solitary confinement and could neither straighten up nor lie down, only stand in a distorted position (119). Guilt is portrayed in Clamence's words as an emotion that deprives one of one's freedom and turns one into a convict of one's internal world, because, like solitary confinement, it does not enable one to forget one's situation even for a minute. Nonetheless, Clamence alludes to his unwillingness to acknowledge his imprisonment in a vicious circle of guilt. At the beginning of his account these hints are vague, implicit, and assimilated in the other thoughts and arguments of the narrator. For example, he claims to have no more friends, only accomplices, among whom is the narratee, and all of whom are blameworthy (80). Clamence clarifies that his privileged interest in the narratee is temporary and that it stems not from any of the latter's unique qualities but from the narrative situation. He views the narratee as a kind of object that is interchangeable in principle and also in practice with any other narratee marked with similar traits. At the end of the account Clamence is to court another narratee, whereas the former is to become another member, unimportant in himself, of humanity.

Shared guilt explains the almost imperceptible alternation of the first person singular (*je*) and plural (*nous*), as if the narrator's account applied to the narratee and only to him, thus implying that the two of them have to cooperate against the rest of the world. This transition gives the impression that the narratee is guilty of the same transgressions as Clamence and that they both share the same interests. Clamence is not troubled by the inconsistency between his friendly address to the narratee and his proclamation that he has no friends, as long as his rhetoric creates the desirable effect: "Mon cher ami, ne leur donnons pas de prétexte à nous juger, si peu que ce soit!" [My dear friend, let us not give them a pretext to judge us, as slight as it might be] (84).

The hints about the goal of Clamence's account—a self-reproach that entitles him to reproach others—gradually become more explicit, clear, and focused. For example, in reply to the analogy that Clamence creates between his own life and the life of a convict in solitary confinement, his interlocutor asks if one cannot live in this condition and yet be innocent.[21] In his answer, Clamence tends to deny this possibility not only with regard to himself but also with regard to humanity: "Chaque homme témoigne du crime de tous les autres, voilà ma foi et mon espérance" [Each man bears witness to the crime of all the others—that is my faith and my hope] (119). He hopes and believes that collective guilt has a potential for assuaging his tormented conscience; but he is aware that this idea may be conceived as abnormal by both the narratee and the reader. Therefore he simultaneously reveals and conceals his manipulations, thus avoiding the antagonism of his narratee, which might bring him to leave Clamence, and of the reader, who may cease reading the novella because of his revulsion.

Pursuing the same rhetorical move stratagem, Clamence calls up Christ to support his argument. In an increasingly cynical tone of voice, Clamence piles insult upon insult at the expense of Christians, insisting that their way of life contradicts the foundations of their belief: "nous sommes tous coupables les uns devant les autres, tous christs à notre vilaine manière, un à un crucifié, et toujours sans savoir" [we are all guilty toward one another, all Christs in our own debased manner, each crucified by the other, and never knowing it] (126). In a way that is wholly contradictory to that of Jesus Christ—who, himself innocent, took it upon himself to bear suffering and torture in order to redeem humanity of its sins[22]—every person crucifies the other; that is to say, we blame the other instead of ourselves and believe that we will thus be purged. True Christians are supposed to consider themselves guilty (since they are tainted by original sin) and try to purify themselves by believing in the Savior. But human beings are capable only of crucifying their own kind, thus repudiating responsibility for their deeds and imputing them others.[23] This is the foundation of collective self-deception, which Clamence strives to make the narratee acknowledge.

In the last meeting held between the narrator and the narratee, the former lays his cards more openly on the table and exposes the rhetorical devices that have guided his narration. For example, he alludes to Plato's well-known Simile of the Cave (*Republic* 7.514a-17a), whose moral is the immense difficulty of people who lived in falsehood to recognize a truth that completely alters their worldview. When the truth is bluntly revealed to the self-deceived, they are dazzled, claims Clamence (130), and therefore it is better to avoid a direct and explicit expression of truth, as in philosophical argument, and instead to tell a story (or a fable), whose truth is diluted with falsehood and which gradually penetrates the realm of consciousness. This type of expression also facilitates the work of the narrator, who finds it equally difficult to accept the bitter truth and who tries in his confession to avoid it to the same extent that he wishes to reveal it. I believe that this is a reasonable way of making sense of the narrator's confession of the difficulty of distinguishing the truth from the falsehood of his account, which amounts to a declaration of his unreliability.[24] In this respect, both truth and falsehood are intended to attract the attention of the narratee (and the reader). Therefore it matters little if he has invented certain details that had never occurred or seasoned his account in order to make it more palatable.[25] Eventually, he contends, falsehood and truth serve the same purpose, but falsehood does so more effectively (130).[26] Thus, by the end of the novella, the oxymoron *bogus sincerity* seems like a suitable description of Clamence's narration.

Clamence feels that the technique that he has chosen for delivering his messages—the endless repetition of his life-story in front of different narratees—enables him to forget the laughter that had haunted him, to restore his self-image, and to regain the position of superiority for which he has yearned.[27] He stresses that he has regained the symbolic summit that distances him from the depths to which the anonymous woman had plunged and to which he had sunk after this incident. Furthermore, he haughtily declares his success in performing "a Copernican revolution" by shifting the narratee's focus from the outside—judging the other—inwards—inspecting his own soul (149-50). However, the narrator opens the door to distrusting his words, not only because the laughter has not totally disappeared and he is still annoyed by doubt (154) but also because his fragile self-image demands constant maintenance, without loosening the grip even for one moment. In fact, his life—including its vicissitudes, progressions, and retreats—has ceased; instead he revolves in an internal circle from which there is no outlet.

The above-mentioned goal of the narrator also clarifies the reason for his request from the narratee to keep his (the narrator's) account from going overboard by restraining his associative digressions. Towards the end of the novella, Clamence reveals that these requests are nothing but another aspect of his play with the narratee: "Ne vous fiez pas trop d'ailleurs à mes attendrissements, ni à mes délires. Ils sont dirigés" [Don't place too much trust in my tendernesses, or in my delusions. They are contrived] (158). What initially looks like the spontaneous digressions of the narrator is actually planned as a rhetorical device to attract the attention of both the narratee and the reader:

> Je m'accuse, en long et en large. Ce n'est pas difficile, j'ai maintenant de la mémoire. Mais attention, je ne m'accuse pas grossièrement, à grands coups sur la poitrine. Non, je navigue souplement, je multiplie les nuances, les digressions aussi, j'adapte enfin mon discours à l'auditeur, j'amène ce dernier à renchérir. Je mêle ce qui me concerne et ce qui regarde les autres. Je prends les traits communs, les expériences que nous avons ensemble souffertes, les faiblesses que nous partageons, le bon ton, l'homme du jour enfin, tel qu'il sévit en moi et chez les autres. Avec cela, je fabrique un portrait qui est celui de tous et de personne. Un masque, en somme, assez

semblable à ceux du carnaval. . . . Le réquisitoire est achevé. Mais, du même coup, le portrait que je tends à mes contemporains devient un miroir. (51-52)

[I accuse myself, from top to bottom. It is not difficult; my memory is now intact. But be careful, my self-accusations do not take the crude form of heavy blows to the chest. No, I sail smoothly, I multiply the nuances, digressions, too; I end up adapting my speech to the listener, leading him to commit himself. I mix my concerns up with what concerns others. I seize on common traits, experiences that we have suffered together, weaknesses that we share, the right tone, the man of the hour at last, as it suffuses me and others. With that, I contrive a portrait that is of everyone and no one. A mask, in fact, quite similar to those of the carnival. . . . The indictment is complete. But at the same time, the portrait that I hold up to my contemporaries becomes a mirror.]

The narrator treats his narratee (and perhaps, indirectly, the readers too) as more intelligent than most other narratees and therefore as someone harder to manipulate, one whose self-confidence is not easily shaken (153). The narratee's laughter is evidence of the difficulty that he finds in accepting the narrator's request from him to confess. It is plausible that the laughter also reminds the narrator of the days in which he felt he was being held in contempt by his surroundings. This difficulty of interacting with the narratee does not bring him, however, into a state of despair but only causes a slight change in the manipulations that he uses in his account. He contends that the characteristics of the specific narratee lead him to elaborate on his behavior. He knows that in order to achieve the desired effect, he cannot ignore the intellect of his skeptical narratee. But he believes that eventually even such a narratee could not avoid relating to what he is saying. Moreover, his words might have a deeper effect on him precisely because he does not automatically accept them but examines and reexamines them. One cannot know whether the narrator is right or wrong in expecting this kind of a response from the narratee and whether his flattery might soften the narratee and make him easier to persuade or, on the contrary, intensify his antagonism.

It has already been claimed that the fictional narratee unknowingly serves as a mediator between the narrator and the reader.[28] The narratee's silence or his laconic responses, as reported by the narrator, turn him into an abstract and undefined character who serves as a sort of medium between the narrator and the reader (see Fitch). It seems that the narrator finds the address to the reader through the mediation of the narratee more convenient and effective than a direct address.[29] A blunt rebuke might distance the reader and not achieve the desired effect. Utterly different is a state in which rebuke and guilt slowly, indirectly, manipulatively, and almost inattentively transpire, as the reader is unaware that the narrator is invading his or her soul. From this point of view, the narratee is nothing but another rhetorical device of Clamence in his devious journey to the reader. The portrait of the "penitent judge" becomes a series of mirrors that reflect each other and in which the reader is able to see his or her own image through the character (or pseudo-character) of the narratee. The narrator makes the reader feel increasingly ill at ease. The former is interested in turning the latter from a passive voyeur who listens to the confession of a fictional other, with neither commitment nor responsibility, nor, moreover, any feeling of blame, into an active accomplice.[30] Like the narratee, the reader too tends to judge and criticize the narrator, as if the latter's story had nothing in common with the former's. But accepting the lesson or insight of the narrator's account redirects the blame back unto the reader and the narratee. If they accept the narrator's "verdict," they are hurled into a dizzying circle of absorbing blame and setting themselves free from it, which is in principle the situation in which the narrator finds himself.

The narrator encourages the narratee and the reader to criticize and blame him before criticizing and blaming others, because in this way they commit, throughout the narration, the same essential error of self-deception that he has committed and of which they too become aware only post factum. The narrator implies that self-deception is a collective existential state that is unavoidable and not wholly releasable, at least not in modern bourgeois society. The individualism, materialism, and pursuit of external achievements that are the foundations of this society make subjects believe that they are what they are not and that they are not what they are. In this existential state, the most one can do is to be aware of one's susceptibility to self-deception and to instill a similar awareness in others, as does Clamence. Paradoxically, his call for the narratee and the readers (after they have fallen into his trap) to avoid repeating his own mistake becomes at the same time more effective (because of the didactic value of experience) and completely ineffective (because his advice is given in retrospect, after they have been induced to err). In any case, the narrator is interested in making the "almost bourgeois" readers involved, responsible and even blameful as they read on, in spite of their habit to regard reading as detached from these concepts.[31]

The readers are not obliged, of course, to accept the decision of the "penitent judge"; they may certainly object to being accused and treated as self-deceived accomplices as well as to the cunning with which the narrator attempts to lead the narratee and the readers to confess their guilt.[32] The narrator is capable of dealing with his fractured self-image only by smirching another, since he believes that a trouble shared is a trouble halved. This may indeed evoke great antagonism in the reader. But from the point of view of the narrator, this antagonism corroborates the main argument of his account. According to him, readers who disapprove of this argument are interested in avoiding an active and involved position when reading about the life of another, and their intellect offers them an easy outlet from this position. Intellect does not lack emotion and motivation, since it expresses the unwillingness of the antagonist readers to deal with the ramifications of acknowledging their own blame. Hence the narrator tries to lure his readers into a trap from which they cannot escape: however readers interpret the narrator, whether they respond to him willingly or unwillingly, in any case they will not be able to elude Clamence's existential truth, according to which each one of us lives falsely, because truth is too bitter and too difficult to deal with.[33]

Is it nonetheless possible to release oneself from Clamence's hermeneutic trap, or does it really have no outlet? The importance of the answer to this question was already intimated at the beginning of this essay. I have indicated that if every human being, just like every narrator, is perceived as unreliable, then the reader has no reason to feel superior to the narrator. Perhaps, as Clamence claims, we are all permanently and inexorably self-deceived, at least as long as we regard ourselves innocent.[34] A narratological ramification of Clamence's argument, if accepted at face value, is that there is no justification for the distinction between reliable and unreliable narrators: all narrators are unreliable, but only some of them, like Clamence, know how to use their unreliability for their own advantage and gain control of the responses of the reader: "J'ai cependant une supériorité, celle de savoir, qui me donne le droit de parler" [I, however, have one advantage, that of knowing, which gives me the right to speak] (152).

But it seems reasonable to claim otherwise.[35] Camus himself proposes in the preface to his important essay *The Rebel* (1951) to shatter the images of the mirror that reflect human evil in ourselves and others (21);[36] one must surpass this mirror and reconstruct the meaning of life from its abysses, thus releasing oneself from feelings of doubt and absurdity. From this point of view, the mirror that Clamence places in front of his readers is perceived not as a vicious circle but as a starting point. Readers who meet Clamence's demands and dare to look in the mirror might see their portrait as changeable and worthy of change. In contrast with the narrator of *The Fall*, the readers are not obliged to believe that this portrait is essentialist, meaning that it is natural and necessary for a human being; in contrast with him, they might be capable of dealing with their tendency to self-deception without asking for an easy but restraining outlet.[37]

Another way for the readers to set themselves free of the no-outlet situation that the narrator attempts to impose on them is by denying the universal validity of Clamence's portrait of humanity (even though, as stated above, Clamence relates to this potential denial as a reinforcement of his argument). Such readers will regard Clamence's account as evidence that the self-image of every person is based on a certain ideal or certain ideals, whose content is not permanent and whose very ideality creates a gap between the person and reality. Such readers might contend that, after all, not everyone is like Clamence: not everyone is completely unaware of the necessity of this gap; not everyone desperately avoids a reexamination of oneself, one's values, and the motives of one's behavior; and not everyone is constantly self-deceived, even if many are motivated to see themselves in a light that blurs their mistakes and weaknesses.[38]

Consequently, the mirror that the narrator places in front of the narratee and the reader is distorted from the start. Hence Clamence's account is not as universal as it pretends to be, although it challenges every reader. *The Fall* points to the impossibility of a simplistic and naïve perception of the readers as automatically and unequivocally superior to the unreliable narrator. Hence this novella makes the readers less conceited and more critical of themselves;[39] it replaces the *static* distance between reader and narrator with a *dynamic* one, in which the interrelations between the two change during the reading process. The readers might feel morally or cognitively superior to the narrator from certain aspects or during certain phases of the reading process, relate to him as their equal from other aspects, and sometimes even feel inferior to him.

Yacobi's thesis for settling textual inconsistencies and incongruities attributes an active role to the readers: they discover the inconsistency and seek the best hypothesis to explicate it. An implicit assumption of this thesis is that reading and interpretation processes are motivated by the readers' need to remove the difficulties in the text in such a way that may set their minds at rest. *The Fall* undermines this assumption, since

the most reasonable explanations to settle its textual inconsistencies—
the one based on the *function* of the account (its goal) and the other
based on the narrator's *perspective* (his unreliability)—leave the readers disquieted. The most significant mask that the narrator wears—
self-flagellation—is removed from him, and the revelation of his unreliability exposes the real purpose of his account: deflating the stability
and composure of the fictional narratee and of the readers. Whether or
not the latter approve of the final conclusion of the narrator, the text
does not allow them to be uninvolved or indifferent.

Thus, whatever the attitude of the readers to the lesson that
Clamence wishes to teach his narratee, *The Fall* focuses on their reevaluation of themselves and their world, or, to use a term of Paul
Ricoeur, on the refiguration of the fictional text (70-76): indeed,
Clamence never addresses the readers directly, and he speaks about
self-deception as a characteristic of human existence in general; nonetheless, from the point of view of the implied author (and perhaps also
of the real author), it is significant that the narrator's account is told in a
fictional text that is directed to real readers.

It is commonly held that reading enables readers to turn their gaze
from themselves to others and thus to detach themselves from responsibility and engagement, which are features of worldly existence. A
well-known representative of this standpoint is the narrator of Dickens's *David Copperfield*, for whom reading fiction is a comfort that
renders him oblivious to his distress for a short while: "[fictional char-
acters] kept alive my fancy, and my hope of something beyond that
place and time. . . . This was my only and my constant comfort" (58-
59). Copperfield's view of literature is not entirely mistaken, of course,
but it seems that the implied author of *The Fall* is aware of the potential
danger of adhering to this position. Reading is perceived in the novella
as a hermeneutic activity that encourages, perhaps more than any other
activity, the formation of self-deception, precisely because it encourages the creation of a reassuring distance between the world of the
readers and that of the narrator and characters.

Returning to our point of departure, we must now inquire to what extent *The Fall* proposes a significant change of focus in the interrelations between the unreliable narrator and the reader. On the one hand, it seems that Camus's novella merely reinforces the traditional treatment of the reader as a detached observer, detective, and judge, because Clamence's manipulations would have no effect on the readers unless they regarded their position as stable and superior to that of the narrator. The primary identification of the unreliability of another remains, even after reading the novella, dependent on the supposed (relative) reliability of the self. On the other hand, the dynamics of unreliable narration can no longer be looked upon merely as a product of changes in the narration (i.e., the narrator is identified by the readers as more reliable at certain points of the text and less reliable at others),[40] for it is also a product of the changes in the position of the readers *with regard to themselves* while reading the text, which may, of course, influence their view of the narrator. The readers are thus not detached from the account, and their position is neither stable nor secure. It is indeed reasonable that they should come to perceive themselves at a certain phase of the account as equal to the unreliable narrator or even inferior to him. Even if they finally manage to restore their previous superior position, the threat to their self-image and the need to overcome it cannot let them remain just as they were before.

From *Style* 40.4 (Winter 2006): 314-333. Copyright © 2006 by Northern Illinois University. Reprinted with permission of Northern Illinois University.

Notes

[*Editor's Note:* Translations appearing in square brackets are provided by the volume editor, unless otherwise noted.]

I am grateful to Shlomith Rimmon-Kenan, Ruth Ginsburg, and Johnathan Stavsky for their comments on different versions of this essay.

1. During the past few decades, the widespread criticism of the key terms of such a conception of (un)reliable narration, like *truth*, *rationality*, and *subjectivity*, has en-

couraged narratologists to reconsider it. Wall, for example, significantly diminishes the gap between some unreliable narrators, such as Stevens in Ishiguro's *The Remains of The Day*, and the reader, claiming that no narrator—or any human being—is entirely reliable, consistent, and rational (esp. 21, 39). Yet even in Wall's interpretation of the novel and its challenges to theories of unreliable narration, the reader must be more self-reflexive than the unreliable narrator in order to recognize the latter's mistakes and give a more coherent interpretation to Stevens's story.

2. Similar expressions can be found in Rimmon-Kenan 102; Wall 30.

3. I share Yacobi's view ("Reader" 7) that the reader is inferior to any narrator in the sense that the former cannot directly approach the objects of the fictional world and has no access to a report of this world other than the one given to him by the latter. However, in my discussion of the reader's superiority to the narrator, I am not referring to this kind of ontological or existential gap but rather to the reader's belief that he or she excels the narrator in his or her moral qualities, cognitive abilities, or both. The argument that readers feel superior is stronger for the unreliable narrator whose cognitive abilities are deficient than for the unreliable narrator whose worldview is deformed (sometimes named "untrustworthy" [Lancer] or "discordant" [Cohn]). In principle, a reader may think that he or she shares with the narrator norms that society sees as deformed and recognize that, according to these norms, both he or she and the narrator are unreliable. Nonetheless, I believe that a reader who deviates from common moral values more often regards his or her own values as "truer" or "more reliable" and places his or her trust in the narrator that others call "untrustworthy." In referring to unreliable narrators I abstain from using *it*, since I share with Zerweck the view that all kinds of unreliable narrators are personified, even though they are not necessarily homodiegetic.

4. I name the situation of the narration "a monological dialogue" because the words of the narratee are never directly provided in the text and everything that the reader is able to know or assume about him relies on the words of the narrator. The latter asks the narratee some questions, tells of his responses to the story, and even asks him to recount a similar story about his own life (71, for instance), but the voice of the narratee is never heard. Hence the text merely imitates a dialogue and never becomes one (see also Fitch). Nevertheless, we shall see that the presence of the narratee stands out, arouses curiosity, and propels the story no less than that of the narrator. Indeed, one may attribute to the narratee the same deafening muteness that is attributed at the beginning of the text to the "gorilla" waiter (6).

5. The fall of the woman, which might be perceived as the central event of the narrative (as regards both its importance and its location in the text), paradoxically promotes the fragmentation of the narrative and its decentralization (see Felman 171-72). On the shattering of self-image, see Brochier and again Felman (169-71), who has a subchapter on the disintegration of the witness.

6. I will later argue that this "individuality" is to a large extent collective, a typical product of a certain kind of society. See also Blanchot. The narrator, just like the narratee, is only ostensibly individual. It is well known that Camus added an afterword to the English version of the novella, one in which he portrays Clamence as the hero of his time—a portrait that embodies the illnesses of an entire generation (see King 87;

Fortier). Blanchot adds that the narrator wears a mask that makes him impersonal, expresses human distresses, and has experiences so general that there is not even one reader who cannot relate him- or herself to him.

7. Fortier remarks that situating the "scenery" of the narrative in Amsterdam, a city crowded with strangers and surrounded by water from all sides, helps the narrator to create an appropriate atmosphere, which will captivate the narratee and get hold of him.

8. Quillard discusses the irony that is expressed by, among other means, the manner that the narrator addresses the narratee. Quillard quotes forms of address that are an anomaly in spoken French, such as "monsieur et cher compatriote," at the end of the first chapter (18). These forms are an evidence of the narrator's disdain towards the narratee in the guise of a polite appeal, in accordance with the norms of polite society. Quillard contends that Camus's irony employs a hermeneutic function similar to that of Socratic irony: it constitutes a dialogue in which the interlocutor must not accept the narrator's words at face value; he must, on the contrary, distrust the seemingly true and put everything in doubt. Hence the narratee may suspect the narrator's familiarity with him.

9. See, for example, Clamence's reference to Dante's *Divine Comedy* (explicitly on 91) as well as to Christ and the New Testament (passim) and to the well-known Dutch painter Van Dyck (139). King points in her essay to structural elements as well as elements of meaning in the novella inspired by Dante's text.

10. He says, for example, "Soyons justes: it arrivait que mes oublis *fussent* méritoires" [To be fair, it turned out that my omissions *were* worthwhile] (54). Clamence directly refers to this peculiarity (8). See also King. Clamence's rhetorical devices mentioned here may be perceived as on the one hand bringing the narrator closer to the narratee (because they are adapted to his intellectual level) and on the other hand distancing him (because they mar the familiar atmosphere that the narrator tries to create).

11. Clamence's narcissism may make the readers wonder whether the narratee exists as a real character or only as a projection of the narrator. Certain characteristics of the narratee differentiate him from the narrator and make it difficult to identify the narratee with one aspect or another of the narrator's soul. Especially prominent is the refusal of the narratee to confess to the narrator, despite the latter's constant pleadings. In this way the role-play persists through the novella: the narrator narrates (and verifies the narratee's attention once in a while), and the narratee listens (and sometimes interrogates, responds, smiles, or protests).

12. For a thorough treatment of the narrator's rhetorical devices, see Brochier.

13. In this context, there are some fascinating connections between *The Fall* and *Oedipus Rex*, some of which are indicated by Blanchot. Oedipus's self-image, like Clamence's, was based during a great part of his life on escaping from the truth (although these are very different kinds of truths). Blanchot claims that both the classical Greek tragedy and the modern novella are centered on a "king" (with or without quotation marks) who reigns securely, until the fact that he has "one eye too many," meaning excessive lucidity, dramatically changes his life and urges him to abdicate.

14. For Clamence's reexamination of his life and the way it is expressed in his narration, see Fitch.

15. Blanchot comments that the fall of the narrator, just like the fall of each of us, has no real beginning. We fall and console ourselves with the assertion of a certain point at which our fall began.

16. On this test, see Fortier. Felman discusses the kind of paradox in which the narrator is unable to experience, comprehend, and narrate the event that he relates.

17. Fortier elaborately notes, in accordance with his structuralist methodology, words in the novella pointing upwards as opposed to words pointing downwards. Everything that goes deep and is thus literally and symbolically related to the fall arouses disgust in the narrator, whereas everything that rises or is associated with the state prior to the fall excites him.

18. The term "stage of existence" is based on the philosophy of the Danish philosopher Søren Kierkegaard, who is counted, just like Camus, among the existentialist philosophers. According to Kierkegaard, there are three such stages: aesthetic, ethical, and religious. The aesthetic stage is identified by Kierkegaard with a hedonistic way of life. Each person chooses one of these stages and may choose another one at every phase of his life. Kierkegaard believes that the religious stage of existence is the highest and that it most fully realizes the goal of human existence. As opposed to this, Camus does not believe any more in the possibility of this stage of existence as a solution to the anguish of modern human being, and in his fictional and philosophical writings he asks to deal with a human world with no God.

19. This idea of changing one circle of existence for another as a result of the revelation of an internal existential contradiction in one of the circles is also drawn from Kierkegaard's thought. Kierkegaard himself relies on Hegelian dialectics with regard to this; however, as opposed to Hegel, he believes that exposing the contradiction does not *necessarily* lead to a change that will solve it, but that every change in the existential sphere is the result of a *chosen* act.

20. For Clamence's immersion in hedonism and the failure of this way of life for him, see Brochier, King, and Fortier.

21. As noted above, all of the narratee's responses are only inferable from Clamence's narration and are never spoken directly.

22. Clamence argues that Christ was not really blameless, because the Massacre of the Innocents would not have taken place had he not come into the world.

23. King justly refers to Clamence as a sort of Antichrist. Like the devil, he too falls from the heights of his vanity, and, like him, he betrays, after his fall, those who have cooperated with him, by his announcement of a universal guilt.

24. See also Zerweck's general statement (citing Wall 23): "[U]nreliable narrators in realist contemporary texts no longer necessarily highlight the unreliability of the fictional narrator *per se*. Instead, they question both 'reliable' and 'unreliable' narration and the distinction we make between them" (163).

25. I disagree with Fitch's claim that the only thing left of the narrator at the end of the novella is his presence, and the attempt to persuade the reader to confess of his own life. Fitch contends that the hermeneutic action at the end shifts from "the text in itself" to "the text for the reader," as the mirror is turned to the latter. Admittedly, the narrator

queries the truthfulness of every detail of his story; nonetheless, I believe that the general frame of the story: a life that is based on lies—a traumatic experience (or traumatic experiences)—disillusionment and guilt is not to be doubted. If the reader doubts these too, he or she will not be able to see the mirror that is directed at him or her. In my view, the mirror effect is created only if the narrator continues to be reflected in it until the end, even though it is no longer turned to him.

26. I agree with Blanchot about the ironic tone, including self-irony, shrouding the entire novella. Unlike Blanchot, however, I think that Clamence has a serious intention (the contrast between "serious" and "ironic" is Blanchot's) to shift the guilt from himself to his narratee. This intention is at the heart of Clamence's motivation to narrate his story.

27. Within this context, Brochier names Clamence an "intellectual terrorist," arguing that intellect serves Clamence to gain power over others and to prove his superiority (121).

28. Fitch claims that the narratee of *The Fall* is the implied reader who has become a fictional character. However, I believe that just as the fictional narratee cannot be identified with the narrator, so he cannot be identified with the reader, although their attributes partly overlap. The specific attributes of the narratee, for example his sex (male), his age (forty years old, more or less), his profession (lawyer), and his origins (Parisian) do not necessarily correspond to those of the real or implied reader. Nevertheless, the responses of the narratee to the words of the narrator, for example his wonder in the face of the narrator's declaration of his desperate need for sympathy ("Je vois que cette déclaration vous étonne" [I see that this statement surprises you] [35]), his questions, for example the question concerning the fateful night to which the narrator hints ("Comment? Quel soir?" [What? Which night?] [36]), and, of course, his "courteous" silence (70), are shared by the implied reader. Like the narratee, the reader too is curious to know what the narrator has to say, is aroused by him to wonder and perturbation, and is "an embarrassed bourgeois," sufficiently established and educated to be bothered by existential questions related to the meaning of life, death, love, freedom, responsibility, and guilt. Were it not for this, why would the narratee continue to listen to the words of the bothersome and egocentric narrator, and why would the reader continue to read them? The rhetorical devices employed by the narrator-actor, who desperately requires an audience, win him one that is much larger than the specific narratee whom he addresses.

29. It is reasonable to argue that the implied author of *The Fall*, not the narrator, is the one who communicates with the reader indirectly, "behind the back" of the narrator. Nevertheless, my opinion is that Clamence's treatment of his narratee as an Everyman who may be exchanged with any other urges the readers to consider themselves included in the narrator's address to the narratee.

30. Fitch stresses that *The Fall* demands from the reader more than what fictional texts usually do: the narrator requests the reader not only to use his or her imagination and identify with the life of the character as it is shaped by the author but also to examine his or her own moral qualities as a person. Unlike Fitch, I believe that *The Fall* is not an unusual text in this respect; its uniqueness is expressed in the rhetorical devices that the narrator employs in order to intensify the involvement of the reader.

31. Camus's novella undermines certain common presuppositions of the interpretation of the genre named "confessional fiction." For example, Nave claims that the aim of fictional confession (like the aim of religious confession) is to achieve atonement, to purge oneself, and to be readmitted into society. She contends that confession as a spontaneous-voluntary act is natural and that therefore it evokes a feeling of truth and lacks the forgery and artificiality of the obligatory confession. Clamence's account, especially the paradoxes that he raises with regard to the goal of the confession and its truthfulness, does not enable us to accept Nave's argument without reserve.

32. Fitch justly notes that the reader is not obliged at all to accept the general arguments of the narrator concerning human beings and the world. Similarly, Fortier claims that, as opposed to the impression that the narrator tries to create, he does not end his story with the upper hand; the narratee does not simply have to accept his worldview. Unlike me, however, they do not propose alternatives to this worldview.

33. A hermeneutic trap similar to the one set by Clamence is attributed to psychoanalysis. Popper argued that if Freud's patients agreed with his interpretation, this agreement was regarded as its confirmation, whereas if they disagreed with it, Freud named this disagreement "resistance," explaining that the patient represses the truth that is a threat to his mental stability. Thus disagreement as well as agreement confirms the interpretation of the psychoanalyst. Therefore, Popper argues, psychoanalytic theory is irrefutable.

34. Felman and Reilly deal with the concrete political and historical context of Camus's novella. Camus debated with Sartre and other prominent scholars of his time about the communist revolution, and he insisted on the injustice of the use of temporary violence and suppression even if it is meant to serve the purpose of creating a just society. Thus, according to Camus, regarding oneself and one's worldview as utterly pure and innocent as opposed to all others, as a communist of his time might have done, is potentially dangerous for society.

35. The attempt of the readers to evade the role that is ostensibly dictated to them by the text is in accordance with Iser's position as regards the constant tension between the two elements that construct the implied reader: textual structure and structured act (36-37). Iser contends that textual structure entails different possibilities of realization or concretization. My essay presents a few of these possibilities for the reading of *The Fall*.

36. Camus's essay *The Rebel* is connected to *The Fall* in many ways. One interesting connection is between Clamence and different types of "metaphysical rebels" whom Camus describes in the preface of *The Rebel*, such as the dandy (43-49).

37. King's critique of Clamence emphasizes that, like other modern rebels whom Camus presents in his essay *The Rebel*, he too engages in a rebellion that has no positive basis that can enable him to surpass himself, and that therefore he fails. The inability to create such a positive basis is connected with his dichotomous worldview, which rejects any doubt and vagueness and concludes that anyone who is not wholly innocent is completely guilty.

38. See also King's criticism, pointing in a direction different from the one proposed above. King emphasizes that Clamence's interpretation of his behavior and its motives is not truer after the trauma that he experienced than it had been before: as

much as he formerly believed himself entirely innocent, the fall makes him believe that all his deeds are purely egoistic. In this way the narrator moves from one extremity to the other and does not succeed in achieving a balanced self-image.

39. See also Reilly: "The text [of *The Fall*] implicitly challenges us to prove him [Clamence] wrong, but this means breaking the prison, not pretending that it isn't there" (137).

40. Manfred Jahn suggests that the analysis of unreliable narration should consider the axis of *development* (that is, an unreliable narrator becoming more reliable as the story develops or vice versa) as well as the axis of *degrees* and the axis of *aspects* of unreliability (85). Jahn's suggestion is an important step towards understanding the dynamics of unreliable narration as proposed in this essay.

Works Cited

Blanchot, Maurice. "La confession dédaigneuse." 1956. *Les critiques de notre temps et Camus*. Ed. A. Blanc. Paris: Garnier, 1970.

Booth, Wayne C. *The Rhetoric of Fiction*. Chicago: U of Chicago P, 1961.

Brochier, Jean-Jacques. *Albert Camus: Philosophe pour classes terminales*. Paris: Balland, 1979.

Camus, Albert. *La Chute: Récit*. 1956. Paris: Gallimard, 1961.

_____. *L'Homme révolté*. Paris: Gallimard, 1951.

Chatman, Seymour Benjamin. *Story and Discourse: Narrative Structure in Fiction and Film*. Ithaca: Cornell UP, 1978.

Cohn, Dorrit. "Discordant Narration." *Style* 34 (2000): 307-16.

Dickens, Charles. *David Copperfield*. 1849-1850. New York: Random, 1969.

Felman, Shoshana. "The Betrayal of the Witness: Camus' *The Fall*." *Testimony: Crises of Witnessing in Literature, Psychoanalysis, and History*. Ed. Felman and Dori Laub. New York: Routledge, 1992. 165-203.

Fitch, Brian T. "The Interpreter Interpreted: *La Chute*." *The Narcissistic Text: A Reading of Camus' Fiction*. Toronto: U of Toronto P, 1982.

Fortier, Paul A. *Une Lecture de Camus: La Valeur des Éléments descriptifs dans l'Oeuvre Romanesque*. Paris: Klincksieck, 1977.

Iser, Wolfgang. *The Act of Reading: A Theory of Aesthetic Response*. London: Johns Hopkins UP, 1978.

Jahn, Manfred. "Package Deals, Exxclusionen, Randzonen: Das Phänomen der Unverläßichkeit in den Erzählsituationen." *Unreliable Narration: Studien zur Theorie und Praxis unglaubwürdigen Erzählens in der englischprachigen Erzählliteratur*. Ed. Ansgar Nünning. Trier: Wissenschaftlicher Verlag Trier, 1998. 81-106.

Kierkegaard, Søren. *Either/Or: A Fragment of Life*. Garden City: Doubleday, 1959.

King, Adele. *Camus*. 1964. Edinburgh: Oliver, 1966.

Lanser, Susan Sniader. *The Narrative Act: Point of View in Prose Fiction*. Princeton: Princeton UP, 1981.

Nave, Hannah. *The Confession: A Study of a Genre*. Tel-Aviv: Papirus, 1988. Published in Hebrew.

Nünning, Ansgar. "Unreliable, Compared to What? Towards a Cognitive Theory of Unreliable Narration: Prolegomena and Hypotheses." *Transcending Boundaries: Narratology in Context*. Ed. Ansgar Nünning. Tübingen: Narr, 1999. 53-73.

Plato. *The Republic*. Trans. and introd. H. K. P. Lee. Harmondsworth: Penguin, 1958.

Popper, Karl. *Conjectures and Refutations: The Growth of Scientific Knowledge*. London: Routledge, 1963.

Quillard, Genevieve. "Mécanismes ironiques et code socioculturel dans *La Chute*." *Le texte et ses langages*. Albert Camus 14. Ed. Raymond Gay-Crosier. Paris: Lettres Modernes, 1991.

Reilly, Patrick. *The Literature of Guilt: From Gulliver to Golding*. Houndmills: Macmillan, 1988.

Ricoeur, Paul. *Time and Narrative*. Trans. Kathleen McLaughlin and David Pellauer. Chicago: U of Chicago P, 1984-1988.

Rimmon-Kenan, Shlomith. *Narrative Fiction: Contemporary Poetics*. 1983. London: Routledge, 2002.

Wall, Kathleen. "*The Remains of the Day* and Its Challenges to Theories of Unreliable Narration." *Journal of Narrative Technique* 21 (1994): 18-42.

Yacobi, Tamar. "Fictional Reliability as a Communicative Problem." *Poetics Today* 2 (1981): 113-36.

_____. "Reader and Norms in Fictional Communication." *Hasifrut* 2 (1985): 5-34.

Zerweck, Bruno. "Historicizing Unreliable Narration: Unreliability and Cultural Discourse in Narrative Fiction." *Style* 36 (2001): 151-76.

Pathologies of Pride in Camus's *The Fall*_____

Robert C. Solomon

What is Hell? Here is one answer: five straight days of conversation with a garrulous, narcissistic, rather depraved lawyer. This is the text, in fact the entire content, of Camus's brilliant quasi-religious novel, *The Fall*.[1] It is, as the title promises, something of a "downer," a tale of horrid descent, a moral parable for our sick and absurd times. And there is another definition of Hell: it is having "fallen," from the heights and happiness to the depths of despair, from success and virtue to failure and depravity, and bitterly, exquisitely remembering it. On this account, there is no hell without a heaven, and it is the contrast between them that makes it so.

Jean-Baptiste Clamence is the garrulous lawyer. He calls himself a "judge-penitent," an ironic but poor description, I will argue, of his current profession. Once a noble and immensely successful "defender of widows and orphans," he now more resembles a black widow spider, waiting as predator for the fly-by tourist in the seediest bar in the seediest section of the seedy inner circle of Amsterdam. His predation consists of entangling the victim, in fact, the reader, in a web of eloquently spun words, demonstrating his unabated skill in presenting, at length, a "brief," protesting simultaneously his guilt and his innocence, and quickly establishing his superiority in the relationship. He is obsessed with his own innocence, "even if we have to accuse the whole human race and heaven itself." But although Clamence (and Camus) offer us a soliloquy on guilt and innocence and judgment and repentance, a more straightforward interpretation of the novel is that it is all about superiority. Clamence describes his superiority through innocence in his earlier Parisian life, and he goes on to demonstrate it through his protestations of guilt in the seedy setting of the Mexico City bar in the bowels of Amsterdam.

Thus one could readily conceive of *The Fall* as a meditation on the "deadly" sin of pride. Pride perhaps need not entail superiority, or felt superiority, but it is certainly entangled with it. And that introduces a host of ethical—not to mention theological—questions. Is pride indeed a sin, or is it only "false" pride and such that are sinful? Is pride necessarily about something in particular (some accomplishment or achievement), or is it, as David Hume argued, ultimately about The Self simpliciter? Does superiority have to be competitive, a "zero-sum game," or can one feel superior without thereby demeaning anyone else? And does superiority entail invulnerability, or is it in fact a set up for a "fall"? It is this last question that defines the plot line in *The Fall*. The implication of Clamence's story is that his fall and his move from Paris to Amsterdam demonstrate the falseness of his sense of earlier superiority and his innocence. It is also a moral lesson for all of us. Insofar as we maintain a sense of our own superiority and innocence we, too, are vulnerable and therefore "false." Instead of pride, we should adopt Hume's "monkish virtue" of humility, and perhaps embrace the Christian view of humanity as both fallen and redeemable.

This interpretation of the book as a meditation on the "falseness" of pride has been ably presented by Phillip Quinn.[2] Quinn is perfectly aware that the Christian symbolism that pervades every page of *The Fall* is but a tease. Camus is an atheist and the philosophical setting of the novel is pointedly devoid of the Christian promise of redemption. Indeed, in the final pages Clamence goes into a feverish rave in which he holds up Christ himself as an example of the falseness he has been "outing" throughout the book. Quinn, of course, is a devout and prolific defender of the Christian promise. Accordingly, he suggests at the end of his review a stark choice, "Christianity or nihilism." He ends by softening this and suggesting that there may be some non-nihilistic yet non-Christian way of thinking about all of this, but in the scope of the novel he finds no possibility of redemption. Thus for Quinn, pride is, as it was for Saint Augustine and Pope Gregory, the worst of the sins. It is never defensible, even where it is warranted. Thus, even the pride of success should be subdued by the humbling force of humility, that all-embracing sense of ourselves as essentially flawed and vulnerable beings.

But if one does not share Quinn's Augustinian Christian viewpoint, the self-image of this pervasive humility might become offensive. An alternative is Nietzsche, whose views on this matter are well known, or Aristotle, in whose ethics pride is a virtue, not a vice. Of course, for Nietzsche or Aristotle, pride may be misplaced. It might be based on literally false self-description, and is thus cancelled out by Aristotle's virtue of "truthfulness." It might be inappropriate to the circumstances or based on defensive resentment, incurring Nietzsche's criticism. But in the case of "false" pride it is not just a feeling of pride that is in question but its objective appropriateness. The ideal of Aristotle's ethics is the *megalopsychos*, the "great-souled man." A *megalopsychos* would be obnoxious today, but perhaps this is because we are all so steeped in Christian culture, which is what Nietzsche was so vehemently on about. But what *megalopsychos* represents is pride as a virtue and as a primary ingredient in happiness. It is not that the *megalopsychos* cannot fail or fall but he (or she) does not dwell on that, focussing rather on the joys of a successful life, including the exercise of the virtues. This is how we should view Clamence in his Parisian incarnation, not as an example of false pride but as a striking example of a *megalopsychos*, a virtuous, contented, and rightfully proud man.

I

The first point to make about Clamence is that, in Paris, he is indeed a truly virtuous, fully contented, enviously successful man. He is indeed, as Camus suggests in his head note from Lermontov, "A hero for our time." The temptation, especially given his own embittered perspective on his own past, is to see Clamence as deeply flawed and as a "two-faced" hypocrite. But insofar as one can "read through" his deceptive self-description, as one must "read through" Meursault's descriptions in *The Stranger* there is no reason for accepting this view of Clamence as deeply flawed and as "two-faced."[3] Indeed, the power of the novel is the "fall" of a nearly perfect human being into bitter despair. If it can happen to him, we are forced to realize, it can happen to any of us. On the other hand, if we can discern some basic flaw, for example hypocrisy, in Clamence's character, then we can attribute his fall and subsequent unhappiness to *that*. And we, who are relatively flawless in that respect, are off the hook.

This temptation to find the tragic flaw or *hamartia* in the tragic hero goes back to Aristotle, who in his *Poetics* insisted that tragedy should be structured around a powerful, lofty hero with some tragic flaw that brings him down. It is important that nothing external does this, although external forces might enter in as an afterthought to solidify the failure wrought by the flaw in character. Aristotle was thinking of such tragedies as Sophocles's *Oedipus*, but the analysis might just as well be applied to more modern tragedies, for instance those of Shakespeare.

Oedipus, we are told, was obstinate, and would not listen to the sage advice of Teiresias and his wife/mother, Jocasta. ("Best to live lightly, as one can, unthinkingly.") Hamlet, we are told, is "a man who could not make up his mind." But should we see either Oedipus or Hamlet as flawed? To be sure, they are human, perhaps all too human. But Oedipus is a king out to cure the curse that is inflicting his people. His obstinacy might be better described as perseverance. And Hamlet, first of all, wanted proof. It is not indecision that made him not accept at face value the murderous moanings of a ghost who pretended to be his father. He then faced insurmountable difficulties, not least of which was the fact that his beloved mother was now married to the man he felt obliged to murder. And his hesitation before murdering Claudius as he prayed, as distinct from his utter impulsiveness when he thought he was killing Claudius behind the arras, had nothing to do with indecision but was an essential part of his plan to send his uncle to hell without redemption.

So what work is the theory of the tragic flaw and Aristotle's insistence that the tragic hero must be lofty—a king or a prince, for instance—doing here? It blocks the likelihood of seeing Oedipus and Hamlet as people like us, not perfect, perhaps, but tragic despite their virtues, not because of their vices. Thus insofar as we buy into Clamence's description of himself before the fall, we find ourselves with a ready rationalization. He fell because he was flawed and because he lived loftier than we do. It is not that his vulnerability is all of our vulnerability. His pride makes him exceptional; Quinn is certainly right about Camus's novel being a morality tale on the pathology of pride. But what is that pathology, if it is not the pathology of pride as such? I would suggest that the pathology of pride, even when it is "true," is rather the pathology of pride fallen, the pathology of that famously bitter emotion of resentment (*ressentiment*). And resentment would like nothing better than to be convinced of the viciousness, even the sinfulness, of those compared to and contrasted with whom it feels humbled. In Clamence's case, the comparison and contrast is with his earlier self.

II

Camus's *The Fall*, like its earlier complement, *The Stranger*, is divided into two parts. In *The Stranger*, the parts are quite clearly divided by Meursault's murder of the Arab. Before that, he was blithely innocent, essentially mindless, whether one takes that to be simply his nature or the result of a duplicitous prior act of "bad faith."[4] After that, he is in prison and on trial, leading to the development of a Self in this hitherto seemingly selfless and wholly unreflective character. The two parts of *The Fall* are not textually separated but are also starkly distinct. The first part, which we discern only through Clamence's jaded descriptions, is his life in Paris as an eminent and successful lawyer. The second part is his subsequent life in Amsterdam as a "judge-penitent," much of which is taken up with re-describing and re-interpreting his prior life in Paris.

Philosophically, the division is essentially the same in both *The Stranger* and *The Fall*. The first part offers us a life that is devoid of reflection and thus happily devoid of judgment and guilt. Throughout,

Meursault seems as incapable of moral judgment as he is unable to muster up the slightest passion. Clamence makes much of the fact that in his role as defense attorney he is neither judge nor judged. Of course, Clamence's life is much more reflective than Meursault's, if by that we mean that he is thoughtful and clearly knows what he is doing. But it is unreflective in a more serious and contentious sense. He may, unlike Meursault, have a keen sense of his life as a whole. Indeed, that is the nature of his pride. But he maintains his innocence and does not take seriously the possibility of failure or his vulnerability. He refuses to see or at least take seriously the palpable presence of other people's envy and resentment. And that innocent sense gives way to part two, in which both characters are held up for judgment by others (and by themselves!) and in which their guilt is made transparent. If the first part is the world of unreflective "lived experience," the second part is the world of reflection, a world defined by self-condemnation. Meursault perhaps manages to escape self-condemnation, though the last line of the novel, about being greeted at his execution by "howls of execration," seems to undercut this, but Clamence gives himself wholly over to it. It is through self-condemnation, in place of his public courtroom victories on the behalf of others, that comes to define his new and depraved sense of excellence and his superiority over all others.

Lived experience and reflection are presented as contraries in Camus's works. They are not just complementary nor do they simply represent the complexity of consciousness. The one interferes with the other. Thus Clamence, despite occasional lyricism about the Dutch weather and the quality of Dutch gin and his superior references to the vulgarity of the bartender, is pretty much oblivious to his surroundings. His life in Amsterdam is "caught up" in reflection. Far from him Queen Jocasta's philosophy—"Best to live lightly, as one can, unthinkingly." He lives heavily, like the gloomy Dutch weather, through embittered and resentful thinking. And through that embittered thinking, he remembers and interprets his earlier seemingly innocent and noble life as so much of a sham. He offers us several metaphors, all of which point to a "double" life. If he had a professional business card, he tells us, it would be Janus-faced, with the slogan, "don't rely on it." Don't rely, in other words, on the apparent face of innocence and nobility, for the face of the Amsterdam devil is on the other side. He tells us that when he looked in the mirror after one of his few humiliating experiences, his smile was "double." The duplicity refers to his presumed hypocrisy, to the alleged fact that he is guilty while pretending to be innocent, to his apparent selflessness that is in fact, he tells us, motivated by the sheerest self-interest and vanity. On the one hand, there is the world of innocence and nobility, the world of Rousseau's (so-called) "noble savage" and Nietzsche's ancient noblemen. On the other hand, there is the world of reflection and guilt, the world of Rousseau's corrupt courtiers and Nietzsche's resentful slaves.

Each of these worlds has its own "truth," although the latter world has a decisive advantage over the former. The reflective life is, as Nietzsche tells us, exceedingly "clever," and it can incisively judge the relatively naïve world of mere experience. From within the innocent world, that is, a world not yet infected by self-doubt and the fear of failure, the truth is simply the goodness of life, the joy of flourishing, and one's own moral and extra-moral excellences. It views the resentment and envy of those who do not share that *joie de vivre*, that sense of flourishing, and those excellences as sad, even pathetic, but it does not take seriously (or perhaps even notice) their condemnation. But this means that it lacks the means to defend itself, that is, to defend itself against accusations of "elitism" and "superiority," for it does not see these as accusations at all. Thus Aristotle presents his ethics "for the best" without succumbing to egalitarianism—though he is keenly aware of the importance of equality within certain well-defined contexts—and he presents his list of virtues or excellences without defending them, as opposed to the "Why be moral?" obsession that defines modern ethics.

Through reflection and resentment, however, "elitism" and "superiority" are damning accusations, and the resentful critic can easily discern ulterior and underlying motives that the noble soul either would not recognize or, if differently described, would not take seriously. Thus an innocent act can be interpreted as a self-serving one, and a generous or heroic act as a selfish one. All philosophy students are familiar with this game. One *feels* no hint of self-interest in a virtuous act, but this may be self-deception. One's subsequent good feelings betray this, for, after all, mightn't the anticipation of those good feelings—or the possibility of bad feelings of guilt or shame—have motivated the act in the first place? There is no defense against such suspicions, for even Kant was willing to acknowledge that we are in no position to know the actual motivation of our actions. Within the innocent world, it might not matter what the motives are. The act—or one's nobility of character—speaks sufficiently for itself. But from the point of view of the resentful world, motives really do matter, for even the best acts and characters can be scrutinized for ulterior motives and the most base actions and personalities can be defended in terms of their good intentions.

To move to the text itself, here is one simple example of how Clamence plays this game with himself—and with us. He first mentions how happily he helps those in need, for example, helping elderly or blind people across busy boulevards. He enjoys exercising these simple virtues so much, he tells us, that he goes out of his way to find opportunities to practice them. In this, he perfectly exemplifies Aristotle's virtuous person, who exercises his or her virtues not out of duty or obligation but because he or she *enjoys* doing so. But it is easy to see the vulnerability of such a virtuous person to the scrutiny of the resentful critic. Taking the enjoyment itself as the motive rather than as a secondary consequence (as Aristotle argues in his *Ethics*, Book X, sect. 5) the resentful critic rejects the protestations of the virtuous person—if he or she bothers to protest at all—to the effect that the action was "for its own sake" and not for any ulterior motive.

Moreover, small details provide further evidence for condemnation. Returning in his narrative to the same situation, Clamence notes that after helping a blind man across the street he doffs his hat, an extra courtesy that the blind man could not possibly have appreciated. It is easy to imagine this. One practices such virtues as courtesy until they become unthinking, second nature. In this incident, the gesture was amusingly inappropriate but certainly innocent for all of that. But from this small oddity, accusations of hypocrisy are quickly forthcoming. It had to be vanity, the argument goes, not a merely automatic gesture. It was showing off, despite the claim to be mere courtesy. Thus the seeming virtue of the entire behavior, not just in this incident but in all such incidents, is undermined. Clamence's former courtesies along with his other virtues are thus displayed for what they "really" were, the acts of a vain and selfish man and, worse, hypocritical and "two-faced," pretending to be one thing while really being another.

The virtuous Parisian cannot defend himself. He has passed through the novel and exists now only in the memories of this bitter resentful man. He and his world are vulnerable. Just as Aristotle and his virtues come off as elitist and far from moral from the perspective of Kant and his cronies, the virtues of the younger Clamence are dismissed as "false" from the perspective of his later incarnation. The world of innocence is always vulnerable when it is viewed from within the world of bitter reflection. Unless, that is, the world of bitter reflection is itself exposed to its own "truths," and its own motives of envy and resentment are displayed for all to see. This is what Nietzsche does. It is also what Camus does, through his ultimately crazed character Clamence. *The Fall* is not a condemnation of pride or superiority, but a condemnation of resentful pride and superiority, pride that refuses to recognize itself as such and superiority that proves itself only by stealth and subversion. In the noble world, one is rightly proud of his or her excellences and accomplishments. In the resentful world one takes pride (if that is the word) not in winning but in bringing the other low. The fall is not due to a tragic flaw at all but rather to conniving and self-deception, in this exceptional case the conniving of Clamence's later self against the former.

III

If the theme of *The Fall* is superiority and pride, the book is not a condemnation of pride or superiority but a condemnation of resentful pride and resentful superiority. It is also about judgment and repentance, which are not irrelevant to the sin of pride, or rather, to false pride, unwarranted pride, and an unwarranted sense of superiority. Such pathologies of pride involve judgment, or rather meta-judgments, that is, judgments about the warrant of emotions. Pride is not, as Hume suggests, merely a pleasant feeling or a pleasant feeling about oneself, which "contains not any representative quality." But he adds, passions may be "accompany'd with some judgment or opinion," and in this sense they may be "contrary to reason" or "unreasonable."[5]

Pride, in particular, is subject to judgment, both within (as constitutive of) the emotion and as meta-judgment about the warrant of the emotion. Ultimately, it is difficult to distinguish these, at least in one's own case. To feel pride is already to judge that one's Self and one's accomplishments are worthy of pride. If others do not or would not agree with that assessment, the possibility of "false" pride, unwarranted by the circumstances, is quite likely. This is how Christian psychology gets its hooks into pride. By starting with a cosmically unflattering comparison and contrast between God the "greater than whom none can be conceived" and mere human beings, even noble, virtuous, and accomplished human beings, it is easy to see how one might conclude that none of our nobility, our virtues, or our accomplishments are worthy of pride. But why should we accept that humiliating comparison? There is a chicken-and-egg problem here: it is only by accepting the Christian (or some comparable) worldview that one is compelled to conclude that nothing about us is worthy of pride, but the feeling of humility and unworthiness may well impel someone to accept the Christian worldview. This concern is something other than the accusation that pride is a sin because it involves the neglect of worship and awe of God (which is a link to another deadly sin, *acedia*, badly translated as "sloth") or that it implies a kind of narcissism and consequent neglect of both God and other people. If one does not accept the Christian worldview the neglect of God is no vice, and one can accept the fact that narcissism is no virtue without so tightly linking it to pride. Clamence, in particular, takes great pride in his virtues, and these consist in turn of his attentiveness and aid to others.

The pathologies of pride begin, no doubt, with false pride, unwarranted pride, a sense of superiority that is misplaced or inappropriate. Thus Aristotle opposes boastfulness to truthfulness and counts it a vice, not a sin, because it is either not true to the facts or it is inappropriate. But the fact that it is a version of pride does not count against it at all. Only that it is—quite literally—false. But Aristotle's vices typically come in pairs, one of excess, one of deficiency, in contrast to the virtues. Excessive pride—that is, pride in more than one deserves—is evident enough. But it does not follow that all pride is excessive or false, that there is nothing for mere human beings to be genuinely proud about. If we tighten our worldview to what Nietzsche called a "this-worldly" perspective, an essentially human perspective, then human virtues and accomplishments are to be judged on their own merits, not in comparison and contrast with god Almighty or the supposedly perfect exemplar of Jesus. Following Nietzsche, Clamence makes his blasphemous attack on Jesus himself, denying him the perfection that he supposedly represents. Within our human framework, we know perfectly well what is worthy of pride and what is not. Genuine accomplishment and virtuous deeds are worthy of pride, and the life that Clamence has led in Paris warrants and justifies pride if anyone's life does.

Severed from the Christian account in which all localized enjoyment of human life is mere vanity (as stated in *Ecclesiastes*), we can even appreciate what is worthy in vanity. Vanity, as opposed to pride, involves advantages and "blessings" that are not due to one's own efforts or virtues but are rather, one might say, matters of luck. One's good looks, for example, without neglecting the pride one might take in good grooming. Or one's natural wit, charm, and intelligence, again without neglecting the pride one might take in hard work and the constant exercise of those gifts. Pride and vanity are thus intertwined, and, again, so long as one doesn't condemn all human enjoyment as vanity and all sense of human virtue and accomplishment as false pride both are to be enjoyed, or rather, to coin an ugly word, they are to be meta-enjoyed, for in pride and vanity we both enjoy our virtues and our blessings and in innocent reflection we enjoy the fact that we enjoy both our virtues and our blessings.

To appreciate the range of such meta-enjoyments, compare what Milan Kundera says about kitsch: "Kitsch causes two tears to flow in quick succession. The first tear says: how nice to see children running on the grass! The second tear says: How nice to be moved, together with all mankind, by children running on the grass! It is the second tear that makes kitsch kitsch."[6] Many human emotions are not only amplified but also transformed through reflection. This may also be true of enjoyment. Reflection on how one is enjoying oneself may not only enhance the enjoyment but transform it into something quite different, self-satisfaction, for example. But it can also undermine it, compromising pleasure or even turning it into pain. Thus the cynic that Camus sometimes seems to play suggests that there is something essentially kitsch-like about our enjoyment of our lives, and that reflection on the meaning of life and "the Absurd" reduces all such enjoyment to self-deception. But the details of life are not absurd, as Camus well knew, and human virtues, accomplishments, and "blessings" are apt subjects for reflection, producing the "positive" emotions of pride and vanity. They need not be matters fit for humiliation.

Thus the corresponding vice of deficiency, in Aristotle's terms, is the Christian virtue of humility, for it is a refusal to enjoy what one deserves to enjoy and is thus detrimental to happiness and the good life. It also leads to an even more serious vice, which Aristotle does not much deign to consider, and that is the viciousness of resentment. For the true "opposite" of pride is not the mere Monkish virtue of humility; it is that bitterness with life and all of its blessings that Nietzsche so strongly if not bitterly criticizes as the weapon of the weak and those who are sick of life.

IV

Simone de Beauvoir writes, "When Gods fall, they do not become mere men. They become frauds." Clamence is not a god, nor did he so think of himself at least until his over-the-top display of megalomania during his fever in Amsterdam. Yet he is clearly something of an *Übermensch*—and this is how he thinks of himself when "on the heights" in Paris. But for an *Übermensch*, Clamence seems unusually vulnerable. That Nietzschean image certainly carries with it the veneer of invincibility, and it quite explicitly excludes the vulnerability to resentment to which all of us are prone. But this is just to say that perhaps that Nietzschean image is itself too overblown, that here Nietzsche himself falls prone to that same "otherworldly" posturing that he so criticizes in the Christian worldview. For is not the image of the *Übermensch* just another comparison and contrast with a superhuman ideal in which we are bound to come out poorly. Indeed, this is what Nietzsche praises as "going under" in the Prologue to *Zarathustra*. This is a kind of self-humiliation, in conscious comparison and contrast with the "superman" that is not unlike the self-humiliation of the weak and mediocre in conscious comparison and contrast with the nobles that Nietzsche criticizes as "slave morality." But we can chalk this up to Nietzsche's never well-hidden misanthropy and nevertheless endorse a good deal of his neo-Aristotelian or in any case aristocratic ethics, an ethics of excellence and of character as opposed to an ethics of universal rules, not to mention of resentment. Accordingly, we can recognize in the Parisian Clamence an extraordinarily enviable and admirable character. He is not invulnerable and obviously he is not invulnerable to resentment, but he is, in his earlier incarnation, as close as any of us can imagine coming to the Western urbane ideals he so clearly embodies.

This is not to say that he is perfect, but his imperfections can be bracketed as those of a macho Parisian man after the Second World War. His treatment of women, for instance, may be abominable by contemporary American standards, but it is probably unfair to apply those standards to Clamence or to Camus or to Parisian society in the fifties. In any case, Camus's intention was clearly to present us with a portrait of a most admirable man, and one can bracket Clamence's insensitivities in this regard as a reflection of Camus's own less than admirable habits with women.

There is a kind of guilt to which all "do-gooders" are vulnerable. It is that sense of never being able to do enough. Anyone who receives more than twenty charity solicitations a month knows what is now sometimes called "donor burn-out," that sense that one's generosity is and always will be overwhelmed by the needs of others. And such guilt can also occupy a more insidious dimension, even closer to the conscience. Compassion demands that we have to share the suffering of others, but it seems that we never feel enough, our suffering is never comparable to the suffering with which we would sympathize. And, of course, there was a kind of guilt to which Camus was particularly prone. It can be summarized in his need to choose between "his country or his mother" in the Algerian war, and his insistence of being "Neither a Victim nor an Executioner" in the Communist struggles that followed. Sartre could write with aplomb about "dirty hands," but Camus would have no part of it. And it is in this context that he invented the ultimately good and guilty "judge-penitent," Clamence.

One might criticize both Clamence's earlier sense of innocence and his later hyper-reflectiveness. First, he seems wholly unself-critical, and then he is too self-critical. Again, I am tempted to suggest that this reflects Camus's own ambivalence regarding innocence and reflection, but this, I think, is essential not only to both of the novels that we have been considering—*The Stranger* and *The Fall*—but to Camus's other works, notably *The Myth of Sisyphus*, his notebooks, and his lyrical Essays as well. How philosophical can one be without falling into the gloom to which philosophy is so prone? "I tried phi-losophy," noted Doctor Johnson, "but cheerfulness kept breaking out." To what extent can one live the life of reflection which, contra Aristotle, both Kierkegaard and Dostoevsky likened to a kind of disease? Does reflection inevitably lead to a sense of one's own inadequacy? Such questions readily lead a good sensualist like Camus either to bed or to the beach, and so, too, Clamence. Well, not to the beach, perhaps, but certainly to the bed and, ultimately, to Clamence's period of debauchery that was still inadequate to shut out the pain of guilty reflection.

I think a more apt diagnosis is that Clamence, if not Camus, indulged in the wrong kind of reflection, reflection that was already tainted with the other-worldly, with comparisons and contrasts to perfection, and consequently with the seeds of failure and resentment. This is the cost of what Nietzsche called the "shadows of God"; our continuing insistence to hold up superhuman ideals of perfection and then declare ourselves failures or frauds in their reflection. Thus the comparison and contrast with a perfect world makes this one seem "absurd," and the comparison and contrast with either God or Christ or the *Übermensch* renders us pathetic, "human—all-too-human." But let us not take this less than perfect aspect of Clamence as his "tragic flaw" either. It is just another aspect of his being human, his being much like us—only better. His fall does indeed point to a capacity that we all share, and Christianity provides just one version of it. In this, again, I think Phillip Quinn is right on the mark, but Camus rightly raises the question of whether the Christian worldview is the only cure—or rather whether it is the cause—of this state of affairs. True, the world of *The Fall* is, despite all of its Christian symbolism, a Godless world in which redemption—or at any rate that kind of redemption—is unavailable. But the despair of the novel cuts at least two ways, only one of which can be read as urging us toward the Christian sense of redemption. The other encourages us to reject that or any worldview whose consequence is that morbid sense of guilt and resentment. One can read

The Fall as a morality tale, but Camus probably intended it as a rejection of Christian morality.

But why did Clamence suffer as he did? What caused his fall? Here Camus does go back to ancient tragedy, not to the "tragic flaw" theory as such but to the more general Aristotelian idea that what brings the hero down is not external circumstances, but in some sense his own self. This is not to say that he has a fatal "tragic" flaw but only that it is in some sense the hero's own doing, and it is just as likely that it will be the result of his virtues as of his vices. This explains the utter triviality of everything Clamence tells us with reference to the "why?" of his fall. Indeed, it is not even clear—nor does it much matter—whether the events he cited are factual or not. He tells us that he heard laughter on the bridge but he could not find its source. Immediately after he hears the laughter of youths on his street but quickly discovers that it is mere camaraderie and has nothing to do with him, as if to suggest that the laughter on the bridge might just as well have had nothing to do with him either. It does not matter, as the echoes of that laughter continue to ring in his head and do their damage. It is not the healthy and happy laughter of amusement or joy but the unhealthy and unhappy laughter of self-humiliation. But this is not to explain anything. It is just another description of his vulnerability.

So, too, he tells us that before that event or non-event on the Pont des Arts there was another incident, also on the bridge, this one the seeming suicide of a young woman. I say "seeming" because Clamence's description makes it none too sure that there was such a woman, or if there was, what happened to her. Clamence's failure to help or do anything, even notify the authorities, becomes one of the threads that ties his narrative together. Although we get the full though very minimal description half-way through the novel, he mentions it, though abstractly, early on. He mentions it again, in bitter reflection, at the very end of his narrative: "'Oh young woman, throw yourself into the water again so that I may a second time have the chance of saving both of us!' A second time, eh, what a risky suggestion! Just suppose, *cher maître*, that we should be taken literally? We'd have to go through with it. Brr . . . ! The water's so cold! But let's not worry! It's too late now. It will always be too late. Fortunately!"

It may be probable that a young woman did take her life on the bridge, and it is certain that Clamence did not do anything whether or not he had good reason to think that she did. But, again, I think that there are good grounds for saying that it doesn't really matter: "But what do I care? Don't lies eventually lead to the truth? And don't all my stories, true or false, tend toward the same conclusion" (p. 119)? His final exclamation makes it quite clear that the damage is being continually done by the poisonous thought that, were such a situation to come about again, he would still be unwilling or unable to do anything about it. Like the laughter, the source of that poisonous thought—in an actual incident or merely in his imagination—is ultimately less important than the self-undermining, humiliating nature of the thought itself. One can imagine the earlier Clamence contemplating, in the absence of any such prior experience, the likelihood of his jumping off the bridge to save a person's life. With his early sense of virtue and his urge to help others, there is little doubt that he would, and saving that young woman would have been true altruism. But that is just what the cynical reflective Clamence cannot understand, and looking back, he can no longer imagine it. So again, it is not as if the incident itself had caused him to lose faith in himself. Somehow he already had, and we are left with just another description of Clamence's vulnerability.

There are several other bits of narrative aimed at explaining this vulnerability, the traffic incident, which Clamence tries to see as insignificant, and his ridicule at the hands of a woman, for which he exacts a brutal revenge, but the vulnerability, we learn, is not to be explained. As in *The Stranger*, we get little help understanding Meursault's slippage into more or less "pure" pre-reflective consciousness, we get little help in *The Fall* understanding the actual mechanisms of Clamence's "fall." Indeed, it is of a piece with his growing sense of failure and fraudulence, of being less than perfect, of being "two-faced" in his masterful way of dealing with the world and his slavish insecurities. It is from the standpoint of this vulnerability that he learns to practice the duplicitous art of the "judge-penitent," which might better be described as his desperate effort to remain proud and feel superior in the face of his ever-increasing humiliation. He learns to "see through" his earlier façade of virtue—as if it were a façade—and finds beneath it all of the signs of duplicity and hypocrisy. But it is the duplicity and hypocrisy of the critic Clamence, not any duplicity and hypocrisy on the part of the innocent Clamence, that is betrayed.

V

Clamence's narrative in *The Fall* is only secondarily intended to tell a story. It is first of all a seduction aimed at his almost silent interlocutor in the bar and ultimately toward the reader. His strategy, as he finally describes it, is to paint a vivid portrait "of all and of no one" and then hold it up to the viewer so it becomes a mirror. The point is to seduce the listener to reflect on and judge himself. Like all seductions, it proceeds by stealth and indirection. It seems to be doing one thing, but it's actually doing another. Clamence's narrative seems to tell a story and be a personal confession of guilt, but it's actually setting a trap. Here is the real duplicity, not innocent Clamence as two-faced but resentful Clamence as seducer, using his charm and his verbal skills to mislead and trap his victims. "Don't rely on it," indeed!

How Clamence does this—or how well he does it—is of considerable interest, but even more tantalizing is why he does it. The "how" gets to the complex dynamic of interpersonal confession, a fascinating question, but the "why" gives us the complex key to Clamence's depraved character. The seduction succeeds by way of getting the victim to scrutinize his own less than perfect behavior with the same cruel persistence and from the same perspective that has undermined Clamence. But why should he do this? What does he get out of it? For even if his accusation of duplicity and selfishness against the earlier Clamence is false and unfair, it accurately characterizes him now. Clamence as we get to know him is a cynic and a narcissist. He always has ulterior motives, and he is always looking to his own advantage. We can be sure that his seemingly tireless efforts to seduce have a pay-off for him, but we are never entirely clear what it is, even when he is willing to tell us—on the assumption that we have by this time been caught in his seducer's web.

My first hypothesis has to do with the benefits of confession as such. Clamence boasts to us, in his feverish rant: "The confession of my crimes allows me to begin again lighter in heart and to taste a double enjoyment, first of my nature and secondly of a charming repentance" (p. 142). But what is the "charm" of repentance? In this God-less world, without the possibility of redemption, it is hard to figure out what can be so charming, unless repentance is in some sense its own reward—as the earlier Clamence says of his virtues. But confession is not just the lightening of one's burden. It is also communication with another person, and confession yields a strategic advantage. He tells us "I was the lowest of the low," and then he imperceptibly passes from the "I" to the "we" and explains, "I have a superiority in that I know it and this gives me the right to speak. You see the advantage, I am sure. The more I accuse myself, the more I have a right to judge you. Even better, I provoke you into judging yourself."

Throughout his narrative, Clamence keeps repeating variations on the Biblical "judge not, that ye not be judged" theme. At this point, his advice seems to be, judge yourself, and that will compel others to judge themselves. But elsewhere, he seems to be defending a gunslinger's Golden Rule, judge others before they judge you, and, at another point, it is the more sage and strategic judge yourself before others judge you. But in the end he finds that all such strategies fail in their ultimate aim, which is to evade judgment, period. Perhaps surprisingly, he does not offer the Nietzschean advice not to judge at all: "I do not want to accuse; I do not even want to accuse those who accuse. *Looking away* shall be my only negation. And all in all and on the whole: some day I wish to be only a Yes-sayer."[7]

But it is clear that judging is what Clamence does. It is the world of his expertise. In the absence of his earlier, enviable role in the justice system and his palpable sense of success and superiority, judging others gives him sustenance and a more subterranean sense of superiority, the dubious superiority that comes with resentment: "Once more I found a height . . . from which I can judge everybody" (p. 142). But then again, he says in his fever-filled rave that "I was wrong, after all, to tell you that the essential thing was to avoid judgment. The essential thing is being able to permit oneself everything, even if, from time to time, one has to profess vociferously one's own infamy." The confession becomes not a means but a cost, a cost of utter licentiousness and self-indulgence. "I have learned to accept duplicity instead of being upset about it."

This licentiousness, "shamelessness" would be a good word for it, is Clamence's ultimate "solution." What it really amounts to is his first replacing pride with shame and then shame with shamelessness, wallowing in it. Clamence boasts, "I yield to everything, to pride, to boredom, to resentment, and even to the fever that I feel delightfully rising at this moment." Hardly an attractive list of "everything," but it is through this utter self-indulgence, this utterly adolescent sense of freedom, that Clamence can declare, "I dominate at last. But forever." Even, "How intoxicating to feel like God the father." But what a sick and phony sense of superiority this is! What a terrible example of "false pride." It brutally exemplifies Nietzsche's characterization of the illusions of superiority in "slave morality." Through resentment, one turns noble values on their head, so that strength becomes weakness and weakness becomes strength. It is when one is most infirm, as Clamence is infirm, that one entertains these illusions of greatness. "I crush everything under the weight of my own infirmity." One suspects the same with Nietzsche.

One might well argue that Clamence maintains his earlier sense of superiority throughout the novel, substituting this perverse and illusory sense for his earlier, admittedly more warranted sense of superiority and pride. But even if one were to make this argument, it comes at a terrible cost. Whereas the earlier Clamence, as a true *megalopsychos* if not an *Übermensch*, simply took pride in his accomplishments and virtues, with considerable benefit to his fellow citizens, the resentful Clamence gains his sense of superiority only at considerable cost to others. True, much of his sense of superiority is wholly "in his head," without much effect on other people, but we gather from his intent to carry out serial seductions that his ravings and illusions are by no means innocent. In other words, despite the accusations of hypocrisy against the earlier Clamence, he was in Paris a genuinely virtuous man. But the resentful, recollecting Clamence is not only cynical; he is exceedingly cruel.

No doubt Camus is being ironic when he makes Clamence an advocate for what I have elsewhere called "the blaming perspective," better known, perhaps, through the harsh moralizing of Camus's one-time friend, Jean-Paul Sartre. (There are a great many sarcastic barbs aimed at Sartre and his "atheist café" friends in *The Fall*, and we remember that its writing was just after their very well-publicized falling out.) Clamence declares his harsh basic principle, "No excuses ever, for anyone," and "I am for any theory that refuses to grant man innocence and for any practice that treats him as guilty" (pp. 131-32). In his earlier incarnation, of course, his philosophy and his legal practice had been all about excuses and extenuating circumstances, excuses of poverty and adversity, excuses of perversity. But here is the author of "Neither Victims nor Executioners" putting words in his character's mouth that would make us all both at once. It is easy enough to see why. The *why* of Clamence's campaign of seduction is nothing less. If everyone is guilty, then, by his dubious logic, he who acknowledges that first has the right to condemn and rise above all of the others. It matters not at all that humanity itself is thus degraded.

The novel also ends on a morbid if familiar note. In the midst of his hysterical raving, Clamence turns to his interlocutor with a desperate plea: "I'm happy, I am happy, I tell you, I won't let you think I am not happy." There should be no doubt that Clamence is *not* happy, and the desperation and defensiveness of his plea makes that quite clear. But it is worth noting that all of Camus's curious characters are happy. Meursault recognizes both in his mundane life and while awaiting his execution that he "had been happy and was happy still." Sisyphus, despite his absurd labor, "must be imagined happy." And in the *Plague*, Dr. Rieux looks anxiously forward to the possible return of the bacillus in "a happy city." Indeed, Camus seems to enjoy putting happiness together with death. "A Happy Death" is the title of his first novel. It is what Meursault has to look forward to. So we should not be surprised that Clamence finishes off his plea with "I am happy unto death." That is the ultimate pathology of pride, that it prefers even death to humiliation, and if one fails at happiness in life, then happiness unto death would seem to be the last desperate hope, the final gasp of a bitter resentment.

Notes

1. Albert Camus, *La Chute* (Paris: Gallimard, 1956). Trans. as *The Fall* by Justin O'Brien (New York: Random House, 1956); all references to the book are to the O'Brien edition and are in parentheses in the text.

2. Phillip L. Quinn, "Hell in Amsterdam: Reflections on Camus's *The Fall*," *Midwest Studies in Philosophy* 16 (1991): 89-103.

3. Albert Camus, *L'Etranger* (Paris: Gallimard, 1942). Trans. as *The Stranger* by Stuart Gilbert (New York: Random House, 1946). All references to *The Stranger* are to the Gilbert edition.

4. David Sherman, "Camus's Meursault and Sartrian Irresponsibility," *Philosophy and Literature* 19 (1995): 60-77.

5. David Hume, *Treatise of Human Nature* (Oxford: Oxford University Press, 1978); Book II, sect. iii, p. 415.

6. Milan Kundera, *The Unbearable Lightness of Being* (New York: Harper and Row, 1984), p. 251.

7. Friedrich Nietzsche, *Gay Science*, trans. Walter Kaufmann (New York: Random House, 1968), §276.

The Popular-Ritual Structural Pattern of Albert Camus' *La Chute*

Evelyn H. Zepp

The traditional image of Camus' works has been largely a classical one: a static system of balance and harmony based on an underlying philosophical principle. There can be no doubt as to the validity of this image; Camus' own writings attest to his classicism. To see that the aesthetic principle of balance and harmony, for example, is at the core of Camus' works, one need only look at many of his titles. These titles reveal how his thought shaped and was shaped by the opposition and balance of pairs.

However, as important as this image is, it may hide other, at least complementary, approaches. In particular, the grotesque and carnival tradition, as presented by Mikhail Bakhtin in *Rabelais and his World* and *Problems of Dostoevsky's Poetics*, is highly relevant to Camus' fictional works, and especially to *La Chute*.

The scope of this study allows us to examine only one aspect of this tradition, but it is a most important aspect. In opposition to the classical canon, the grotesque canon presents the unfinished, the incomplete, that which lacks clear, individualized outlines or borders. Bakhtin states: "The essence of the grotesque is precisely to present a contradictory and double-faced fullness of life. Negation and destruction (death of the old) are included as an essential phase, inseparable from affirmation, from the birth of something new and better."[1] A "classical" duality will involve a pair in total opposition—each pole clearly separated and distinguished from the other. A "carnival" duality will involve a pair in which each "pole" is inseparable from the other, depends on it, and shares some of its qualities. This form of duality—the simultaneous awareness and interdefinition of two "poles"—is the basic carnival vision; Bakhtin finds that it creates "two-in-one images" which "seize and capture a phenomenon in the process of change and transition and . . . fix both poles of evolution within a phenomenon in their continuous, creative, renewing changeability: death is foreseen in birth and birth in death . . . discrowning in coronation, etc."[2]

The two-in-one image is a consistent structural principle in Camus. Perhaps the most obvious example is the image of the sun in *L'Etranger*, which is an inextricable web of the principles of both light and dark, of life and death (both fundamental carnival couples). The two-in-one image also takes the form of doubles, both as separate characters and as mirror images of a principal character. Meursault is reflected in the young reporter: "Et j'ai eu l'impression bizarre d'être regardé par moi-même."[3] [And I had the bizarre impression that I was looking at myself.] As mirror image, Meursault and Clamence both see themselves as dual entities: Meursault, "je me suis regardé dans ma gamelle de fer. Il m'a semblé que mon image restait sérieuse alors même que j'essayais de lui sourire" [I looked at myself in my mess tin. It seemed to me that my features remained solemn even while I was trying to smile] (*L'Etranger*, p. 1183); Clamence, "Mon image souriait dans la glace, mais il me sembla que mon sourire était double."[4] [My image smiled in the mirror, but it seemed to me that my smile was double.] These two examples propose a divided consciousness, but one in which the two poles are two-in-one: split yet inseparable. Indeed, the absurd itself and the divided consciousness it involves are fundamentally a "carnival" rather than a "classical" duality. They are what Julia Kristeva calls a *dyad* ("dont les deux termes étant en communication entre eux, constituent un système de code" [whose two terms, communicating with each other, constitute a system of code]).[5] The poles of the absurd do not form a dichotomy, a classical duality, but rather exist in tension, in a continual state of interaction. Camus writes in *Le Mythe de Sisyphe* that the absurd is "une confrontation et une lutte sans repos";[6] "elle ne peut se diviser. Détruire un de ses termes, c'est la détruire tout entière" [a confrontation and a struggle without rest; it cannot be divided. To destroy one of the terms is to destroy the whole thing] (*Le Mythe*, pp. 120-21); "L'absurde est essentiellement un divorce. Il n'est ni dans l'un ni dans l'autre des éléments comparés. Il naît de leur confrontation . . . l'absurde n'est pas dans l'homme . . . ni dans le monde, mais dans leur présence commune" [The absurd is essentially a divorce. It is found in neither one nor the other of the compared elements. It is born in their confrontation . . . the absurd is not in man . . . nor in the world, but in their common presence] (*Le Mythe*, p. 120).

These are just a few examples of carnival duality in Camus. It is in *La Chute*, however, that this carnival principle is seen most clearly. The two-in-one image itself appears in numerous ways. For example, Clamence refers to the imaginary signs (*enseignes*) which would reveal the ambivalent carnival truth, the true dual nature, of individuals: "Imaginez des cartes de visite: Dupont, philosophe froussard, ou propriétaire chrétien, ou humaniste adultère, on a le choix, vraiment. Mais ce serait l'enfer!" [Imagine visiting cards: Dupont, cowardly philosopher, or Christian landlord, or adulterous humanist, take your choice. But it would be hell!] (*La Chute*, p. 1499). Emblematically for the whole text, Clamence's own "sign" would be a clear two-in-one entity: Janus. "Je connais la mienne en tout cas: une face double, un charmant Janus" [I know mine in any case: a double face, a charming Janus] (*La Chute*, p. 1499). Of course, the ultimate form of the ambivalent Janus in the text is the *juge-pénitent*.

In addition to the two-in-one image, at a deeper level in the text, there is a structure built on a whole carnival process of ambivalence, involving multilevel space, the carnival ritual *par excellence* of crowning-discrowning, and ultimately, the whole communicative process of *La Chute*—its dialogical prose and the unique relationships it creates. The scope of this study allows us to examine only one of these: the carnival ritual process of crowning and discrowning.

One of the spatial orientations of *La Chute*—up and down—is intimately tied to what Bakhtin identifies as the most important carnival process, crowning and discrowning. In this carnival ritual, a king is chosen from the crowd at the beginning of the carnival, treated with full honors until the end of the carnival, and then stripped and beaten. This ritual process of crowning and discrowning an impostor-king expresses the carnival truth of constant change and flux: "The basis of the ritual performance of crowning and discrowning the king is the very core of the carnivalistic attitude to the world—*the pathos of vicissitudes and changes, of death and renewal.* Carnival is the festival of all-destroying and all-renewing time" (Bakhtin, *Dostoevsky*, p. 102). The popular wisdom of carnival uses the trappings of official power and wisdom to express the essential "double-faced fullness of life" (Bakhtin, *Rabelais*, p. 62), an awareness which negates power at the same time as it affirms it. Thus, carnival is fundamentally an attack on official power, seriousness, and hierarchy.

In *La Chute*, which is in many ways a struggle for (verbal) power, crownings and discrownings take place on multiple levels—with Clamence, with the interlocutor, and with the reader. In every instance, an attempt to seize power, to be outside the flux of change, or to be part of official, one-sided seriousness is countered by the double carnival vision—crownings are inevitably followed by discrownings. We shall begin by examining the evident cases within the text.

The title of the work has all too often been read only within the framework of Christian symbolism. The "fall" is, however, the essence of the process of discrowning and also its ultimate topographical representation—the concrete shifting from top to bottom which is an integral part of grotesque imagery. There are a number of incidents in the book which appear to be "falls" in the carnival sense rather than in the Christian.

Clamence begins his recital of his days in Paris with a description of what is essentially a "crowned" state. His successful life has been a participation in the carnival "feast": "J'allais de fête en fête. Il m'arrivait de danser pendant des nuits, de plus en plus fou des êtres et de la vie" [I went from party to party. I managed to dance away entire nights, more and more crazed by beings and life] (*La Chute*, p. 1490), and also a crowning by the festival crowd: "une joyeuse salutation s'élevait vers moi" (*La Chute*, p. 1488); "La vie, ses êtres et ses dons venaient au-devant de moi; j'acceptais ces hommages avec une bienveillante fierté. En vérité à force d'être homme, avec tant de plénitude et de simplicité, je me trouvais un peu surhomme" [Life, its creatures and its gifts passed in front of me; I would accept these tributes with a benevolent pride. In truth, by dint of being human, with such fullness and simplicity, I was a bit of a superman] (*La Chute*, p. 1490). Indeed, Clamence actually uses the word *reign* numerous times in his description of his "crowned" state: for example, "je régnais librement, dans une lumière édénique" [I reigned freely, in an Edenic light] (*La Chute*, p. 1489).

This "crowned" state contains within itself, however, the necessity of discrowning. Clamence's dislike, even terror, of depths, caverns, etc.—of "down" elements—is an instinctive realization of the necessary "fall" before him. His experience on the Pont des Arts comes at the moment in which he feels "un vaste sentiment de puissance" [a vast sensation of power] (*La Chute*, p. 1495), that is, when he feels most secure in his official, "crowned" state. He is unseated by an outburst of carnival laughter: "ce rire n'avait rien de mystérieux, c'etait un bon rire, naturel, presque amical, qui remettait les choses en place" [That laughter had nothing mysterious about it, it was a good laugh, natural, almost friendly, that restored things to their places] (*La Chute*, p. 1495). This is carnival laughter; it upsets official seriousness (Clamence's claim to power) and its one-sided truth. Henceforth, Clamence feels himself to be "double."

The process of discrowning is continued by a second important event, the narration of Clamence's confrontation with a motorcyclist in the midst of a Parisian traffic jam. This experience is even more clearly a carnival discrowning, since it involves a gathering of the people on a modern (and comic) version of the "carnival square." Clamence is stripped of his position by the crowd, and even subjected to the typical blows of discrowning: "Mais j'étais à peine sur la chaussée que, de la foule qui commençait à s'assembler, un homme sortit, se précipita sur moi, vint m'assurer que j'étais le dernier des derniers . . . je reçus un coup violent sur l'oreille. . . . Je m'étais laissé battre sans répondre. . . .

Je me revoyais . . . sous les regards ironiques d'une foule d'autant plus ravie que je portais, je m'en souviens, un costume bleu très élégant. . . . Je m'étais en somme dégonflé publiquement" [But I had scarcely put my foot on the ground when out of the crowd that was beginning to assemble a man emerged, threw himself on me, assuring me that I was the lowest of the low. . . . I received a violent blow on my ear. . . . I had let myself be struck without responding. . . . under the ironic gaze of a crowd especially delighted because I was wearing, as I recall, a very elegant blue suit. . . . I was in short publicly deflated] (*La Chute*, pp. 1502-3).[7]

Clamence's subsequent "fall" from his successful place in Parisian society is a continuation of this process of discrowning by and before the crowd: "je me sentais vulnérable, et livré à l'accusation publique. Mes semblables cessaient d'être à mes yeux l'auditoire respectueux dont j'avais l'habitude. Le cercle dont j'étais le centre se brisait. . . . Oui, ils étaient là, comme avant, mais ils riaient. . . . J'eus même l'impression, à cette époque, qu'on me faisait des crocs-en-jambe. Deux ou trois fois, en effet, je butai, sans raison, en entrant dans des endroits publics. Une fois même, je m'étalai" [I felt myself vulnerable and open to public accusation. My peers ceased in my eyes to be the respectful audience I was accustomed to. The circle of which I was the center was broken . . . Yes, they were there, as before, but they were laughing. . . . I even had the impression, during this time, that my limbs had turned into fangs. Two or three times, in fact, I stumbled for no reason, going into public places. Once even I fell flat on my face] (*La Chute*, p. 1515).

This discrowning process is not final, however, as it is only one thread in the complex web of time sequences, places, and narrative voices in the text. Crownings and discrownings take place at all levels. For example, the discrowning process we have been tracing is paralleled in the narrative by Clamence's new attempt to gain power in the Amsterdam bar. Another example, drawn from the past, the crowning of a new pope in the prisoner of war camp, illustrates clearly the carnival duality, the simultaneity, of both sides of the process. As Clamence is "crowned," he discrowns the official church. His coronation as "pope" is clearly intended to counterbalance the faults of the "official" Pope and Church, and at the same time lays bare the power structure and fear which inform the Church and its rituals—fear of damnation, necessity of confession, etc. (Clamence later speaks of his "sacrements" of menace, dishonor, and the police, the means through which "je prêche dans mon église de *Mexico-City*, j'invite le bon peuple à se soumettre" [I preach in my church of *Mexico-City*, I invite the good people to submit] —*La Chute*, p. 1546). At the same time, this crowning, and Clamence's attempt to impose a new official hierarchy, not only invite but necessitate another discrowning—this time of Clamence himself. No one part of the ritual crowning-discrowning process may be separated from the other—discrowning is inherent in crowning and vice versa. Clamence's rejection of the flow of time and its necessary changes—the continuity of this process—is the element which more than any other places him outside the carnival spirit.

Thus, this incident of the crowning of the new pope in the prisoner of war camp is also important as an illustration of Clamence's fundamental alienation from the carnival spirit, and builds the case for his final (in the text) discrowning, the one to be carried out by the reader. More than any other, at the outset his crowning as pope seems to be within the true carnival spirit: it presupposes a reversal of official procedures and hierarchy, since the one chosen is the one with "le plus de faiblesses" [the most weaknesses] (*La Chute*, p. 1540), and a community of the people: "Il nous déclarait qu'il fallait un nouveau pape qui vécût parmi les malheureux, au lieu de prier sur un trône . . . un homme complet, avec ses défauts et ses vertus [qui] acceptât de maintenir vivante, en lui et chez les autres, la communauté de nos souffrances" [He proclaimed to us that it was necessary to find a new pope who lived among the unfortunate, instead of praying on a throne . . . a complete man, with his faults and his virtues who would be willing to keep alive, in himself and others, the community of our sufferings] (*La Chute*, p.

1540). But Clamence is unable to maintain the carnival spirit, destroying the carnival equality as he drinks the water of a dying comrade.

Thus, all of Clamence's attempts to regain his "kingdom," to place himself outside the body of the people, to maintain the official, static world of his "crowned" state, must lead to discrownings. As Bakhtin demonstrates in *Rabelais and his World*, those who will not enter into the carnival spirit are subject to beatings, dismemberment, and death at the hand of the people. At the end of *La Chute*, Clamence envisages such a death: "on me décapiterait, par exemple. . . . Au-dessus du peuple assemblé, vous éléveriez alors ma tête encore fraîche, pour qu'ils s'y reconnaissent et qu'à nouveau je les domine" [I would be decapitated, for example. . . . Above the gathered crowd, you would then raise my still warm head, so that they could recognize themselves and I could again dominate them] (*La Chute*, p. 1551).

Even at the moment of his death, though, Clamence can see himself only as dominant. His vision parallels his assertion at the end of the text: "Je règne enfin, mais pour toujours. J'ai encore trouvé un sommet. . . . J'attendrai donc vos hommages à *Mexico-City*, aussi longtemps qu'il le faudra. . . . Je trône parmi mes vilains anges, à la cime du ciel hollandais, je regarde monter vers moi, sortant des brumes et de l'eau, la multitude du jugement dernier" [I finally reign, but forever. I have found a summit. . . . I will await your tributes in *Mexico-City*, as long as it takes. . . . I sit on my throne beside my naughty angels, atop the Dutch heavens; emerging from the mists and the water, I watch the multitude of the last judgment] (*La Chute*, pp. 1548-49). Clamence's real "sin" is his resistance to the carnival vision of life, his attempt to escape the constant flux of the human condition, which he must share with everyone else. He epitomizes the "official" world, which would stop time and change, which insists on rigid hierarchy. Thus, this final (in the text) crowning attempted by Clamence must again invoke a subsequent discrowning, present in the response, the laughter, of the interlocutor: "Ne riez pas! Oui, vous êtes un client difficile" [Do not laugh! Yes, you are a difficult client] (*La Chute*, p.

1548). The interlocutor, rejecting through his laughter Clamence's final "self-revelation" as one more attempt to seize power, here begins the process of distancing from Clamence and his "confession" which extends to the reader and leads to *his* discrowning of Clamence. It should not be forgotten that the discrowning process which Clamence has been aiming at the interlocutor: "je vous provoque à vous juger vous-même" [I provoke you into judging yourself] (*La Chute*, p. 1548), is also intended for everyone: "Avec cela, je fabrique un portrait qui est celui de tous et de personne. Un masque en somme, assez semblable à ceux du carnaval, à la fois fidèles et simplifiès. . . . Mais, du même coup, le portrait que je tends à mes contemporains devient un miroir" [With that, I create a portrait which is that of everyone and of no one. A mask, in fact, quite similar to those of the carnival, at once faithful and simplified. . . . But at the same time, the portrait that I hold up to my contemporaries becomes a mirror] (*La Chute*, p. 1547). However, Clamence's attempt to discrown his "contemporaries" traps him in a dual process. By revealing his "carnival mask," Clamence may have indeed achieved his purpose of forcing the interlocutor to judge himself, but he has also revealed himself as an impostor. The reader's distrust is only compounded when, at the very end of the book, he learns that the interlocutor is also a lawyer, "de la même race" [of the same race] (*La Chute*, p. 1551) as Clamence. The interlocutor is no longer the everyman, the substitute for the reader, he has been all along. The process of identification between Clamence, interlocutor, and reader furthered throughout the text disintegrates here. The reader is distanced from both characters, and, in particular, begins his own discrowning process of Clamence the impostor.

The multilevel carnival situation created prevents the *arresting* of the temporal progression of crownings and discrownings; Clamence cannot achieve a static position in the presence of the carnivalized reader. Time begins again at the end of the text, as the snow begins to fall (the first movement breaking into the closed world of the text—Clamence's walks around Amsterdam are merely closed circles), and

Clamence, thrust back into time, will in turn be judged and discrowned once again. The ritual process of the "carnival logic of an impostor's *elevation*, his comical *discrowning* by the whole folk on the square, and his *downward* fall" (Bakhtin, *Dostoevsky*, p. 141) coincides with the movement of *La Chute* and induces reader involvement in the text at a very concrete level. Facing Clamence's last assertion of superiority at the end of the book, it is the reader who will carry out the next act of discrowning, beyond the bounds of the text.

Let us add that the reader need not be aware of the carnival background nor of the specific crowning-discrowning structure in order to react as indicated. This ritual process is an integral part of our cultural heritage. One need only look at the plot structure of many situation comedies—unmasking and dethroning an impostor—to recognize its contemporary validity and appeal. The importance of laughter in this process, a question the limitations of this study do not allow us to explore here, should also be recognized.

Finally, it will be apparent as well to what extent this movement of crowning and discrowning is tied to the processes of communication taking place (between Clamence and the interlocutor, between Clamence and himself—as narrator and character, between Clamence and the reader, and between the text and the reader), and especially to the dialogue form. Every word becomes two-fold and ambivalent, or "two-in-one"; it "crowns" (asserts) itself and "discrowns" (negates) the word of the other. (We have already noted, for example, how Clamence appropriates the challenge of the man at the motorcycle incident into his own discourse.) The discursive (dialogical) process of the text is thus infinitely complicated, much more so than a simple monologue/dialogue opposition might reveal. The analysis of the dialogical word is another area of analysis opened by the exploration of the carnival tradition and the application of its different concept of duality in Camus.

Our exploration of the carnival ritual process of crowning/discrowning suffices, however, to show us that carnival duality creates a work quite different from one structured around classical duality. *La*

Chute is a work based on relationships and continuous processes, rather than on the static confrontation of fixed images, characters or ideas. Its dualities may be perceived as constituting a system of "dyads," with a constant interaction of their "poles" rather than their fixed, static opposition. Such an approach to Camus works as forming a web of dynamic processes, rather than static statement or closed poetic universes, is a necessary corrective to his classical image and can only further the appreciation and understanding of Camus the artist.

From *Modern Language Studies* 13.1 (1983): 15-21. Copyright © 1983 by Susquehanna University. Reprinted with permission of Susquehanna University.

Notes

[*Editor's Note:* Translations appearing in square brackets are provided by the volume editor, unless otherwise noted.]

1. *Rabelais and his World*, trans. Helene Iswolsky (Cambridge: M.I.T. Press, 1968), p. 62. Further references will be indicated in the text as *Rabelais*.

2. *Problems of Dostoevsky's Poetics*, trans. R. W. Rotsel (Ann Arbor: Ardis, 1973), p. 137. Further references will be indicated in the text as *Dostoevsky*.

3. Albert Camus, *L'Etranger* in *Théâtre, Récits, Nouvelles* (Paris: Gallimard, 1962), p. 1186. Further citations from *L'Etranger* will be indicated in the text.

4. Albert Camus, *La Chute* in *Théâtre, Récits, Nouvelles*, p. 1495. Further citations from *La Chute* will be indicated in the text.

5. *Sémeiotiké: Recherches pour une sémanalyse* (Paris: Seuil, 1969), p. 156.

6. Albert Camus, *Le Mythe de Sisyphe* in *Essais* (Paris: Gallimard, 1965), p. 121. Further citations from *Le Mythe* will be indicated in the text.

7. The importance of this incident in the development of Clamence *"juge-pénitent"* should be stressed. It is especially noteworthy that the words flung at him by his adversary are now the words which shape his confession: "je me tiens devant l'humanité entière, récapitulant mes hontes, sans perdre de vue l'effet que je produis, et disant: 'j'étais le dernier des derniers'" [I hold myself in front of all humanity recounting my shame, without losing from view the effect that I produce, saying: "I am the worst of the worst"] (*La Chute*, p. 1547). Clamence's profession as *juge-pénitent* is a reaction of wounded vanity; Clamence, the Clamence of the present narration, has incorporated the words of the other into his own discourse in order to answer them. Bakhtin calls this process, a development of the carnival ritual of crowning/discrowning, *dialogism*. It can be demonstrated that Clamence's whole narration is a dialogical discourse which reflects a continuous, inseparable process of crowning/discrowning.

A Story of Cain:
Another Look at "L'Hôte"

Elwyn F. Sterling

Within the large body of criticism devoted to the fiction of Albert Camus, "L'Hôte" has received surprisingly little attention. Peter Cryle has argued that early critical bias caused a subsequent neglect of all of the *nouvelles* in *L'Exil et le Royaume*.[1] In the case of "L'Hôte," the relative scarcity of comment may also stem from a fairly broad consensus that the *nouvelle* expresses indirectly the author's own attitude or ethical dilemma in the face of the burgeoning Algerian conflict[2] and thereby deals with an historical episode too narrowly defined in space and time to have more than passing significance. This judgment may have been reinforced by the apparent simplicity of the story's fictional situation (Brée, p. 132).

At first glance, the situation does appear simple. A schoolteacher, Daru, is ordered for administrative reasons to shelter an Arab prisoner overnight and to deliver him the next day to the appropriate authorities. The prisoner is a murderer who must certainly expect to be sentenced to prison, if not to be executed, for his crime. Some critics have viewed Daru as a compassionate and humane man who is caught by chance in ethically painful circumstances that require a clear-cut choice between wholly antithetical options (Thody, p. 191; Majault, p. 114; Perrine, p. 52; Guers-Villate, p. 231). These options are variously seen as being between orders and freedom, the French administration and the Algerian rebels, or loyalty to his own kind and a "broader human fraternity" (Fortier, p. 538; Perrine, p. 53; Rhein, p. 125). Moved by understanding and a generous sympathy for the Arab's plight, determined to be neither "master nor slave" and to maintain his innocence (Maquet, p. 176), the schoolmaster points out two paths to his prisoner: one leads to Tinguit and prison, the other to the nomads and freedom. By leaving the choice of path to the Arab—who finally takes the prison road—Daru refuses to judge his fellow man and thereby establishes the value of freedom (Guers-Villate, p. 233). For many analysts, the host's noble offer has been doubly and tragically misunderstood. Some believe that the Arab has misunderstood because neither he nor Daru can speak the other's language (Brée, p. 133; Rhein, p. 125)—despite rather lengthy conversations and an explicit response in Arabic by the latter at one point;[3] others argue that he is too "primitive" to grasp the schoolteacher's meaning and to "choose prison deliberately" (Cryle, p. 135; Thody, p. 191; Guers-Villate, p. 231). Moreover, an "invisible witness" has misunderstood the nature of Daru's act (Maquet, p. 126; Rhein, p. 125). When the schoolmaster returns to the classroom, he finds a message on the blackboard that implicitly condemns him to solitude, exile, or even death as an ironic compensation for his compassionate revolt (Brée, p. 133; Majault, p. 114). This would-be "saviour" of his fellow man is ultimately "crucified" (Gadourek, p. 215).

The foregoing summary clearly shows the narrowly focused and essentially positive light cast on the schoolteacher's behavior by some analysts of "L'Hôte." If an occasional dissenting voice has noted Daru's guilty conscience or questioned the ethical validity of his refusal to choose (Minor, p. 79; Simon, p. 289; Durand, p. 1113), a majority of critics have concentrated on the apparently either-or nature of the dilemma of choice without considering the protagonist's negative motives. No less neglected has been the theme of murder, which is central to much of Camus's fiction. And yet in the world of the author, *chaque endroit a son envers* [Each place has its reverse]: a more balanced view should take into account the negative, as well as the positive, aspects of the story and thereby better clarify the complex ambiguities of innocence and guilt in a situation that has not only political but also profoundly human implications. Fortunately, Camus revealed his own awareness of the story's negative dimensions by considering "Cain" as a possible title (p. 2048). This essay proposes to examine some of the analogies that exist between the account of the "first murder" and the events of "L'Hôte" as a means of exploring further its ethical significance and of suggesting some of the metaphysical overtones implicit in the *nouvelle*.[4]

One striking similarity between the two accounts comes to mind immediately. In both cases, a violent act of passion sets events in motion. As Cain slew Abel, the Arab has slain his cousin with a bill-hook in what might be considered an instinctive form of revolt against "une divinité cruelle et capricieuse" (*Essais*, p. 445) that was menacing him with suffering and perhaps death. At issue, in this desert suffering from a searing drought where "les moutons mouraient alors par milliers et quelques hommes ça et là, sans qu'on puisse toujours le savoir" [the sheep were then dying by the thousands as well as some men here and there without anyone always knowing] (p. 1612), was a debt of grain, the sustenance of life itself. If the Arab does not rebel against the French—a detail perhaps included to underline the broader significance of the account—his neck bears the mark of revolt as the result of being led at the end of a cord.[5] He has "un front buté . . . un air à la fois inquiet et rebelle" (p. 1613). Structurally, as in the biblical story, "la première révolte coincide avec le premier crime" [the first revolt coincides with the first crime] (*Essais*, p. 443). The analogy is of course incomplete because it lacks that element of choice given to Cain by the Lord prior to the killing, an element that lends to Abel's murder a flavor of premeditation:

> The Lord said to Cain, "Why are you angry and why has your countenance fallen? If you do well, will you not be accepted? And if you do not do well, sin is couching at the door; its desire is for you, but you must master it."
>
> Cain said to Abel his brother, "Let us go out to the field." And when they were in the field, Cain rose up against his brother and killed him.[6]

More than Cain, the Arab has clearly committed a *meurtre de fatalité*[7] not entirely dissimilar to the one perpetrated by Meursault. As a reason for killing his cousin, he can only answer, "il s'est sauvé. J'ai couru derrière lui" [He ran away. I ran behind him] (p. 1619). Because the act is more ambiguous than Cain's, because guilt is obvious but a measure of innocence is not excluded, the murder elicits a degree of sympathy for its perpetrator.[8] In a sense, the Arab is both a victim and an executioner, in need of understanding and vulnerable to condemnation. Yet he is already a "son of Cain," in his own way, when forcibly led to the schoolteacher's door. Not only has he killed; he has slain one of his own.

Until the Arab's arrival, Daru, the schoolmaster, has been living on the margin of human society, as did Meursault.[9] The school is physically located halfway up a steep slope "à quelques kilomètres de l'endroit où le plateau commençait à descendre vers le sud" [at some kilometers from the spot where the plateau begins to slope toward the south] (p. 1612). Some three kilometers separate it from the nearest European inhabitants. Nameless, faceless natives inhabit the plateau but certainly not the immediate vicinity. Simultaneously isolated from men and involved in intermittent human commerce, Daru reigns over his own private Eden. As a Frenchman, his position is superior in every way to that of the area's few native inhabitants. As the schoolmaster, he is the sole fount of knowledge and the high priest of French culture. As the representative of the French administration charged with distributing rations of grain to men who would otherwise starve, he literally holds the power of life and death. If Daru is aware that he (and his future guest, for that matter) counts for nothing when measured against the eternally sterile aridity of the desert (p. 1617), he has come, in the face of la misère des autres and in the midst of his own dénouement, to feel himself "un seigneur" [a lord] (p. 1612). In fact, however, everything about Daru's situation implies that it is a precarious point d'équilibre from which he may slip and fall at any time. If he is "content" in this country that is cruel to human inhabitants, its paradisiac quality depends for him on its solitary nature where "rien ne rappel[l]e l'homme" [nothing recalls man] (p. 1615). The presence of men makes the land still more "cruel à vivre" (p. 1612). Only in the desert, in the midst of a nature devoid of men, does the notion of "avoir raison" take on meaning, as Camus put it in *Noces* (*Essais*, p. 87). Let men appear and things are no longer unequivocally subject to logic, no longer clearly right or wrong: they become relative and ambiguous.[10] Daru's fortunate position of a lord in paradise balances on his marginal state of exile.

The Arab's arrival shatters Eden's peaceful silence because it forcibly involves Daru in an area of human affairs where acts can have simultaneously good and bad consequences, where refusal can become, at the same time, a murderous form of consent to judgment.[11] The situational irony rests on Daru's solipsistic way of thinking: significantly, the story is told wholly from his point of view. Seen from this perspective, he has two choices: to keep the Arab overnight and deliver him to the prison at Tinguit in accordance with Balducci's orders, or to refuse to deliver him. The first option casts him in the role of a policeman and even a judge. The schoolmaster finds the role unpalatable[12] because it violates his personal code of honor. Daru is "un homme" (p. 1616) in the sense peculiar, at least in Camus's view, to the Algerian ("L'Été à Alger," *Essais*, p. 72) and rebellious against injustice. This, rather than sympathy for and understanding of the Arab's plight, causes him to untie the cords that bind the prisoner's hands. To deliver him to prison implies condemnation and even consent to his death, either through execution or because, as Daru knows, neither he nor the Arab can truly survive outside of the desert (p. 1617). The second option is repugnant because it makes the teacher, in a way, an accomplice of a murderer and thus implies a certain consent to the crime: "tout ça me dégoûte, et ton gars le premier" [all that disgusts me, and your guy first of all] (p. 1616). There are, of course, other points of view: Balducci's, the Arab's, and, ultimately, that of the "invisible witness."

The *gendarme* too is "un homme" who feels shame over the cord that he has had to use, but he has sacrificed his personal qualms of honor to the conviction that "on ne peut pas les laisser faire" [We cannot let them get away with it] (p. 1616). He too appeals for Daru's sympathy and understanding. Furthermore, he asks Daru to be, in a sense, what was implicitly asked of Cain outside of the garden of Eden, i.e., his brother's keeper: first, of his French brethren in the face of an imminent uprising—"Si tu veux nous lâcher, à ton aise, je ne te dénoncerai pas" [If it pleases you to give up on us, I will not denounce you] (p. 1616); and second, of the Arab who is *wanted* by the agitated inhabitants of his village.[13] But as the sacrifice of Cain did not find favor in the eyes of the Lord, neither does Balducci's in the eyes of Daru. Like the old man-servant of *Le Malentendu*, the schoolmaster prefers, in his self-conceived role of "seigneur," not to intervene in the affairs of men: "Une colère subite vint à Daru contre cet homme, contre tous les hommes et leur sale méchanceté, leurs haines inlassables, leur folie du sang" [A sudden anger arose in Daru against this man, against all men and their dirty malice, their inexhaustible hatreds, their violent madness] (p. 1615). Not unexpectedly, then, Daru rejects Balducci's fraternal appeal for sympathy and understanding: "il l'avait renvoyé d'une certaine manière, comme s'il ne voulait pas être dans le même sac" [He had put him off in a certain way, as if he did not want to be in the same bag] (p. 1621). He likewise rejects the unspoken and spoken appeals for fraternity that come to him from the Arab.

The latter is not unintelligent and insensitive. If, like the Algerian of *Noces*, like Meursault, and indeed like Cain, he does not regret his crime, he is evidently aware that the act of murder has set him apart from men.[14] He asks Daru why he would eat with him, averts his eyes when Daru asks him in a hostile tone why he has killed, stiffens and again turns his eyes aside when asked if he is afraid, is overheard moaning before going to sleep, and, when awakened, shows in his eyes an initial appearance of madness and fear. In fact, the absent-minded, distracted expression that remains after he recovers his self-control (pp. 1619-21) recalls the attitude of Meursault throughout his trial and suggests an awareness that he is guilty and no doubt intends to pay. He too is "un homme" and does not seek those opportunities to escape that the teacher incessantly provides; instead, with an attitude that recalls Meursault's feelings towards his lawyer (p. 1173), he asks for fraternal support and understanding: "Viens avec nous, dit-il" [Come with us, said he] (p. 1619). But Daru does not answer, remaining deaf to the appeal. From his point of view, a fraternal response would imply complicity and tacit consent to a barbarous act. It is not through understanding of the Arab's anguish, then, that he provides opportunities for flight, but through a wish to be alone again "sans avoir rien à décider" [without having to decide anything] (p. 1618). Ill at ease in the Arab's presence simply by virtue of the latter's humanity, he is also bothered because to sleep in the same room "lui imposait une sorte de fraternité qu'il refusait dans les circonstances présentes" [imposed a sort of fraternity on him that he refused in the present circumstances] (p. 1620). Daru's rejection of sympathy for and understanding of the Arab's plight is a conscious decision. Like the Lord confronting Cain, he refuses to accept his share of responsibility for the crimes of men: "Et il maudissait à la fois les siens qui lui envoyaient cet Arabe et celui-ci qui avait osé tuer" [And he cursed at the same time his people who were sending him this Arab and this one who had dared kill] (p. 1621). His quandary will remain bounded by his own *angoisse*, and he will, in effect, "tourner en rond" (p. 1621) in a metaphorical circle of his own construction in search of a way out.

Viewed from his perspective, Daru apparently finds an *issue* in nonintervention. As the Lord did not intervene to prevent Cain's crime[15] and "le sacrifice d'Abel" (*Essais*, p. 445), but left the choice to Cain, the schoolmaster will leave the choice to the Arab. For the latter, the options presented by the schoolmaster are dual: to follow the route to prison and a metaphorical, it not literal, form of death—since neither he nor the teacher can really live outside of the desert—or to take the road that will lead to the nomads and make him into a biblical "fugitive and a wanderer on the earth." In either case, Daru has condemned the murderer, as the Lord did Cain, to the condition of a *solitaire*, a stranger among men. He has also placed his mark upon the Arab, for if the latter had to be led to the school at the end of a cord, he will now take the route of self-sacrifice in response to the teacher's failure to use "un langage clair" and point the way.[16] But Daru's lordly sense of ethical preëminence—suggested by the physical "éminence" of the geographical place of decision (p. 1622)—is only momentary. From the point of view of the "invisible witness"—whether the native inhabitants of the plateau, the narrator, or Daru's own conscience—the teacher has not found a definitive way out. For the witness, Daru is but a man among men; his refusal to choose is itself a choice; he is not a "meurtrier innocent." Seen from that perspective, by refusing sympathy and understanding, he, like Cain, has chosen badly.

There was another *issue*, and the schoolmaster could have been, in a way, his brothers keeper. What does the Arab ask when taken out into the desert, as Cain led his brother into the field, if not for fraternal company on the road? With an air of panic reflected on his face, he turns to Daru with a final appeal, "Écoute" (p. 1623). But the latter, pot-bound in his self-conceived role of "seigneur," gives nearly the same reply that the old man-servant gave to another *angoissé* at the end of *Le Malentendu*: "Non, tais-toi. Maintenant, je te laisse" [No, be silent. Now I leave you] (p. 1623). Daru thus abandons the Arab and, in effect, banishes him from his presence. Yet the Arab has also left his mark on the teacher, and the latter descends from his "summit" with a heavy heart. The refusal to understand has become a form of consent to judgment and condemnation. Back in the schoolroom, Daru will be forced to recognize the reality of his own humanity. Traced on the board by an awkward hand, whether his own or that of another, are the words, "Tu as livré notre frère. Tu paieras" [You have handed over our brother. You will pay for this] (p. 1623).[17] Daru has "fallen" into lucidity and must face the fact that he too, by refusing to understand, has become a "son of Cain." Henceforth, he must bear his share of responsibility for the crimes of men. Because he did not wish to be in the same "sack," he too is condemned to wander, a fugitive over the face of the earth: "Dans ce vaste pays qu'il avait tant aimé, il était seul" [In this vast country that he had loved so much, he was alone] (p. 1623). As in the case of Cain, the punishment may be greater than he can bear.

Notes

[*Editor's Note:* Translations appearing in square brackets are provided by the volume editor, unless otherwise noted.]

1. *Bilan critique: l'exil et le royaume d'Albert Camus* (Paris: Minard, 1973), p. 11. For other analyses of "L'Hôte," see Germaine Brée, *Camus* (New Brunswick: Rutgers University Press, 1959); Laura G. Durand, "Thematic Counterpoint in *L'Exil et le Royaume*," *French Review*, 47, 6 (May 1974); Yvonne Guers-Villate, "Rieux et Daru ou le refus délibéré d'influencer autrui," *Papers on Language and Literature*, 3 (Summer 1967); Joseph Majault, *Camus: révolte et liberté* (Paris: Editions du Centurion, 1965); Albert Maquet, *Albert Camus: The Invincible Summer* (New York: George Braziller, 1958); and Anne Minor, "The Short Stories of Albert Camus," *Yale French Studies*, 25 (Spring 1960).

2. See, for instance, Cryle, p. 120; Philip Thody, *Albert Camus: 1913-1960* (New York: Macmillan, 1961), p. 191; Carina Gadourek, *Les Innocents et les coupables: essai d'exégèse de l'ouvre d'Albert Camus* (The Hague: Mouton, 1963), pp. 214-15; Edwin P. Grobe, "The Psychological Structure of Camus's 'L'Hôte,'" *French Review*, 40, 2 (December 1966), 361-62; Conor Cruise O'Brien, *Camus* (London: Fontana/Collins, 1970), p. 69; Laurence Perrine, "Camus' 'The Guest': A Subtle and Difficult Story," *Studies in Short Fiction*, 1 (1963), 58; Philip H. Rhein, *Albert Camus* (New York: Twayne, 1969), p. 125; John K. Simon, "Camus' Kingdom, the Native Host and an Unwanted Guest," *Studies in Short Fiction*, 1 (Summer 1964), 289.

3. Albert Camus, *Théâtre, Récits, Nouvelles*, Bibliothèque de la Pléiade (Paris: Gallimard, 1962), p. 1617. Subsequent page references to this text will be to this edition.

4. The metaphysical overtones, blasphemous in their implications—cf. Albert Camus, *Essais*, Bibliothèque de la Pléiade (Paris: Gallimard, 1965), p. 436—may explain the rejection of "Cain" as a title in favor of "L'Hôte." The latter title, no less ambiguous than "Cain," also established referential continuity with *Le Malentendu*. Like the Arab, Jan realizes that he will not leave the house as "un hôte indifférent" (p. 158). Camus considered other possible titles: *Les Hauts Plateaux et le condamné, Sous la neige*, and *La Loi* (p. 2048). We may speculate that he eventually rejected these because of their excessive specificity or poverty of metaphorical suggestiveness.

5. The Arab refused to ride on the horse in an earlier manuscript version (p. 2050).

6. *The Holy Bible: Revised Standard Version* (Cleveland: The World Publishing Company, 1962), pp. 3-4.

7. In an earlier manuscript version, the Arab attributed it to God's will (p. 2052).

8. Cf. "Un esprit pénétré de l'idée de l'absurde admet sans doute le meurtre de fatalité; il ne saurait accepter le meurtre de raisonnement" (*Essais*, p. 416).

9. "Préface à l'édition universitaire américaine," p. 1928.

---

10. In an earlier manuscript version, Daru chose exile in the desert precisely to avoid such ambiguities (pp. 2050, 2052).

11. This is a recurrent Camusian motif. In an earlier version, Daru withdrew to the desert to escape the need to say no, to judge, and to destroy (p. 2052).

12. Cf. the similar attitude of Meursault, Tarrou, Diego, and Clamence.

13. For an indication of the possibly violent justice awaiting the Arab from his own, see Grobe, p. 362.

14. Likewise, Meursault, about to extend his hand to the examining magistrate, withdraws it upon recalling that he has killed a man.

15. Cf. the role of the old manservant, a probable surrogate for God, vis-à-vis Martha's crime and the murder of Jan in *Le Malentendu*.

16. The Arab thus becomes, after a fashion, the keeper of the schoolteacher. His choice of the prison road possibly eliminates any condemnation of Daru by his fellow French for refusing to deliver the prisoner.

17. Cf. Constance Rooke, "Camus' 'The Guest': The Message on the Blackboard," *Studies in Short Fiction*, 14 (Winter 1977), 78-81.

RESOURCES

1913	Albert Camus is born on November 7 in Mondovi, Algeria, to Lucien Auguste Camus and Catherine Sintès.
1914	October 11, wounded at the First Battle of the Marne, Lucien Camus dies. Catherine takes Albert and his older brother Lucien to Belcourt, a working-class district of Algiers, where they live with her mother, Marie Catherine Sintès, and her two brothers in a three-room apartment without electricity or running water.
1918	Camus enrolls in primary school, where he is mentored by Louis Germain, to whom he will later dedicate his Nobel Prize speech.
1924	Camus enrolls as a student in the Grand Lycée in Algiers.
1930	Camus experiences his first symptoms of tuberculosis and is forced to interrupt his studies at the Grand Lycée.
1930-1936	Camus studies philosophy at the University of Algiers. Jean Grenier serves as his mentor.
1934	June, Camus marries Simone Hié.
1935	Camus joins the Algerian Communist Party.
1936	Camus divorces Simone Hié. *Révolte dans les Asturies (Revolt in Asturias)*, which he writes in collaboration with fellow members of the Théâtre de l'Equipe, is banned from performance but published. July-September, tours Central Europe and Italy.
1936-37	As an actor for Radio Algiers, Camus tours towns in Algeria.
1937	May, *L'Envers et l'endroit (The Right Side and the Wrong Side)*, dedicated to Jean Grenier, is published. The Algerian Communist Party expels Camus when he opposes its decision to end its campaign for indigenous civil rights. July, Camus visits Paris for the first time.
1937-1939	Camus writes for the socialist newspaper *Alger-républicain*.

1938	May, *Noces* (*Nuptials*) is published. October, Camus publishes a favorable review of Jean-Paul Sartre's *La Nausée* (*Nausea*) in *Alger-républicain*.
1939	June, publishes a series of articles exposing the dire economic effects of colonialism in the Kabylia region of Algeria.
1940	Camus moves to Paris to work for *Paris-Soir*. December, marries Francine Faure.
1942	July, *L'Etranger* (*The Stranger*) is published. December, *Le Mythe de Sisyphe* (*The Myth of Sisyphus*) is published. Recurrence of tuberculosis. August, Camus stays in the French mountain village of Le Panelier.
1943	September, Sartre publishes a twenty-page essay on *L'Etranger* in *Cahiers du sud*. November, Camus becomes a reader for the Gallimard publishing house. December, Camus becomes editor of the underground newspaper *Combat*.
1944	Meets André Gide, Sartre, and other prominent intellectuals. August, *Le Malentendu* (*The Misunderstanding*) is staged.
1945	August, in *Combat*, Camus becomes the only prominent figure in the West to condemn the bombing of Hiroshima. September, twins, Catherine and Jean, born to Albert and Francine Camus. October, *Lettres à un ami Allemand* (*Letters to a German Friend*) is published. September, *Caligula* is staged.
1946	March-June, Camus travels to the United States and Canada. November, *Ni Victimes ni bourreaux* (*Neither Victims nor Executioners*) is published.
1947	Camus protests French suppression of a revolt in Madagascar. June, *La Peste* (*The Plague*) is published. June, Camus ends his connection to *Combat*.
1948	May, Camus visits Great Britain. October, *L'Etat de siège* (*State of Siege*) is staged.

1949	Summer, Camus travels to South America. Urges clemency for Greek communists sentenced to death. December, first performance of *Les Justes* (*The Just Assassins*).
1950	June, *Actuelles: Chroniques, 1944-1948* is published.
1951	October, *L'Homme révolté* (*The Rebel*) is published to generally negative reviews, including a scathing attack by Francis Jeanson in *Les Temps modernes*.
1952	Camus visits Algeria. August, public break with Jean-Paul Sartre.
1953	June, *Actuelles II: Chroniques, 1948-1953* is published. June, as director of the Festival of Angers, Camus stages his own adaptations of *La Devotion à la croix* (*Devotion to the Cross*) by Pedro Calderón de la Barca and *Les Esprits* (*The Wits*) by Pierre de Larivey.
1954	March, *L'Eté* (*Summer*) is published. November, Camus travels in Italy. He issues an appeal for seven Tunisians sentenced to death.
1955	March, Camus's adaptation of *Un Cas intéressant* (*An Interesting Case*) by Dino Buzatti is staged. April-May, Camus visits Greece. May, Camus begins writing a column for *L'Express*.
1956	January, Camus visits Algeria in an unsuccessful attempt to mediate a truce. May, *La Chute* (*The Fall*) is published. September, Camus's adaptation of William Faulkner's *Requiem for a Nun* is staged. November, Camus speaks out against Stalinist repression in Hungary. He discontinues his column at *L'Express*.
1957	March, *L'Exil et le royaume* (*Exile and the Kingdom*) is published. December, Camus is awarded the Nobel Prize for Literature. "Réflexions sur la guillotine" ("Reflections on the Guillotine") is published.
1958	June, *Actuelles III: Chronique Algérienne, 1939-1958* is published. Camus travels in Italy.

1959	January, Camus's adaptation of Fyodor Dostoevski's *The Possessed* is staged.
1960	Camus dies on January 4 when a car driven by his friend and publisher Michel Gallimard crashes into a tree in the Burgundy town of Villeblevin.
1963	*Carnets: Mai 1935-février 1942* (*Notebooks 1935-1942*) is published.
1965	*Carnets: Janvier 1942-mars 1951* (*Notebooks 1942-1951*) is published.
1971	*La Mort heureuse* (*A Happy Death*) is published.
1978	*Journaux de voyage* (*American Journals*) is published.
1981	*Correspondance 1932-1960* is published.
1989	*Carnets: Mars 1951-décembre 1958* (*Notebooks: 1951-1958*) is published.
1994	*Le Premier Homme* (*The First Man*) is published.
2006	The first two volumes of a four-volume edition of the complete works of Albert Camus are published in the prestigious *Bibliothèque de la Pléiade*.
2007	*Correspondance 1946-1959* is published.
2008	Volumes three and four of the complete works of Camus are published in the *Bibliothèque de la Pléiade*.

Works by Albert Camus

Long Fiction
La Mort heureuse, wr. 1936-1938, pb. 1971 (*A Happy Death*, 1972)
L'Étranger, 1942 (*The Stranger*, 1946)
La Peste, 1947 (*The Plague*, 1948)
La Chute, 1956 (*The Fall*, 1957)
Le Premier Homme, 1994

Short Fiction
L'Exil et le royaume, 1957

Drama
Révolte dans les Asturies, pb. 1936 (with others)
Caligula, wr. 1938-1939, pb. 1944, pr. 1945 (English translation, 1948)
Le Malentendu, pr., pb. 1944 (*The Misunderstanding*, 1948)
L'État de siège, pr., pb. 1948 (*State of Siege*, 1958)
Les Justes, pr. 1949, pb. 1950 (*The Just Assassins*, 1958)
Caligula, and Three Other Plays, pb. 1958
Les Possédés, pr., pb. 1959 (adaptation of Fyodor Dostoevski's novel; *The Possessed*,
    1960)

Nonfiction
L'Envers et l'endroit, 1937 ("The Wrong Side and the Right Side," 1968)
Noces, 1938 ("Nuptials," 1968)
Le Mythe de Sisyphe, 1942 (*The Myth of Sisyphus*, 1955)
Lettres à un ami Allemand, 1945 (*Letters to a German Friend*)
Actuelles: Chroniques, 1944-1948, 1950
L'Homme révolté, 1951 (*The Rebel*, 1956)
Actuelles II: Chroniques, 1948-1953, 1953
L'Été, 1954 (*Summer*, 1968)
Actuelles III: Chronique Algérienne, 1939-1958, 1958
Carnets: Mai 1935-février 1942, 1962 (*Notebooks: 1935-1942*, 1963)
Carnets: Janvier 1942-mars 1951, 1964 (*Notebooks: 1942-1951*, 1965)
Lyrical and Critical Essays, 1968 (includes "The Wrong Side and the Right Side,"
    "Nuptials," and "Summer")
Journaux de voyage, 1978 (*American Journals*, 1987)
Correspondance 1932-1960, 1981

Carnets: Mars 1951-décembre 1958, 1989 (*Notebooks: 1951-1958*)
Correspondance, 1939-1947, 2000
Camus à "Combat": Éditoriaux et articles d'Albert Camus, 1944-1947, 2002 (*Camus at "Combat": Writing, 1944-1947*, 2006)
Correspondance 1946-1959, 2007
Notebooks: 1951-1959, 2008

Bibliography

Aaronson, Ronald. *Camus and Sartre: The Story of a Friendship and the Quarrel that Ended It*. Chicago: University of Chicago Press, 2004.

Abecassis, Jack I. "Camus's Pulp Fiction." *MLN* 112.4 (1997): 625-40.

Amoia, Alba. *Albert Camus*. New York: Continuum, 1989.

Apter, Emily. "Out of Character: Camus's French Algerian Subjects." *MLN* 112.4 (1997): 499-516.

Beer, Jill. "Le Regard: Face to Face in Albert Camus's 'L'Hôte.'" *French Studies* 56.2 (2002): 179-92.

Birchall, Ian. "The Labourism of Sisyphus: Albert Camus and Revolutionary Syndicalism." *Journal of European Studies* 20.2 (1990): 135-65.

Blanchard, Marc. "Before Ethics: Camus's *Pudeur*." *MLN* 112.4 (1997): 666-82.

_____. "Goodbye, Sisyphus." *South Central Review* 15.1 (1998): 8-18.

Bloom, Harold, ed. *Albert Camus*. New York: Chelsea House, 1989.

Blythe, Hal, and Charlie Sweet. "Speaking in 'Tongues': Psychoses in 'The Renegade.'" *Studies in Short Fiction* 25.2 (1988): 129-135.

Brée, Germaine. *Camus*. New Brunswick, NJ: Rutgers University Press, 1959.

_____. *Camus and Sartre: Crisis and Commitment*. New York: Delacorte, 1972.

_____, ed. *Camus: A Collection of Critical Essays*. Englewood Cliffs, NJ: Prentice-Hall, 1962.

Bronner, Stephen Eric. *Camus: Portrait of a Moralist*. University of Minnesota Press, 1999.

Carroll, David. *Albert Camus the Algerian: Colonialism, Terrorism, Justice*. New York: Columbia University Press, 2007.

_____. "Camus's Algeria: Birthrights, Colonial Injustice, and the Fiction of a French-Algerian People." *MLN* 112.4 (1997): 517-549.

Cervo, Nathan. "Camus's *The Plague*." *The Explicator* 52.2 (1994): 111-13.

Champagne, Roland A. "The Ethics of Hospitality in Camus's 'L'Hôte.'" *French Review* 80.3 (2007): 568-78.

Cohen-Solal, Annie. "Camus, Sartre and the Algerian War." *Journal of European Studies* 28.1-2 (1998): 43-50.

Cohn, Robert Greer. "The True Camus." *The French Review* 60.1 (1986): 30-38.

Cruickshank, John. *Albert Camus and the Literature of Revolt*. New York: Greenwood, 1978.

Davis, Colin. "Camus's *La Peste*: Sanitation, Rats, and Messy Ethics." *Modern Language Review* 102.4 (2007): 1008-20.

Duran, Jane. "The Philosophical Camus." *The Philosophical Forum* 38.4 (2007): 365-71.

Duvall, William E. "The Nietzschean Temptation in the Thought of Albert Camus." *History of European Ideas* 11 (1989): 955-62.

Ellison, David R. *Understanding Albert Camus*. Columbia: University of South Carolina Press, 1990.

Fitch, Brian. *The Fall: A Matter of Guilt*. New York: Twayne, 1995.

_____. *The Narcissistic Text: A Reading of Camus' Fiction*. Toronto: University of Toronto Press, 1982.

Foley, John. *Albert Camus from the Absurd to Revolt*. Montreal, Quebec: Queens University Press, 2008.

Freeman, Edward. *The Theatre of Albert Camus*. London: Methuen, 1971.

Gay-Crosier, Raymond, ed. *Albert Camus, 1980*. Gainesville: University Press of Florida, 1980.

Golomb, Jacob. "Camus's Ideal of Authentic Life." *Philosophy Today* 38.3 (1994): 268-77.

Gordon, Jeffrey. "The Triumph of Sisyphus." *Philosophy and Literature* 32.1 (2008): 183-90.

Griem, Eberhard. "Albert Camus's 'The Guest': A New Look at the Prisoner." *Studies in Short Fiction* 30.1 (1993): 95-99.

Grobe, Edwin P. "The Psychological Structure of Camus's 'L'Hôte.'" French Review 40.2 (1966): 361-62.

Hakutani, Yoshinobu. "Richard Wright's *The Outsider* and Albert Camus's *The Stranger*." *The Mississippi Quarterly* 42.4 (1989): 365-78.

Hallie, Philip. "Camus's Hug." *The American Scholar* 64.3 (1995): 428-36.

Harrow, Kenneth. "*Caligula*: A Study in Aesthetic Despair." *Contemporary Literature* 14 (1973): 31-48.

Hawes, Elizabeth. *Camus, a Romance*. New York: Grove, 2009.

Henry, Patrick. "Albert Camus, Panelier, and *La Peste*." *Literary Imagination: The Review of the Association of Literary Scholars and Critics* 5.3 (2003): 383-404.

Hochberg, Herbert. "Albert Camus and the Ethic of Absurdity." *Ethics* 75.2 (1965): 87-102.

Hopkins, Patricia. "Camus's Anti-Shaman." *Rocky Mountain Review of Literature* 48.1 (1994): 33-44.

Horowitz, Louise K. "Of Women and Arabs: Sexual and Racial Polarization in Camus." *Modern Language Studies* 17.3 (1987): 54-61.

Hughes, Edward J., ed. *The Cambridge Companion to Camus*. Cambridge, England: Cambridge University Press, 2007.

Hurley, D. F. "Looking for the Arab: Reading the Readings of Camus's 'The Guest.'" *Studies in Short Fiction* 30.1 (1993): 79-94.

Judt, Tony. *The Burden of Responsibility: Blum, Camus, Aron and the French Twentieth Century*. Chicago: University of Chicago Press, 1998.

Just, Daniel. "Literature and Ethics: History, Memory, and Cultural Identity in Camus's *Le Premier Homme*." *Modern Language Review* 105.1 (2010): 69-86.

Kellman, Steven G. *The Plague: Fiction and Resistance*. New York: Twayne, 1993.

_____. "Singular Third Person: Camus' *La Peste*." *Kentucky Romance Quarterly* 25 (1978): 499-507.

_____, ed. *Approaches to Teaching Camus's The Plague*. New York: Modern Language Association, 1985.

King, Adele, ed. *Camus's L'Etranger: Fifty Years On*. New York: St. Martin's Press, 1992.

Knapp, Bettina L., ed. *Critical Essays on Albert Camus*. Boston: G. K. Hall, 1988.

Krapp, John. "Time and Ethics in Camus's *The Plague*." *University of Toronto Quarterly* 68.2 (1999): 655-76.

Lazere, Donald. *The Unique Creation of Albert Camus*. New Haven: Yale University Press, 1973.

LeBlanc, John Randolph. "Art and Politics in Albert Camus: Beauty as Defiance and Art as a Spiritual Quest." *Literature and Theology* 13.2 (1999): 126-48.

_____. "Memory and Justice: Narrative Sources of Community in Camus's *The First Man*." *Philosophy and Literature* 30.1 (2006): 140-57.

_____ and Carolyn M. Jones. "Space/Place and Home: Prefiguring Contemporary Political and Religious Discourse in Albert Camus's *The Plague*." *Contemporary Political Theory* 2.2 (2003): 209-30.

Letemendia, V. C. "Poverty in the Writings of Albert Camus." *Polity* 29.3 (1997): 441-60.

Lottman, Herbert R. *Albert Camus: A Biography*. New York: Doubleday, 1979.

_____. *The Left Bank: Writers, Artists and Politics from the Popular Front to the Cold War*. Chicago: University of Chicago Press, 1981.

Luppé, Robert de. *Albert Camus*. Trans. J. Cumming and J. Hargreaves. London: Merlin, 1966.

McBride, Joseph. *Albert Camus: Philosopher and Littérateur*. New York: St. Martin's Press, 1992.

McCarthy, Patrick. *Albert Camus: The Stranger*. New York: Cambridge University Press, 2004.

McGregor, Rob Roy. "Camus's 'The Silent Men' and 'The Guest': Depictions of Absurd Awareness." *Studies in Short Fiction* 34.3 (1997): 307-23.

Maquet, Albert. *Albert Camus: The Invincible Summer*. Trans. Herma Briffault. 1958. New York: Humanities, 1972.

Marcus, Amit. "Camus's *The Fall*: The Dynamics of Narrative Unreliability." *Style* 40.4 (2006): 314-37.

Margerrison, Christine. *Ces forces obscures de l'âme: Women, Race and Origins in the Writings of Albert Camus*. Amsterdam: Rodopi, 2008.

Margerrison, Christine, and Mark Orme, eds. *Albert Camus in the 21st Century: A,* Amsterdam: Rodopi, 2008.

Muhlestein, Daniel K. "A Teacher and His Student: Subversion and Containment in Camus's 'The Guest.'" *Studies in Short Fiction* 36.3 (1999): 223-36.

O'Brien, Conor Cruise. *Albert Camus of Europe and Africa.* New York: Viking, 1970.

Onimus, Jean. *Albert Camus and Christianity.* Trans. Emmett Parker. Tuscaloosa: University of Alabama Press, 1970.

Oxenhandler, Neal. *Looking for Heroes in Postwar France: Albert Camus, Max Jacob, Simone Weil.* Hanover, NH: University Press of New England, 1996.

Parker, Emmett. *The Artist in the Arena.* Madison: University of Wisconsin Press, 1965.

Plant, Bob. "Absurdity, Incongruity and Laughter." *Philosophy* 84 (2009): 111-34.

Quilliot, Roger. *The Sea and Prisons: A Commentary on the Life and Thought of Albert Camus.* Trans. Emmett Parker. Tuscaloosa: University of Alabama Press, 1970.

Reid, David. "The Rains of Empire: Camus in New York." *MLN* 112.4 (1997): 608-24.

Rhein, Phillip H. *Albert Camus.* Boston: Twayne, 1989.

Rizzuto, Anthony. *Camus: Love and Sexuality.* Gainesville: University Press of Florida, 1998.

Sagi, Avi. *Albert Camus and the Philosophy of the Absurd.* Trans. B. Stein. Amsterdam: Rodopi, 2002.

_____. "Is the Absurd the Problem or the Solution? *The Myth of Sisyphus* Reconsidered." *Philosophy Today* 38.3 (1994): 278-84.

Scherr, Arthur. "Camus's *L'Etranger.*" *Explicator* 59.3 (2001): 149-53.

Showalter, English, Jr. *Exiles and Strangers: A Reading of Exile and the Kingdom.* Columbus: Ohio State University Press,1984.

Solomon, Robert C. "Pathologies of Pride in Camus's *The Fall.*" *Philosophy and Literature* 28.1 (2004): 41-59.

Sprintzen, David A. *Camus: A Critical Examination.* Philadelphia: Temple University Press, 1988.

Sprintzen, David A., and Adrian van den Hoven, trans. & ed. *Sartre and Camus: A Historic Confrontation.* Amherst, NY: Humanity Books, 2004.

Sterling, Elwyn F. "Albert Camus's Adulterous Woman: A Consent to Dissolution." *Romance Quarterly* 34.2 (1987): 155-63.

_____. "Albert Camus' *La Peste*: Cottard's Act of Madness." *College Literature* 13.2 (1986): 177-85.

_____. "A Story of Cain: Another Look at 'L'Hôte.'" *French Review* 54.4 (1981): 524-29.

Stern, Daniel. "The Fellowship of Men That Die: The Legacy of Albert Camus." *Cardozo Studies in Law and Literature* 10.2 (1998): 183-98.

Stoltzfus, B. F. "Caligula's Mirrors: Camus's Reflexive Dramatization of Play." *French Forum* 8.1 (1983): 75-86.

Strauss, George. "A Reading of Albert Camus' *La Mort heureuse*." *Neophilologus* 59.2 (1975): 199-212.

Sugden, Leonard W. "Albert Camus: The Temptations of East and West." *Dalhousie Review* 52 (1972): 436-48.

Tarrow, Susan. *Exile from the Kingdom: A Political Rereading of Albert Camus*. University, AL: University of Alabama Press,1985.

Thody, Philip. *Albert Camus: A Study of His Work*. New York: Grove, 1959.

_____. *Albert Camus 1913-1960*. New York: Macmillan, 1961.

Todd, Olivier. *Albert Camus: A Life*. Trans. Benjamin Ivry. New York: Knopf, 1997.

Willhoite, Fred H. *Beyond Nihilism: Albert Camus's Contribution to Political Thought*. Baton Rouge: Louisiana State University Press, 1968.

Winegarten, Renee. "Camus Today." *The New Criterion* 11.7 (1993): 35-42.

Wixon, Kathryn A. "Negotiating a Maze: Rereading *La Chute* as a Narration of Space." *Modern Language Studies* 23.2 (1993): 74-83.

Woolfolk, Alan W. "The Dangers of *Engagement*: Camus' Political Esthetics." *Mosaic* 17.3 (1984): 59-70.

Zaretsky, Robert. *Albert Camus: Elements of a Life*. Ithaca, NY: Cornell University Press, 2010.

_____. "Silence Follows: Albert Camus in Algeria." *Virginia Quarterly Review* 86.1 (2010): 214-22.

Zepp, Evelyn H. "The Popular-Ritual Structural Pattern of Albert Camus's *La Chute*." *Modern Language Studies* 13.1 (1983): 15-21.

CRITICAL
INSIGHTS

About the Editor_____

Steven G. Kellman is Professor of Comparative Literature at the University of Texas at San Antonio, where he was the university's first Ashbel Smith Professor. He was Fulbright Distinguished Professor of American Literature at Sofia University and Fulbright Senior Lecturer at Tbilisi State University and has also taught at the University of California campuses at Berkeley and Irvine as well as Bemidji State University and Tel-Aviv University. Kellman is the author of *Redemption: The Life of Henry Roth* (2005), *The Translingual Imagination* (2000), *The Plague: Fiction and Resistance* (1993), *Loving Reading: Erotics of the Text* (1985), and *The Self-Begetting Novel* (1980). He has also edited or coedited books on Camus's *The Plague* (1985), DeLillo's *Underworld* (2002), Leslie Fiedler (1999), Gass's *The Tunnel* (1998), Nabokov's stories (2000), Scorsese's *Raging Bull* (1994), and translingualism (2003), as well as M. E. Ravage's memoir *An American in the Making* (2009). He is coeditor, with John Wilson, of *Magill's Literary Annual*. A widely published critic and essayist, Kellman is the recipient of the National Book Critics Circle's 2007 Nona Balakian Citation for Excellence in Reviewing as well as of the *Baltimore Sun*'s 1986 H. L. Mencken Award. He has served three terms on the NBCC's board of directors and is the organization's vice president for membership. He was elected into the Texas Institute of Letters.

About *The Paris Review*_____

The Paris Review is America's preeminent literary quarterly, dedicated to discovering and publishing the best new voices in fiction, nonfiction, and poetry. The magazine was founded in Paris in 1953 by the young American writers Peter Matthiessen and Doc Humes, and edited there and in New York for its first fifty years by George Plimpton. Over the decades, the *Review* has introduced readers to the earliest writings of Jack Kerouac, Philip Roth, T. C. Boyle, V. S. Naipaul, Ha Jin, Ann Patchett, Jay McInerney, Mona Simpson, and Edward P. Jones, and published numerous now-classic works, including Roth's *Goodbye, Columbus*, Donald Barthelme's *Alice*, Jim Carroll's *Basketball Diaries*, and selections from Samuel Beckett's *Molloy* (his first publication in English). The first chapter of Jeffrey Eugenides's *The Virgin Suicides* appeared in the *Review*'s pages, as have stories by Rick Moody, David Foster Wallace, Denis Johnson, Jim Crace, Lorrie Moore, and Jeanette Winterson.

The Paris Review's renowned Writers at Work series of interviews, whose early installments include legendary conversations with E. M. Forster, William Faulkner, and Ernest Hemingway, is one of the landmarks of world literature. The interviews received a George Polk Award and were nominated for a Pulitzer Prize. Among the more than three hundred interviewees are Robert Frost, Marianne Moore, W. H. Auden,

Elizabeth Bishop, Susan Sontag, and Toni Morrison. Recent issues feature conversations with Jonathan Franzen, Norman Rush, Louise Erdrich, Joan Didion, Norman Mailer, R. Crumb, Michel Houellebecq, Marilynne Robinson, David Mitchell, Annie Proulx, and Gay Talese. In November 2009, Picador published the final volume of a four-volume series of anthologies of *Paris Review* interviews. *The New York Times* called the Writers at Work series "the most remarkable and extensive interviewing project we possess."

The Paris Review is edited by Lorin Stein, who was named to the post in 2010. The editorial team has published fiction by Lydia Davis, André Aciman, Sam Lipsyte, Damon Galgut, Mohsin Hamid, Uzodinma Iweala, James Lasdun, Padgett Powell, Richard Price, and Sam Shepard. Recent poetry selections include work by Frederick Seidel, Carol Muske-Dukes, John Ashbery, Kay Ryan, Mary Jo Bang, Sharon Olds, Charles Wright, and Mary Karr. Writing published in the magazine has been anthologized in *Best American Short Stories* (2006, 2007, and 2008), *Best American Poetry*, *Best Creative Non-Fiction*, the Pushcart Prize anthology, and *O. Henry Prize Stories*.

The magazine presents three annual awards. The Hadada Award for lifelong contribution to literature has recently been given to Joan Didion, Norman Mailer, Peter Matthiessen, John Ashbery, and, in 2010, Philip Roth. The Plimpton Prize for Fiction, awarded to a debut or emerging writer brought to national attention in the pages of *The Paris Review*, was presented in 2007 to Benjamin Percy, to Jesse Ball in 2008, and to Alistair Morgan in 2009. In 2011, the magazine inaugurated the Terry Southern Prize for Humor.

The Paris Review was a finalist for the 2008 and 2009 National Magazine Awards in fiction and won the 2007 National Magazine Award in photojournalism. *The Los Angeles Times* recently called *The Paris Review* "an American treasure with true international reach," and the *New York Times* designated it "a thing of sober beauty."

Since 1999 *The Paris Review* has been published by The Paris Review Foundation, Inc., a not-for-profit 501(c)(3) organization.

The Paris Review is available in digital form to libraries worldwide in selected academic databases exclusively from EBSCO Publishing. Libraries can contact EBSCO at 1-800-653-2726 for details. For more information on *The Paris Review* or to subscribe, please visit: www.theparisreview.org.

Contributors_____

Steven G. Kellman is Professor of Comparative Literature at the University of Texas at San Antonio. He is the author of *Redemption: The Life of Henry Roth* (2005), *The Translingual Imagination* (2000), *The Plague: Fiction and Resistance* (1993), *Loving Reading: Erotics of the Text* (1985), and *The Self-Begetting Novel* (1980). He has also edited or coedited books on Camus's *The Plague* (1985), DeLillo's *Underworld* (2002), Leslie Fiedler (1999), Gass's *The Tunnel* (1998), Nabokov's stories (2000), Scorsese's *Raging Bull* (1994), and translingualism (2003), as well as M. E. Ravage's memoir *An American in the Making* (2009). He is coeditor, with John Wilson, of *Magill's Literary Annual*. A critic and essayist, he is the 2007 recipient of the National Book Critics Circle's Balakian Citation for Excellence in Reviewing. He has served three terms on the NBCC's board of directors and is its vice president for membership.

Scott McLemee is a critic and essayist living in Washington, DC. His work has appeared in *Bookforum, The Nation, Dissent, New Politics, The New York Times*, and numerous other journals, and his weekly column "Intellectual Affairs" appears in the online publication *Inside Higher Ed*. He has edited three collections of writings by the Caribbean historian and theorist C. L. R. James. In 2004, he received the Nona Balakian Citation for Excellence in Reviewing from the National Book Critics Circle, on whose board of directors he served from 2008 to 2011.

Katherine Stirling is an editor at *Vanity Fair* and has written for *The New Yorker* and *The Times Literary Supplement*.

Christine Margerrison is a research associate in the Department of European Languages and Cultures, University of Lancaster (UK). She is the author of *"Ces Forces Obscures de l'âme": Women, Race and Origins in the Writings of Albert Camus* (2008) and a coeditor, with Mark Orme and Lissa Lincoln, of *Albert Camus in the 21st Century* (2008). She also has coedited, with Andy Stafford, Naaman Kessous, and Guy Dugas, *Algérie vers le cinquantenaire de l'indépendance: Regards critiques* (2009).

Brent C. Sleasman is an Assistant Professor in the Department of Theatre, Communication, and Fine Arts at Gannon University in Erie, Pennsylvania. His work has appeared in *Communication Annual* (the journal of the Pennsylvania Communication Association) and the *Sage Encyclopedia of Identity*. He is an associate editor for the *Journal of Camus Studies*, sponsored by the Albert Camus Societies of both the United Kingdom and the United States.

Henry L. Carrigan, Jr. is assistant director and senior editor at Northwestern University Press. He was formerly North American publisher at Continuum International Publishing. Carrigan has written about Günter Grass, Hermann Hesse, Heinrich von Kleist, Robert Musil, Thomas Mann, Franz Kafka, W. G. Sebald, and Robert Walser for several national newspapers and magazines.

Matthew H. Bowker is a visiting Assistant Professor of Interdisciplinary Studies at Medaille College in Buffalo, New York. He holds a Ph.D. in Political Philosophy from the University of Maryland, College Park, where his 2008 dissertation ("Albert Camus and the Political Philosophy of the Absurd") focused on the psychosocial dimensions of absurdity in the thought of Camus. Bowker's research examines the concept of absurdity from philosophical, psychoanalytic, and political perspectives.

Philip Hallie, a specialist in ethics, taught philosophy at Wesleyan University for thirty-two years. His books include *The Paradox of Cruelty* (1969), *Lest Innocent Blood be Shed* (1979), *From Cruelty to Goodness* (1981), *Tales of Good and Evil, Help and Harm* (1997), and *In the Eye of the Hurricane: Tales of Good and Evil, Help and Harm* (2001). He died in 1994.

Robert Zaretsky is Professor of History at the Honors College, University of Houston. He is author or coauthor of several books on modern France, most recently *Albert Camus: Elements of a Life* (2010) *and France and its Empire Since 1870* (2010). His essays appear in *Le Monde Diplomatique, Foreign Policy, The American Scholar, Virginia Quarterly Review, Chronicle of Higher Education, International Herald Tribune*, and *The New York Times*. With his coauthor John Scott, he is writing an account of James Boswell and the Enlightenment, a sequel of sorts to their earlier book *The Philosophers' Quarrel* (2009).

Patricia Hopkins is Associate Professor of French Emerita at Texas Tech University. She is coeditor, with Wendell M. Aycock, of *Myths and Realities of Contemporary French Theater* (1985).

George Strauss lived in Bathurst, New South Wales, and wrote about Albert Camus and André Gide.

Yoshinobu Hakutani is Professor of English and University Distinguished Scholar at Kent State University. His recent books and editions include *Cross-Cultural Visions in African American Literature: West Meets East* (2011), *Haiku and Modernist Poetics* (2009), *Art, Music, and Literature 1897-1902* by Theodore Dreiser (2007), *Cross-Cultural Visions in African American Modernism: From Spatial Narrative to Jazz Haiku* (2006), and *Haiku: This Other World* by Richard Wright (with Robert L. Tener) (2000). His current project is *Crossroads of Cultures: East-West Literary Imagination*.

Avi Sagi teaches philosophy at Bar-Ilan University, Israel, and is the founding director of its Program of Hermeneutics and Cultural Studies. He also is a senior researcher and faculty member at the Shalom Hartman Institute in Jerusalem. Sagi publishes extensively on continental philosophy, philosophy of ethics and religion, contemporary Jewish philosophy, and philosophy of literature. In addition to the monograph *Albert Camus and the Philosophy of the Absurd*, his books include *Religion and Morality* (with Daniel Statman), *Kierkegaard, Religion and Existence: The Voyage of the Self*, and *Jewish Religion after Theology*.

John Randolph LeBlanc is Associate Professor of Political Science at the University of Texas at Tyler, where he teaches political philosophy and public law. He is the author of *Ethics and Creativity in the Political Thought of Simone Weil and Albert Camus* (2004) and of several articles on the ethical-political implications and possibilities of artistic creativity in Camus and his readers. He is currently working on a book-length study of Edward Said's political theory and, with Carolyn M. Jones, preparing a collection of essays on the intersections of religion and politics.

Carolyn M. Jones Medine is Associate Professor in the Department of Religion and the Institute for African American Studies at the University of Georgia. Her research interests are in postcolonial and postmodern theory, African American literature and spirituality, and African American women's—particularly southern women's—literature. She has written numerous articles on the work of Toni Morrison and others.

Amit Marcus completed his postdoctoral research at the universities of Freiburg and Giessen. He is the author of *Self-Deception in Literature and Philosophy* (2007) and of essays on unreliable and self-deceived narration as well as on "we" fictional narratives.

Robert C. Solomon held the position of Quincy Lee Centennial Professor of Philosophy and Business at the University of Texas at Austin, where he taught from 1972 until his death in 2007. A specialist in nineteenth-century German philosophy and twentieth-century Continental philosophy, he published more than forty books, including *True to Our Feelings: What Our Emotions Are Really Telling Us* (2006), *Dark Feelings, Grim Thoughts: Experience and Reflection in Camus and Sartre* (2006), *The Joy of Philosophy* (1999), *About Love: Reinventing Romance for Our Times* (1988), *From Hegel to Existentialism* (1987), and *Existentialism* (1974).

Evelyn H. Zepp is Professor Emerita of French at the University of Wisconsin-Parkside, where she taught for thirty-one years and served as department chair and secretary of the faculty. She has published on Albert Camus, Julia Kristeva, and Marguérite Duras.

Elwyn F. Sterling taught in the Department of Romance Languages and Literatures at Colgate University for forty years before retiring in 1990. In addition to articles on Camus's short fiction, and drama, he published on narrative technique in French fiction of the seventeenth, eighteenth, and nineteenth centuries. He died in 2006.

Acknowledgments

"The *Paris Review* Perspective" by Katherine Stirling. Copyright © 2012 by Katherine Stirling. Special appreciation goes to Christopher Cox, Nathaniel Rich, and David Wallace-Wells, editors at *The Paris Review*.

"Camus's Hug" by Philip Hallie. From *The American Scholar* 64.3 (Summer 1995): 428-435. Copyright © 1995 by the author. Reprinted by permission of *The American Scholar*.

"Silence Follows: Albert Camus in Algeria" by Robert Zaretsky. From *Virginia Quarterly Review* 86.1 (2010): 214-222. Copyright © 2010 by Robert Zaretsky. Reprinted with permission of Robert Zaretsky.

"Caligula: Camus's Anti-Shaman" by Patricia Hopkins. From *Rocky Mountain Review of Language and Literature* 48.1 (1994): 33-44. Copyright © 1994 by *Rocky Mountain Review of Language and Literature*. Reprinted with permission of *Rocky Mountain Review of Language and Literature*.

"A Reading of Albert Camus' *La Mort Heureuse*" by George Strauss. With kind permission from Springer Science+Business Media: *Neophilogus* 59.2 (1975): 199-212. Copyright © 1975 by Springer Science+Business Media B.V.

"Richard Wright's *The Outsider* and Albert Camus's *The Stranger*" by Yoshinobu Hakutani. From *Mississippi Quarterly* 42.4 (1989): 365-378. Copyright © 1989 by Mississippi State University. Reprinted with permission of Mississippi State University.

"Is the Absurd the Problem or the Solution? *The Myth of Sisyphus* Reconsidered" by Avi Sagi. From *Philosophy Today* 38 (Fall 1994): 278-284. Copyright © 1994 by DePaul University. Reprinted with permission of DePaul University.

"Space/Place and Home: Prefiguring Contemporary Political and Religious Discourse in Albert Camus's *The Plague*" by John Randolph LeBlanc and Carolyn M. Jones. From *Contemporary Political Theory* 2.2 (2003): 209-230. Copyright © 2003 by Palgrave Macmillan Ltd. Reproduced with permission of Palgrave Macmillan Ltd.

"Camus's *The Fall*: The Dynamics of Narrative Unreliability" by Amit Marcus. From *Style* 40.4 (Winter 2006): 314-333. Copyright © 2006 by Northern Illinois University. Reprinted with permission of Northern Illinois University.

"Pathologies of Pride in Camus's *The Fall*" by Robert C. Solomon. From *Philosophy and Literature* 28.1 (2004): 41-59. Copyright © 2004 by The Johns Hopkins University Press. Reprinted with permission of The Johns Hopkins University Press.

"The Popular-Ritual Structural Pattern of Albert Camus' *La Chute*" by Evelyn H. Zepp. From *Modern Language Studies* 13.1 (1983): 15-21. Copyright © 1983 by Susquehanna University. Reprinted with permission of Susquehanna University.

"A Story of Cain: Another Look at "L'Hôte" by Elwyn F. Sterling. From *The French Review* 54.4 (1981): 524-529. Copyright © 1981 by American Association of Teachers of French. Reprinted with permission of American Association of Teachers of French.

Stranger), 175; and tuberculosis, 5, 19, 21, 50; and World War II, 6, 19, 49, 51, 86, 211; and Richard Wright, 170; on writing, 15, 107; writing style, 71

Capital punishment, 14, 21, 93, 127

Carrigan, Henry L., Jr., x, 319

Carroll, David, 94

Catherine (*A Happy Death*), 159

Caves du Vatican, Les (Gide), 147

Certeau, Michel de, 205

Cherea (*Caligula*), 143

Children, 14, 75, 89, 105, 113, 125

Christianity, 51, 104, 144; and absurdity, 59, 86; in *Caligula*, 132; in *Crime and Punishment*, 149; in *The Fall*, 239, 241, 258, 267, 272; in "The Guest," 292; in *The Outsider*, 176; in *The Plague*, 75

Chute, La. See *Fall, The*

Clamence, Jean-Baptiste (*The Fall*), 10, 87, 108; and duality, 281; and self-image, 258, 263, 270; as an unreliable narrator, 233

Cold War, 21, 38

Colonialism, 31, 34, 91, 102, 202; in *The First Man*, 84; in "The Guest," 294; in *The Plague*, 204, 219; in *The Stranger*, 74

Combat (newspaper), 20, 118

Communism, 19, 21-22, 103; in Algeria, 122; in *The Rebel*, 53; in "The Renegade," 38; in the Soviet Union, 107. *See also* Soviet Union

Communist Party, 19, 21-22, 122; in *The Outsider*, 171

Cormery, Jacques (*The First Man*), 34

Cottard (*The Plague*), 210

Coulomb, Jean, 25

Crane, Stephen, 171

Create Dangerously: The Immigrant Artist at Work (Danticat), 13

Crime, 147, 174, 178, 241, 293

Crime and Punishment (Dostoevski), 147, 174

Cruickshank, John, 86, 88

Cryle, Peter, 291

Damon, Cross (*The Outsider*), 170

Daniel, Jean, 35

Danticat, Edwidge, 13

Daru ("The Guest"), 291

David Copperfield (Dickens), 249

Death, 133, 147, 178, 283, 287, 292

Death penalty. *See* Capital punishment

Derrida, Jacques, 201

Despair, 58, 67, 107, 122, 258

Djebar, Assia, 32, 95

Dostoevski, Fyodor, 51, 55, 58, 147

Dreiser, Theodore, 171

Duality, 108, 219, 280; in *The Fall*, 108, 264, 266, 274

Duff, R. A., 189

Eliade, Mircea, 133

Emigrants, The (Sebald); and exile, 73

Esslin, Martin, 82

Été dans le Sahara, Un (Fromentin), 36

Ethics. *See* Morality

Etranger, L'. See *Stranger, The*

Eva (*The Outsider*), 177

Exile, 73, 77

Exile and the Kingdom (Camus), and Algeria, 36, 40

Existentialism, 5, 68, 174, 201; in *The Fall*, 238; and Blaise Pascal, 57; in *The Plague*, 207; and Jean-Paul Sartre, 20, 84

Express, L' (magazine), 121, 126

critical reception, 32, 90; and death, 120; and exile, 73; form and style, 11; and nature, 80; Nazi symbolism, 69.

Plato, 242

Possessed, The (Camus), 23

Possessed, The (Dostoevski), 58, 102

Postmodernism, 49

Premier Homme, Le. See *First Man, The*

Pride, 258, 266

Pétré-Grenouilleau, Olivier, 36

Quilliot, Roger, 87, 147, 164

Quinn, Phillip, 259, 272

Rambert (*The Plague*), 74

Rawls, John, 212

Raymond (*The Stranger*), 177

Rebatet, Lucien, 83

Rebel, The (Camus), 21, 124, 227, 247; and absurdity, 53, 137, 190; and alienation, 201; critical reception, 88

"Reflections on the Guillotine" (Camus), 15

Reluctant Fundamentalist, The (Hamid), 11

"Renegade, The" (Camus), 7, 36, 40

"Return to Tipasa" (Camus), 26

Ricoeur, Paul, 48, 249

Rieux, Dr. Bernard (*The Plague*), 8, 14, 75, 213, 223

Rings of Saturn, The (Sebald), 78

Rousseau, Jean-Jacques, 264

Saddok (*The First Man*), 34

Sagi, Avi, x, 84, 91, 320

Said, Edward, 4, 31, 93, 202, 208

Sandel, Michael, 212

Sarkozy, Nicolas, 3

Sarocchi, Jean, 32, 148

Sartre, Jean-Paul, 20-21, 51, 85, 118; break with Camus, 5, 27, 63, 88; and existentialism, 84; and *The Fall*, 278; and Richard Wright, 170

Scherr, Arthur, 87

Scipio (*Caligula*), 142

Sea and Prisons, The (Quilliot), 87

Sebald, W. G., 67; and the Holocaust, 70; writing style, 67, 71

Selwyn, Henry (*The Emigrants*), 76

Shamanism, 133

Shilts, Randy, 12

"Short Guide to Towns Without a Past" (Camus), 39

Sickness Unto Death, The (Kierkegaard), 58

Sleasman, Brent C., x, 319

Solomon, Robert C., xii, 321

Sontag, Susan, 11, 67

Soviet Union, 7, 22, 53, 107. *See also* Communism

State of Siege, The (Camus), 21

Stavrogin, Nicholas (*The Possessed*), 102, 105

Sterling, Elwyn F., xi, 321

Stirling, Katherine, vii, 319

Stranger, The (Camus), 170; and Arabs, 94; critical reception, 85; and death, 5, 19; and duality, 281; and evil, 69; form and style, 11, 180, 262; reception, 8

Strauss, George, xi, 320

Styron, William, 11

Suetonius, 132

Tarrou, Jean (*The Plague*), 15, 120, 213

Temps modernes, Les (magazine), 21, 88

Terrorism, 34, 92, 103, 125

Themes and motifs; absurdity, 5, 25, 48,

72, 82, 86, 127, 135, 173, 188, 281;
alienation, 4, 42, 68, 73, 76, 78, 114,
153, 172, 207; androgyny, 140; art,
13, 107, 226; children, 14, 75, 89,
105, 113, 125; colonialism, 31, 34,
74, 84, 91, 102, 202, 204, 219, 294;
crime, 147, 174, 178, 241, 293;
death, 133, 147, 178, 283, 287, 292;
despair, 58, 67, 107, 122, 258;
duality, 108, 219, 264, 266, 274, 280;
exile, 73, 77; freedom, 120, 136, 143,
154, 240, 291; grotesque, 280;
happiness, 147, 149, 278; home, 70,
74-75, 80; language, 10, 101, 107,
144, 202-203, 209, 216, 234, 240,
275, 292; love, 153, 177, 207, 212,
223; memory, 77; morality, 18, 21,
52, 60, 72, 86, 91, 103, 130, 133,
188, 196, 263, 270; mothers, 23, 50,
73, 103, 175, 261; nature, 79, 135,
172; pride, 258, 266

Todd, Olivier, 86
Trocmé, André, 113
Tuberculosis, 5, 19, 21, 50, 163

Veillard (*The First Man*), 34

Wall, Kathleen, 231
Walser, Robert, 76
Walzer, Michael, 129
Willhoite, Fred, Jr., 90
Wilson, Colin, 87
World War II, 6, 19, 51, 80, 112, 203,
211; influence on Camus, 49, 86; in
The Emigrants (Sebald), 77; in *The
Rings of Saturn* (Sebald), 79

Yacobi, Tamar, 231, 248

Zagreus (*A Happy Death*), 150
Zaretsky, Robert, ix, 320
Zepp, Evelyn H., xii, 321